Custom Auto Interiors

Don Taylor and Ron "The Stitcher" Mangus

California Bill's
Automotive Handbooks

Front and Back Cover Photos
This wild and beautiful '33 Ford roadster
belongs to Connie and Jack Bockelman
of Prescott, Arizona, long-time customers
of Ron's shop. Featuring an Alloway
body, it was Connie's idea to create the
integrated molding around the seats that
flows into the center console. The interior
is totally custom made. The contoured
hand-built seats were created to flow
with the body. Door panels are designed
to integrate with the seats and sweep
into the front panels. Curved kick panels
house speakers. The finishing touch
features hidden rear speakers that play
through a vertical slot at the side of
the seats.

Publishers
Helen V. Fisher
Howard W. Fisher

Editor
Howard W. Fisher

Cover and Interior Design
Gary D. Smith
www.performancedesign.net

Cover Photography
E. John Thawley III
www.thawleyphoto,com

Interior Photography
Don Taylor

Copyright © 2005 by Don Taylor & Ron Mangus

Published by
California Bill's Automotive Handbooks
P.O. Box 91858
Tucson, AZ 85752
520-547-2462

Distributed by
Motorbooks International
729 Prospect Avenue
P.O. Box 1
Osceola, WI 54020-0001
800-458-0454

ISBN-13 978-1-931128-18-6
ISBN-10 1-931128-18-9

Printed in China

4 5 6 7 8 9 10 - 11 10 09 08 07

**Library of Congress
Cataloging-in-Publication Data**

Taylor, Don, 1936 Oct. 10-
      Custom auto interiors / by Don Taylor and
        Ron Mangus.
      p. cm.
      Includes index.
      ISBN-13 978-1-931128-18-6
      ISBN-10 1-931128-18-9
      1. Automobiles—Upholstery. 2. Automobiles—
        Customizing.
      I. Mangus, Ron, 1955-   . II. Title.
      TL256.T385   1998
      629.2'77—dc21   98-12059
          CIP

Notice: The information in this book is true and complete
to the best of our knowledge. It is offered without
guarantees on the part of the author or California Bill's
Automotive Handbooks. The author and publisher
disclaim all liability with the use of this book.

This is a book on advanced auto upholstery design and
techniques. Basic instructions on how to upholster an
automobile are provided in California Bill's *Automotive
Upholstery Handbook:* ISBN-13 978-1-931128-00-1.

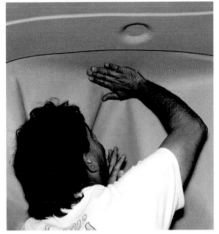
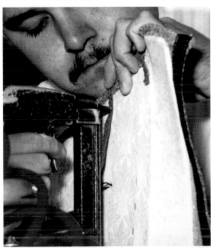
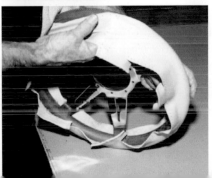

Table of Contents

About the Hands-on Authors

Don "at the bench" hand-sewing "fox edging" to the back cushion of a rumble seat for a 1932 Cadillac V-16 convertible coupe. Today, seats with "fox edging" have been replaced with molded polyfoam.

Don Taylor grew up in the auto trimming business: his father was a trimmer, Don is a trimmer, and his two sons were trained as trimmers as they grew up. As an expert author, Don created the *Automotive Upholstery Handbook* for California Bill's and six automotive books on engine rebuilding, restoration and paint and body work for HPBooks.

In 1979, with his brother Alan, Don created numerous van conversions. And they created several exciting vehicles, including Toyota's "Yamahauler" (later made into a Revell model), and the "Huskyhauler," the Husqvarna Motorcycle team's mobile garage. One interesting job was trimming a steam-powered taxicab with seating for the physically handicapped. It was done for the Federal Department of Transportation (DOT) through San Diego Steam Power Systems. The vehicle was displayed for a year at the Smithsonian Museum with a Taylor-Made sign.

Just prior to hanging up his trimmer's tools for a 14-year "retirement," Don's work on the interior of a 1932 Auburn Coupe won Best of Class, People's Choice, and Best of Show awards at the International Auburn/Cord/ Duesenberg Show.

Currently, in addition to book-authoring and illustrating, Don is temporarily "un-retired," working again with his brother's Alan Taylor Company restoration and custom trim facility in Escondido, California. Collectible cars in the shop as this was written included three Bugattis, three Rolls-Royces, a Bentley and a 1932 Cadillac V-16 convertible.

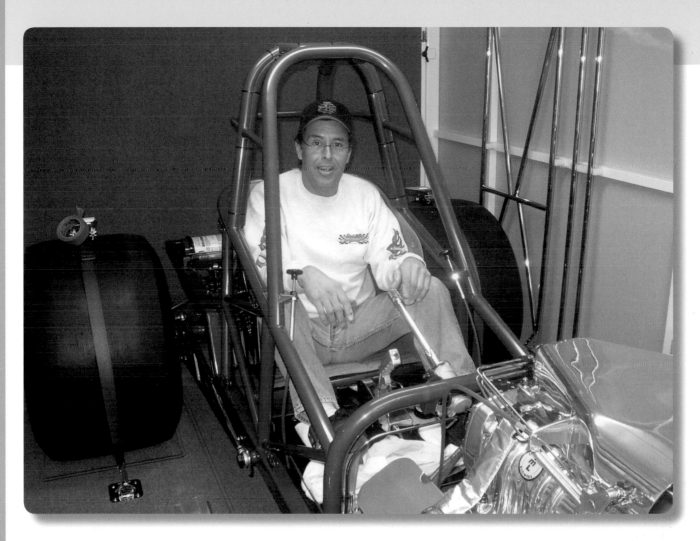

Ron Mangus started his stitching career in 1969 with his brother, Ernie Yanez, who provided special effort in getting Ron started right. He started Custom Auto Interiors in Bloomington, California in 1989.

Ron's name has become famous as the stitcher who creates fabulous interiors. A roadster with his interior won America's Most Beautiful Roadster at the 1992 Oakland Roadster. His work has received numerous Best Interior Awards at a variety of car shows. He has created interiors for: Boyd's Hot Rods, Tim Allen, Billy Gibbons of ZZ Top, Pete Chapouris of PC3G, Linda Vaughan (Miss Hurst), Thom Taylor, Bruce Meyers, Kenny Bernstein, Robby Gordon, Sammy Hagar, Michael Anthony, Cory McClenathan and James Brubaker of Universal Studios.

During the latter part of the 1990s the street rod and hot rod magazines have been filled with featured cars showing off his interiors.

How-to articles showing Mangus' techniques and expertise have appeared in *Hot Rod*, *Rod & Custom*, *Street Rodder*, *Truckin'* and *American Rodder*. His interiors continuously appear in cars featured in these and other street rodding and hot rod magazines. He also developed a line of auto trim essentials and sells these through his "Stitcher Stuff" catalog.

1 • Designing and Planning Your Interior

In the world of hot rod building the last people to lay hands (and sometimes eyes) on the car are the trimmers. If the owner has an infinite amount of time and money, the trimmers can sometimes give him or her what they're looking for—a show winner.

Ms. Owner and Mr. Builder will have planned down to the last 1/32 inch where everything mechanical will be located while depending on the ability of the trimmer to solve the problem of where the seats will go. Mr. or Ms. Owner could save a bundle of money, weeks of time, many phone calls and numerous headaches with just a little bit of preliminary planning of the interior while the car was in the building stage.

We've seen cars come into the shop where the brake pedal was beautifully located, but so far left of the driver's seat that it had to be operated with the driver's left foot. Foot-operated dimmer switches are very often located so the kick panel will cover them. Wires are almost always run through a location convenient to the person doing the wiring rather than with any thought of how they might be affected by the upholstery. You can bet that fingers will be pointing everywhere if a $1500 headliner has to come out to replace a 15-cent domelight wire! Planning the interior must be part of the whole planning process and should begin as soon as you have the body.

Interior Planning

Locating the Seats

Photo 1. The fun of rod-building is your ability to do anything you want. There really are no rules, so wherever you go with it, it's OK. Here, the designer named the car "Black Rose" and has embroidered a headliner panel with a beautiful black rose logo.

As this is a planning project, locating the seats—and all of the interior parts—should be started as early in the process as possible.

Whatever planning you can do to prevent having to relocate parts will be the best "thinking" time you've ever spent. Much of the following should be done with the body off the frame.

The oldest, and still best, method of locating the seats is simple trial and error. If you have a seat picked out, maybe the one that came with the car, or an aftermarket such as Recaro, Cerullo, Glide Engineering, or Tea's Design, stick it into the car and begin making adjustments. Leave the tracks and any other adjusting mechanisms connected. Get into the car, sit down and take a look around. How much headroom do you have? Where is your left elbow in relation to the door? Is your body centered along the steering column? Do you have room to raise your knees without bumping into the steering wheel? If you plan on having a center console, is there enough room? How's the view out the windshield and side windows?

Now, we must complicate everything. Consider where your headliner will be. It could be anywhere from 1 to 3 inches below the shell. Next comes carpeting and insulation, usually a combined thickness of over 1 inch. Together, these can eat up as little as 2 inches of headroom but sometimes upwards of 5 inches. By adding strips of plywood under the base of your seat and gluing squares of cardboard to the roof with contact spray adhesive, you can get an almost exact idea of where your seat will be located in relation to the headliner and carpet.

If you find yourself having to slide down onto your tailbone to get enough headroom then something must be done about the seat. In the body of the book we tell you just how to do that.

There are several tricks you'll learn on how to drop the seat to give added headroom. (You can get an inch just by raising the front a bit and adjusting the back

to compensate.) And, if an inch or two is not enough, then we'll talk about fabricating new frames.

Finally, you'll learn how to build a seat from plywood and polyfoam for that complete custom fit.

If it looks like you'll be building a plywood and polyfoam seat, get a 5/8- or 3/4 inch piece of plywood and about 3 inches of polyfoam and rig up a trial seat. By blocking up here and there you'll get a good idea of where your body's going to eventually come to rest.

The final location of the seat should put you in a position where you have at least 2 inches of headroom; you can operate all the controls comfortably; the center of the steering wheel aligns with the middle of your chest; and your left elbow is about 9 inches below the top edge of the door panel. That 9 inches is an arbitrary, but standard, location. Consider it a "starting" location—especially if you're a little shorter or taller than average. When you've finished reading the chapter on seat building you'll know how to make adjustments beyond what we've described here.

Locating Controls

Clutch, Brake and Dimmer Switch

As upholsterers, we're not about to begin a discussion on mechanics or engineering of your clutch and brake pedals. We can, however, make a few suggestions and reminders to help you locate these two vital parts and still have a comfortable ride.

The relationship between the seat and steering wheel has a lot to do with how accessible the clutch and brake pedals are to your feet. If you're sitting too close to the steering wheel, you may bump your knee against it when you lift your foot to actuate one of the

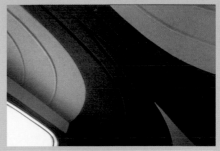

Photos 2-4. Headliner designs become more and more involved as imaginations search further and further for originality.

Photos 5-7. The stock door handle on this Willys coupe fell right under the armrest. It needed to be lowered about 2 inches. The final solution: put a Volkswagen door pull in the center of the pleated insert.

Photo 8. Speaker wires from this amplifier run too close to the emergency brake (arrow). A screw-down plate covers the raw edges of the carpet around the base of the brake lever. Screws for this plate would penetrate the speaker wires if this loom were not rerouted. Even with no screw problems, the wires are rubbing against the brake—a sure bet for a future short.

Photos 9 & 10. Sometimes it's impossible to arrange things to suit the upholsterer. Here, the frame and rollbars of this racing roadster present problems the trimmer must solve. Ron's team did a good job of solving them.

pedals. So now the depth of the seat back and the distance the seat can travel on its tracks (if there are any) must be considered.

Again, in the seat-building section we discuss how to expand or reduce seat-back thickness to gain added leg room. If seat adjustment is not going to give you the needed leg room, consider changing the steering-wheel or steering-column angle.

When locating the clutch pedal, consider what your kick panel design will be. Often, a rod builder will expect to locate one or more sound-system speakers here. If the speaker has a lot of depth from cone to magnet, then the kick panel will have to protrude past the front-door pillar. This could interfere with clutch travel. If you then try to add a manual dimmer switch (the foot-operated style) you'll be in all kinds of trouble.

So, with seat in place (this will give a good idea of what you'll be doing with your quarter panels), locate the clutch, brake, dimmer switch and speakers. Then you won't have to worry about jury-rigging some kind of solution later

Emergency Brake

Here's another one of those things you can really mess up. "Boy, look how nice the emergency brake will fit right here on the tranny!" Yes, it will fit just fine—until your wife gets in the car and moves the seat forward. Now the brake is useless! Unless the emergency brake will be located within a console, be sure the seat placement will not interfere with its use. This may mean setting the seat up on the frame of the car (without the body) and making sure there's plenty of travel room for the brake. If you fail to do this, your only solution may be to cut a corner out of the seat!

Door Handles

Door handle (and window crank) placement is a direct extension of door panel design. Some builders will want the door handle incorporated into the armrest. Others will want that beautiful aluminum billet handle to be completely visible. There are those who may elect to have a button in the console. These decisions are all yours. What matters now is that you make them. It's always a tragedy to build a door panel only to find the window crank hits the armrest.

This is a touchy situation at this early stage of rod development. It presupposes you have a design in mind that's completely finalized. Most often, this is not the case. Nevertheless, you need to be aware that this decision (door handle and window crank placement) must be made before you begin assembling the door panel. Because it is a relatively easy project to relocate a door handle, this project can be left to the last minute—even after the door panel is well under way.

The window crank is not an easy fix. Maybe that's why most rod builders install power windows! Locating a button is much easier than relocating a mechanical window mechanism. Be alert to these two important aspects of interior planning.

Wiring

Unlike assembly-line manufact-ured cars that employ snap-in trim finishing, custom car builders cement almost all of the interior parts to the car. On the family Ford or Toyota you can pop the headliner out in about 30 minutes, then install it in another 20. On a one-piece leather headliner in a '39 coupe, it's there to stay. If it must come out, then putting it back is the same as making a whole new headliner. This works the same with carpeting and about 1/3 of the many panels that make up a custom interior. Therefore, accessing the car's electrical wiring could be a very expensive project unless a little forethought is employed.

Secondly, wiring must be routed through places you know will be safe. We've run into situations where a wiring loom passes right under the future location of a seat track. Too often, while drilling holes for panel attachment, the trimmer drills right into a bundle of wires. If you plan your interior right along with the rest of your planning, these problems can be avoided.

Try to run your wiring where you will be able to access it without ripping out interior parts. As in the headliner problem described above, install a plastic or copper tube for the domelight wire to travel through. Then, if it ever needs to be removed, you can simply pull it out and feed another in.

If your car has a driveshaft tunnel, it's easy to make a false side on the tunnel, out of chipboard, through which wiring can be run. The carpet can then be cemented down, yet the wire loom is not sealed in for life. It will take imagination and early planning to assure yourself that future repairs will be as painless as possible.

Locating Peripherals

Sound System

The largest peripheral in a street rod is the sound system; locating all of its very large parts can challenge the best planner. Often, the way the interior is designed and planned can enhance the system rather than cause an upholstery nightmare. Note the solution to the speakers behind the seats in the truck featured on page 95, photo 20. By designing the seats with a novel "megaphone," sound is passed out

Photo 11. In the panel section of the book, we'll show you how to make this raised type of design. It works really neat!

Photo 12. We added this illustration just because Don thought the way the instrument panel was blended into the modesty panel was one of the best he'd seen. What a very clean appearance it gives.

Photos 13 & 14. Here's a roadster that might be considered the ultimate in "high-tech" interior appearance. This is, indeed, the "hard" look.

through the sides of the seats!

Select your components early on. Their size will most often determine their location. Standard practice usually indicates the amplifier will reside under a seat—unless you decide the seat must sit directly on the floor to increase headroom. So, here you are again, mocking up your interior long before the body has been fastened to the frame. You just can't go wrong by doing this. Don't simply measure and say, "Yeah, that's good."

With your measuring tape you find there are 3 inches of clear space under the passenger's seat and the amplifier you want is 2-1/2 inches tall. Excellent. Buy the amp now and stick it under seat. Then plunk your heaviest friend into the seat and see what kind of clearance you have. Your friend "Big Ed" doesn't "bottom out" on the top of the amp and everything's just fine. Suppose, however, you didn't buy the amp now but waited until you were ready for it. Guess what? It went out of production last month and its replacement unit is 3-1/2 inches tall. Now "Big Ed" is going to have a "Big Amp" poking him in the bottom every time he rides with you.

Speaker placement can be just about anywhere. We suggest that you don't place them in the doors. This is not to do with upholstery but because of the abuse they take each time the door closes. The farther the speaker is from the hinge-point of the door, the greater abuse it suffers each time the door is closed. Just a free piece of advice.

On page 58, photo 11, note the location of the speakers in the Willys roof and how it was finished off on page 77. This was an interesting solution but a bit dangerous. Above, we discussed wiring under the headliner and the possibility of having to replace it. What happens if one of these speakers blows? Replacing it will be a major problem.

If the speakers you want to use are too deep to be incorporated into a side or quarter panel, don't give up. Why not think about creating a panel design where the speaker is the focal point of that design? Later in the book you'll learn how to make all kinds of curved surfaces on flat panels. Let the speaker stick out. Build the panel up around it, making it appear as a meteor falling with flame trails behind.

Planning should not make you give up something you want. It lets you have what you want without having to pay the price of tearing something apart later on.

Lighting

The lighting can be as simple as determining where you'll use a domelight or courtesy light, to as complicated as installing neon accent lights or fiber optics. In the case of the latter, extensive planning is called for.

Aftermarket dome and courtesy lights are so many and varied that very little planning or thought need be given to them. However, you must again consider the wiring and accessibility problems. Some halogen courtesy lights get smoking hot. Avoid placing them in the rear quarter panels too close to the seat. Don did this once and melted the vinyl seat facing. Not good.

This holds true also for accent lights behind valances that are focused onto the headliner. Be sure your accent lights are very low wattage and remember that cloth will scorch at the same temperature that vinyl will start to melt.

If you plan to use neon or fiber optics in your car, we suggest you employ an expert in this field as part of your planning process. Sometimes these folks are hard to find, but their talent will be repaid many times over in problems not encountered. Your best and least expensive help will come from factory reps.

Select and purchase the products you wish to use. Then, look for that 800 number on the package where the company sends you for technical help. Call and ask where the nearest rep is located. He or she will usually come out for free and help you with your setup.

Conclusion

Too often, the upholsterer is left to solve problems that should never have occurred. If you're the upholsterer you can't help but agree with this statement. If you're the car designer you can save the upholsterer a lot of time (and your money) by planning the interior while you're planning the mechanical and electrical. This way, the future car will function as a whole. If you leave everything to the upholsterer, then some of the interior will quickly be recognized as an afterthought.

Designing the Interior

Ron says, "The most important part of rod design is to maintain a basic, overall theme throughout the car." This means settling on an overall theme—as we describe in the next paragraph—then keep everything working together toward that concept. Overall, simply avoid mixing styles. Don't wear tennis shorts with your dinner jacket. Simple.

Themes have different names among different rodding groups, but most will recognize such names as "retro," "period," or "nostalgia" as design concepts of the '40s and '50s. These cars imitate the styling concepts that were popular in those years.

Interiors in these cars were generally made of leather or vinyl. Little, if any fabrics were used. Of the many vinyls, Uniroyal's Naugahyde brand has become synonymous with the name vinyl. Naugahyde and other vinyl interiors were affectionately called tuck-and-roll or pleated-and-rolled interiors. This comes from the cotton, hand-filled pleats (Polyfoam has not been around forever, you know.) and the big rolled front edge of the seat—sometimes called a French roll.

On the other side of the rodding community are the "high-tech" or "techno" rods. These cars incorporate every body style imaginable with every modern convenience the aftermarket can think up. Interiors in these cars are referred to as the "hard" look or "soft" look. These "looks" will incorporate leather, vinyl, tweed and velours (although velours seem to be losing some popularity).

The "soft" look can be defined as "that which is wrinkled." However, the wrinkles must be in the right places. Unintended wrinkles still represent poor craftsmanship. The soft look tries to represent, within the car, the same look your leather sofa represents within your living room.

The "hard" look is a bit of a misnomer. The materials are still soft and full, but the design is sculpted and chiseled. These are the grooves, panel-on-panel, and raised surfaces that all work together to make the interior of your car look as if it might have been chiseled from a solid block.

Now we see, more and more, these two looks being combined together. Look at the '49 Mercury in photos 15-17. Here the two styles work together to produce an awesomely beautiful interior.

Working up a Design

The way most people design their interiors is to go to dozens of rod meets, runs and shows. There they see every conceivable interior, good, bad and ugly. They take hundreds of pictures, which they file away to look at when it comes time to work up their own design. Usually the concept comes first.

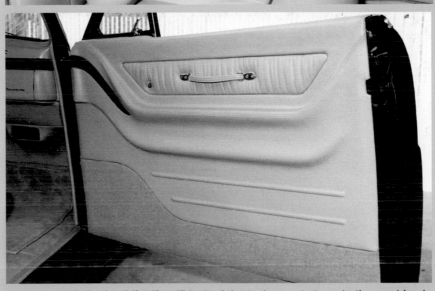

Photos 15-17. Contrast the "hard" look of the techno-rod above to the combined "hard" and "soft" look combo in the '49 Mercury. The seats look as if they could be used in your living room. Note how the design of the interior sweeps and swirls, flowing the console into the dash and then out into door panels. This is a truly gorgeous interior.

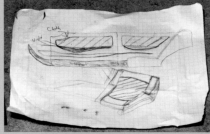

Photo 18. This couple, planning their new interior, brought along a color sample of their paint scheme. Ron has taken them out into the sunlight to look at sample books. Never make your fabric color selection under fluorescent lights. There are dramatic color differences between what you see under artificial light and natural light. Mercury-vapor lamps in some parking lots give totally different colors to some materials and colors.

Photos 19 & 20. One of our project cars in this book is a '57 Ford coupe. Here is the original sketch the owner brought to the shop and the resulting panels.

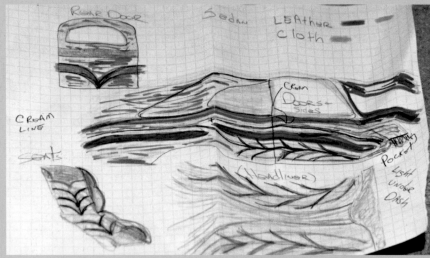

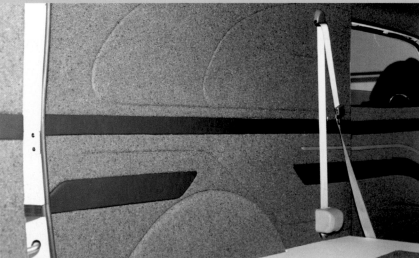

Photos 21 & 22. Another customer sketch and the results. You can see some of the changes incorporated between the idea and the execution. Changes can be made anywhere along the line so long as you're happy deviating from your original design.

"Boy, my next car's going to be a retro—complete with a flathead engine and wide whites." Right there, the design starts to lock in. "I'm selling this !@#$ tomorrow and building something with air conditioning, leg room and a sound system I can hear!" Well, you've got a pretty good idea of what she wants and consequently, what the basics of her interior will be.

Now it comes down to what features you want and what you can afford. Stand by for "sticker shock" when you look at the price of leather. Leather still requires a great deal of hand work in the manufacture. Then, a lot of that very expensive cowskin winds up on the cutting-room floor. Remember: the cow is not square. Therefore, neither is its hide. However, the buyer is charged for every square inch of that hide. This includes the unusable portions of the neck, leg and tail area. Then, there are always nicks, cuts and abrasions from fights, barbed wire, cactus and sagebrush. These must be worked around, taking lots of hourly shop time and wasting very expensive leather. So, right off, know that leather is king and you'll pay a king's ransom for it.

Vinyl was invented to replace leather. The very first "imitation" leather was little more than what was otherwise called oilcloth. A thin, plasticized petroleum product was bonded to a cloth back and stamped with a leather-like grain. This was given the name leatherette and hailed as the greatest technical advance in man's creature comforts since sliced bread. Unfortunately it tended to self-destruct within months. In those days parents left children in the car unattended. To amuse him or herself, the child sat and picked the plastic film off the cloth, trying for ever larger unbroken pieces.

In the '50s vinyl and polymers were invented and "artificial leather" became a reality. Ultraviolet light could still do what an unattended child once did but that too was overcome in the '60s with increased UV protection. Today, the vinyl industry can produce a material that the untrained eye and hand cannot distinguish from leather. A recent brand name that has an excellent "finger" (how it feels and works) is a vinyl called Mellowhide. If it is not available in your area, call one of the fabric houses in the suppliers list.

With both vinyl and leather there is a seemingly infinite variety of colors to choose from. And if you can't find the exact shade you need, both can now be dyed to match any color your mind can imagine. We discuss this later in the book beginning on page 184.

Because of this great variety of color, you can now match vinyl or leather with the same color and tone of tweed. The combination of these two materials represents about 95 percent of the techno or high-tech look interiors. Again, suppliers for these products can be found in the suppliers list if not in your own area.

Having decided the theme of your car, attended dozens of meets and rallies, viewed and photographed dozens of interiors, it's time then, for you to get out the kids' crayons or colored pencils and go to work. You don't have to be a great artist or even a good artist. Just start sketching out ideas you've begun to think of as what you'd like to have in your car. Later, we'll show you how to turn those sketches into reality. Meanwhile, look at photos 19-22, page 12, to see the two sketches and the interiors they became.

Summary

The most important part of designing an interior is to maintain some type of theme that relates to a period or style. You'll want your nostalgia rod to have plenty of nostalgia and look like it was built "way back when." Your high performance, luxo-cruiser, techno rod should give that sculpted look saying, "here's real high-tech styling!"

Photo 23. This '49 Ford "Retro-Rod" looks as if it just rolled out of a '50s trim shop. Ron is particularly proud of this car. It was commissioned by Billy Gibbons of the ZZ Top band.

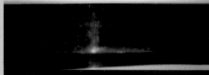

Photo 24. This owner incorporates his initial into the design.

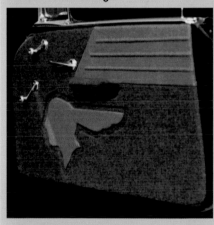

Photos 25 & 26. This builder wants to show off his Pontiac logo...or a Chevy "Bowtie."

2 • Pattern Making

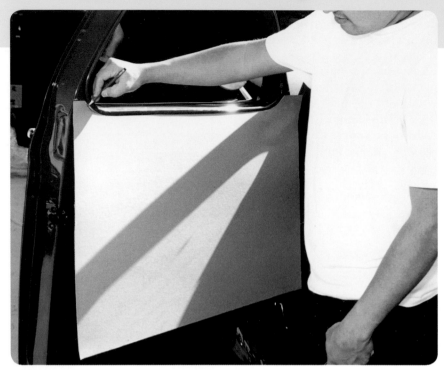

Photo 1. Juanito, the youngest member of the crew, will make a door-panel pattern for our '41 Willys coupe. He begins with a large piece of chipboard, temporarily cemented to the door. This keeps it in place while he marks some of the contours around the garnish molding.

Photos 2 & 3. A little more cement will hold the chipboard tightly to the door. When doing this, allow the cement to dry well before bringing the two pieces into firm contact. If the cement is wet when you "contact" the two pieces and allow them to dry together, when you peel the chipboard off, most of it will stay on the door. Go light with the cement and let it dry well before "contacting" the two.

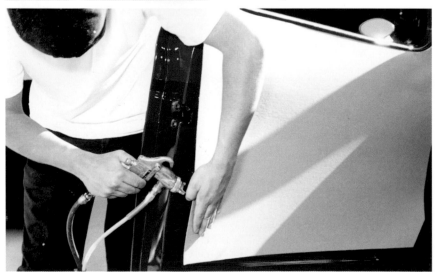

It's common practice in the street rod and custom car fabrication business to bring the car to the trim shop as a hollow shell. All panels, trim, covering, seats, windshield and backlite are gone—or never existed—in the case of a car built from scratch. You, the trimmer, are expected to make everything that will go into the car as trim or upholstery.

As a trimmer of family cars or a hobbyist, you're accustomed to having something to wrap a cover around. Now you have to make that "something" first. In the past, if you had to replace a door panel or kick panel, you either had a broken one to work from or a left panel to copy over to a right panel. Here you have no panel at all.

To make anything from "scratch," such as a door panel, a heel pad, luggage panel or any other, you must first make a pattern of the area you wish to panel. This chapter shows you the simple steps to do this.

We're going to learn how to make a pattern for a panel that fills an open space. This includes door panels, kick panels, quarter panels and any panel that will be upholstered before it is installed. We can think of several panels that are covered after being installed, but we'll get to those later. The most fundamental panel made in the trim shop is the door panel. So let's begin our description there.

Making a Pattern for a Door Panel

Our first demonstration will be to make a pattern of the driver's door panel on a really nice '41 Willys coupe. Our guide for this demonstration is Juanito, who specializes in making patterns for the shop. Juanito begins by selecting a full piece of chipboard and squeezing one edge of it under the garnish molding. He then outlines the edge of the garnish molding with a pencil line and cuts away the selvage under the molding. This cut is fairly rough at this point because he knows he must go back and refine it later. With the chipboard well located, Juanito cements it in place. Because this is a temporary hold, he only uses a small amount of adhesive.

When the chipboard is secure, Juanito begins to locate areas that will be closely defined. Our illustration shows him beginning by marking out an area around the door latch. Next, he moves up to the garnish molding where he will refine his line. The following steps are the most important in pattern making, so follow closely.

Juanito cuts off a scrap of chipboard with a good straight line. He applies a full measure of adhesive to both the pattern-piece and the scrap. He then presses the straight edge of the scrap to the straight edge of the garnish molding and presses the scrap home. Now he has an exact edge which will eventually be transferred to a piece of panelboard for the finished door panel.

This is the lesson to take away in this chapter. To make a pattern for any type of panel, you begin by securing a large piece of chipboard to the area. You then add scraps of chipboard around the edges until you have the exact shape of the panel. These are the basics of all pattern making. Now, let's return to Juanito and see how he finishes this pattern.

To get the basic line of the curve in the rear corner of the garnish, Juanito "guestimates" where the line is and pencils it in. He cuts away the excess and tries fitting it. He will trim away the excess two or three times before

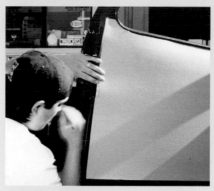

Photo 4. Juanito has now marked out the cut for the door latch. Here is a good demonstration of the ease of cutting and fitting in this location. With chipboard, if you cut away too much, simply cement a new piece in place and cut again. If you were using panelboard (wood or Masonite) you would have ruined the whole piece.

Photo 5. Juanito's initial cut around the garnish was rough. Now he refines it with a scrap pressed tightly to the bottom edge of the molding. This is cemented in place.

Photo 6. Here we have a close-up of "guestimating" the contour of the molding below the piece of chipboard. Juanito will cut and fit until his piece is perfect. Then, as before, he'll cement it in place.

Photo 7. The same piece must also fit the front edge of the door.

Photo 8. Everything is fitted and cemented tight. We now have a perfect fit around the garnish molding.

Photo 9. Juanito turns his attention to the bottom of the panel. He has cemented a second piece in place, making sure the bottom of the pattern is in perfect alignment with the bottom edge of the door. Notice the approximate 2 inches of overhang at the front edge of the door and how Juanito handles this in the next photographs.

Photo 10. Another straight piece of scrap edges the front of the door. Juanito will then trim away the chipboard beneath the front edge. This gives him plenty of cementable surface and contributes to the strength of the pattern.

Photo 11. The panel has been completely edged. Juanito checks once more for fit.

Photo 12. Assured that his fit is perfect, Juanito lays the pattern on a piece of 1/8 inch panelboard, marks around the pattern and cuts out the panel. By flipping the pattern over, he can cut a panel for the passenger's door. The pattern will be marked as a '41 Willys door panel pattern and saved for future use, should another Willys come into the shop.

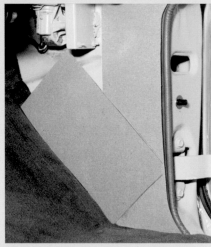

Photo 13. We're off and running on the creation of a '57 Ford kick panel. The door panel and quarter panels have been made using the technique described for the Willys. Here, we have established a front edge around the windlace and started building the pattern by laying a piece along the carpet edge. Had the carpet not been installed, we would have had to make allowance for it—otherwise the finished panel would have been too large.

Photo 14. Here the completed panel pattern is laid out for marking and cutting. Six pieces of chipboard were used to make this pattern.

he considers it ready. He then cements it in place.

He continues in this fashion all the way around the molding. If this curve was less tight, perhaps a 10 inch radius, he could cement small, straight strips around the edge. With such a tight radius, however, straight strips would present too many angles. To finish the top of the panel Juanito repeats the above process at the other end of the garnish.

In photo 9 we see him move to the bottom of the panel. He has glued another piece in place and is checking to see how it fits along the bottom. With careful work, the edge of the chipboard will align with the bottom of the door. Juanito works carefully and gets a good alignment. On observation, however, he sees that the chipboard does not reach to the jamb edge of the door.

To make the pattern the correct size and shape in this area, Juanito again cuts scraps of chipboard and cements them to the main body of the pattern. He makes sure the edge of the chipboard aligns with the edge of the door. Again, he follows the same process for the front edge of the door, photo 10.

Let's review the basics once more. Begin with a large piece of chipboard that is somewhat smaller than the area you're going to pattern. Then, cement small scraps around the edge, aligning the scrap edge with the edge of the piece you're patterning. The result will be an exact duplicate of the area.

To see how the door panel turned out, look at photo 42 on page 30. Could it be any more perfect?

Making a Pattern for a Kick Panel

A kick panel is a lot like a door panel—most of it is straight angles with one or two curves. Our quick demonstration is a passenger's side kick panel for a '57 Ford coupe. The first step was to make a piece that fits around the windlace. Again, Juanito made this pattern.

You'll notice in the photograph that he fit the curves by guessing their shape and trimming away the excess. If he were less skillful he would have cemented a straight piece along the edge of the windlace, then fit the curved areas with scrap. Even in custom shops, however, speed is important and craftspeople are hired for their abilities to do the job quickly.

The forward edge of the kick panel is defined by cementing a rectangular scrap to the piece that defines the windlace edge. There are no further curves, so Juanito can simply cement straight pieces of scrap around the perimeter of the panel to reach the desired shape. As before, the pattern is transferred to a piece of panelboard and a new kick panel is produced.

Custom Panel Patterns

Work on our '41 Willys is going to be featured a lot in this book. In fact, we'll be following it through to completion. The sound system has been installed behind the seats and mounted into a big sheet of 1/2 inch plywood. The customer wants a single panel to cover the area. Let's watch Juanito work.

He begins with a single sheet of chipboard and roughs out a hole for the speaker and CD player. Notice how he makes no attempt to make the edges fit around these parts. He'll come back to that later. By adding another sheet of chipboard, he gets all the way across the back of the car.

In the photos you can see he begins to glue scraps around the cutouts to fit snugly around the components. Nothing looks neat or finished. That's not important.

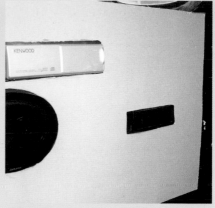

Photo 15. If it fit any better…The panel board Ron is using here was bought at a "fire sale." It is interior mahogany panelboard with a vinyl overlay. It was probably used in a kitchen or bath application originally. It works great for all kinds of auto applications.

Photo 16. In the back of our Willys, the customer installed a big stereo system with all of its components. We must make one large panel to cover the whole back of the car. Juanito, as before, begins with a full sheet of chipboard. Here, he's cutting out for the speaker. It will be a rough cut now and refined later.

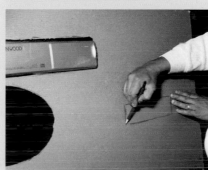

Photo 17. We come in for a close-up here to see Juanito marking his next cuts. You also get a chance to see how rough the cuts really are. As mentioned, they will be refined later.

Photo 18. Here's the finished cut around this component.

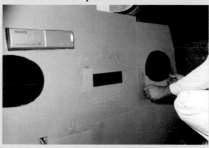

Photo 19. Juanito has finished getting the width of the panel. It has taken about 12 sheets of chipboard. Now, he begins smoothing the edges around the components. We call this refining the pattern.

Photo 20. Here's the fully refined pattern. Notice the many pieces all work together to give a finished product. It looks terrible but it fits perfectly.

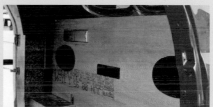

Photo 21. A perfect fit creates a perfect panel. Not only are all of the cuts around the components accurate but note the cuts around the battery box and transmission tunnel. They, too, are within the most discriminating tolerances. Turn to page 50, the bottom photo, to see how it looks upholstered.

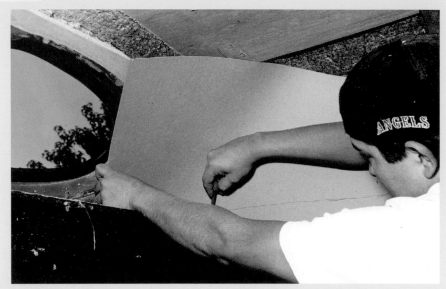

Photo 22. Juanito must now make a compound curved pattern to fit in this quarter between the rear window and the door jam. This will become part of the base for a one-piece headliner—a trick you'll also learn in the coming chapters. He begins, as before, with some rough-out markings.

Photos 23 & 24. Juanito makes a pattern for a pattern. He has elected to use a smaller piece of chipboard to get the contour of the rear-window edge.

What is important, is everything fits snugly and all curves are smooth. In the final photograph you can see the finished panel. It fit the first time. No trimming was necessary. Why? Because all the trial-and-error was in the pattern making, not in the finished product.

Compound Curved Panels

One of the great advantages of this build-up style of pattern making is that you can make one flat piece fit into a compound curve. Let's see how Juanito handles this problem in the headliner area of the Willys.

The trimmer will need a panel to fit in the area between the rear window and the door jamb. This panel will be secured with glue and staples. Later, it will be covered with foam and become part of the headliner. It must, therefore, be a smooth piece with no breaks or cracks.

As for any other panel, Juanito begins with a large, main piece to build on. He rough-trims around the rear window. This is followed by cutting a half-moon shape in the area where the tightest radius is found. If you want to jump ahead to page 19 you can see how this area is filled in.

When the main body piece is secured, Juanito begins to add pieces as before. This time, however, they create a compound curve rather than a single flat or curved surface. When everything is satisfactory, Juanito pulls out the pattern, transfers it to "waterboard" (waterproof panelboard). Because it will become part of the underlayment for the headliner, Juanito glues and staples it into place.

If you've ever tried to do this kind of pattern making with a piece of vinyl, holding it in place and cutting out the shape, you're going to love this simple process!

Making Patterns from Old Upholstery

Although this subject was well covered in the *Automotive Upholstery Handbook*, I think a brief review is in order. Often, as trimmers, we find it easier to use the old cover for a pattern than to try and fit to the old seat or panel. The important thing, however, is that we do not incorporate into the new cover any previous mistakes or flaws from the old.

To use an old cover for a pattern, we begin by naming each piece (such as, bottom pleat, top pleat, front facing, back facing) and all the others. As you recall, we then mark each panel in chalk, pencil or pen with the initials of its piece such as BP, TP, FF, BF. This way you can easily remember which piece is which.

With a razor blade, scissors or sharp knife, cut away each piece by splitting the seam. Never trim away the selvage edge! This is where the "witness marks" are located and you'll need these to realign each piece. In fact, after you've carefully split the seam and separated the pieces, go back and re-establish each of the witness marks. We do this by cutting larger notches over the existing ones, or just noting where the notch is with a chalk mark.

Now the pieces you have cut out can be used as patterns. In photographs 30 and 31 you'll see Pete use big cylinder-shaped pieces of steel to hold his patterns in place. These or lead weights, masking tape, staples, clamps or anything you can think of may be used to hold the pattern in place. After marking around the pattern, remember to locate the witness marks. Be sure you've allowed enough for a selvage (sewing) edge. Sometimes the selvage edge will fold under itself. This must be straightened to make a correct edge.

After cutting out the new piece there are still a couple of

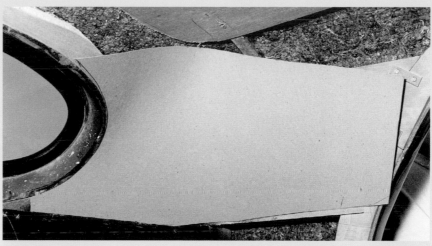

Photo 25. The shape of the rear window has been well defined and added to the main pattern piece.

Photo 26. Note the top of the pattern and compare it to the previous photo. The top has been cut out to accommodate the contour of the roof. In addition, three more pieces of chipboard have been added. To get the shape of the door, Juanito will mark the chipboard from the backside. The top panel you see in this and the previous photos began life as a pattern. It was made just like our earlier demonstration of the door panel.

Photo 27. The piece of black material that Juanito is transferring the pattern to is waterproof panelboard. In the shop we simply refer to it as "waterboard." It's used where little stress is met. In the early days (1930s to '50s) it was used for all paneling—both OEM and aftermarket. Its greatest advantage at that time was its ability to accept being sewn. Its disadvantage was that it was really not very waterproof. After a number of exposures to the wet, it would warp—quite badly. Today, we still sew to it, but our cements are so good we seldom need to.

Photo 28. Here's our waterboard panel glued and stapled into place. It will make a great back-up for our headliner. When we get to the headliner chapter you'll see the interesting way we "fill in the blanks."

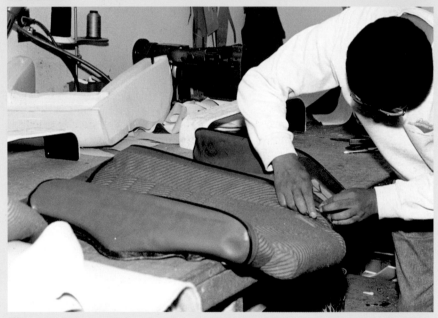

Photo 29. Although the new seat cover will look nothing like this factory cover, Pete can use it for part of his pattern. Using a razor blade, he begins to remove the vinyl facings from the fabric centers. Before he's finished, the cover will be in all of its component parts, ready to be used as patterns.

Photo 30. This pattern piece is almost beyond use. It's the center of a motorcycle seat. Although nearly destroyed, there's enough for Pete to use for his pattern. It saves a lot of time when you can do this. In any shop, time equals money.

things you must do to ensure a good fit. Lay the new piece onto the seat or panel in the area from which it originated. If it's a side facing, lay it over the side facing area. Now check to be sure it fits correctly in this area. You may have to trim a little or, if you didn't quite get the original piece flat enough, you may find your piece too small. If you sewed it this way you'll have a sloppy fit. So, if the new piece is too small, or in some way does not fit perfectly, make a new piece.

Another area of fitting will be to see if both sides of the new piece are the same where applicable. In our last two photographs, Pete is working on a motorcycle seat. Both sides of the seat must be the same. Therefore, each piece that Pete cuts out must be folded in half to be sure each side has the same shape. If it doesn't, a little must be trimmed from each side to make an accurate match. We try never to cut more than 3/8 inch from each side to make this match. If you find you need to cut more than 1/2 inch, consider making another piece that will have a more accurate fit prior to trimming. If both sides of the panel are the same, you'll have a fine fitting cover when everything is sewn together.

Summary

There's nothing more intimidating than a totally empty shell of a car for which the owner expects an award-winning interior—if you have no idea of where to start. You must start with making patterns for the work you'll do. It's so much cheaper and easier to use chipboard than trying to cut a wood or Masonite panel to fit into that little space. By starting with a large piece of chipboard in the center (or aligned with an edge) then cementing smaller pieces to it that align with all the other edges, you have a pattern that is guaranteed to fit. You can make patterns for door panels, kick panels, luggage panels and quarter panels. You can make patterns for places where panels would not normally be. You can even make patterns for compound curves. We'll demonstrate this technique further when we begin building modesty panels.

In the coming chapters you'll see how we make patterns for headliners, convertible tops, making seats from scratch and all kinds of other interesting tricks to make fitting easy and accurate.

Don't forget that you can make patterns from old covers. Just be sure you work for total accuracy by noting where your witness marks are. Make sure you use a correct seam allowance, and that the finished piece properly fits the area it will cover.

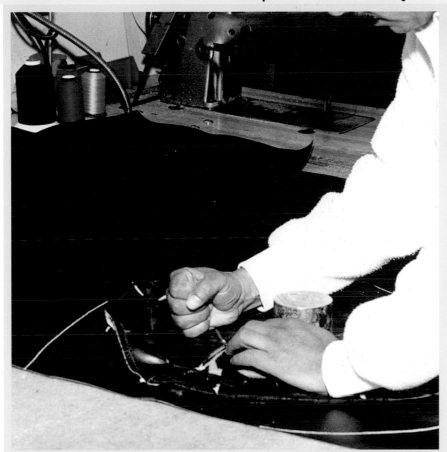

Photo 31. Here's a neat trick. To transfer a mark from a pattern piece to a body piece, make a heavy chalk mark on the back of the pattern. Then, with your hand (here a fist) slap down hard on the pattern. The chalk line on the bottom of the pattern will transfer to the body piece. Pete did this to locate some of the seam lines.

Ford 1932 roadster custom bucket seats with hard-look door panels. Leather, of course!

3 • Fabricating Armrests

Upon first glance you might think this chapter is a bit out of place and that building door and quarter panels should come first. Logically, that should work. You make the door panel, then the armrest and attach it to the panel. When we deal with the world of custom trim, however, the above is not always the way it works. Often, the armrest is an integral part of the door-panel design. Sometimes it's even the basis of the design. Given this importance, we feel it best to demonstrate how the armrest is made. Then in the next chapter, while we explain the fabrication of the door panel, we can include how the armrest is incorporated into the design. In custom upholstery the design concept is almost always the main consideration. That's why it's so exciting.

Designing the Armrest

As we suggested earlier, the customer may have a design concept when he or she comes to the shop. Often it will be more than a concept—it could be a complete treatment. Short of the complete treatment, as the trimmer, you can help the customer with some of the design ideas. The first is one of practicality.

The standard location for an armrest is about 9 inches below the window garnish and about 1/3 the length of the panel forward of the jam-edge of the door. This, of course, is based on "average" size people and a "standard" car. Given a customer who is considerably shorter or taller than average or a car whose door looks like it was lifted from a '30 Bugatti limousine, you'll need to make adjustments for the armrest

Photo 1. Usually, we show the finished product at the end. This time we want you to know what the finished product will look like before you start working on it. This will help you understand where we're going.

Photo 2. From the customer's design, George Torres has developed a pattern for the base of the armrest frame. He stapled two pieces of panel board together so he can stack-cut both bases at the same time. The armrests he's making are for the rear quarter panels. The front door panels are quite different in shape. If all four armrests were the same, George would cut all four at the same time.

location.Usually, this is done by sitting the customer in the car on something representing the seat but well located in respect to where the finished seat will be—then locating the armrest directly beneath his or her left elbow. If husband and wife or owner and significant other are far different in size, be sure to "average" the location so both will be comfortable.

The second consideration must be the location of the inside door handle. You might wish to incorporate the door handle into the armrest. Access can be from the top or bottom. Usually, if access is from the bottom, the trimmer will try to design the armrest so the door handle is not visible. This is almost impossible when the door handle is accessible from the top. Remember, however, as we discussed earlier in the first chapter, if you don't want the door handle in the armrest you can relocate it.

Because you're building this armrest from scratch, other than location restrictions, any idea you or the customer wish to develop can be built from the following instructions. So, let your imagination run wild. Design something to make your car stand out from the rest. Look at all the pictures in this book for ideas you can incorporate. Look for ideas the fabric or color may suggest. Consider molding the armrest to continue the sweep of the instrument panel—or even the pattern in the seat back. You are limited only by what you can think. We'll make the rest easy by showing you how it's done.

When you have your design in mind, sketch it onto a piece of paper. If you have trouble drawing things, use graph paper. Graph paper is divided into grids of equal size where each piece of the grid can represent a certain dimension. Thus, if one square of the grid equals 1 inch, then a 35 × 29 inch door panel could be drawn 35 squares wide and 29 squares high. Now your drawing is the

Photo 3. At Ron's shop, they use a saber saw to do all the cutting. You can also use a band saw or jig saw. If you elect to use a saber saw, use a fine-tooth blade to eliminate as much splintering as possible.

Photo 4. George even sands both pieces at the same time to ensure they both have the same shape when they're finished.

Photo 5. Here's the result of what George has just done. By simply flipping one piece over, it's a mirror image for the other side. Be sure you mark each piece as right and left or passenger and driver. Failure to do this might result in making two identical armrests!

Photo 6. George now makes a pattern for the top piece. He fits it so there is about 1 inch of overhang on the base. This allows for chipboard and foam covering.

Photos 7 & 8. Again, George stack-cuts the plywood for the tops. Note the two screws holding the wood to the bench and the two pieces together. This is a quick clamping device and nothing's going to move around.

Photos 9 & 10. It's difficult to see in these photographs, but be sure to allow 1/4 inch between the top of the base and the top on which you rest your elbow, to allow for the 1/4 inch foam you'll be using. Glue and staple the two pieces together.

Photo 11. Notice the angle George is grinding into the top. This will allow for a good fit of the chipboard and give plenty of gluing surface.

Photos 12 & 13. Here are good photos of the finished armrest frames. The two areas of special interest are the bevel on the top pieces and the offset of 1/4 inch to allow for the foam covering over the top of the armrest.

Photo 14. George begins the process of shaping the armrest with chipboard. First he cements both the chipboard and the armrest frame.

Photos 15-18. Carefully align and center the chipboard over the armrest frame then press the edges into place. Finish by pressing the chipboard down onto the base so there is at least 1 inch of contact all the way around.

same proportional shape as the door panel.

Onto this outline you can draw the shape of your armrest (and any other design features you wish). Just count the squares and you'll know the size of your armrest. For example, if your armrest is 13 squares long and 5 squares high, the finished armrest will be 13 inches long by 5 inches tall. Suppose, however, you've decided two squares will equal 1 inch. Then 13 squares will equal 6-1/2 inches while five squares equal 2-1/2 inches. If this stuff got any easier you wouldn't need a book! Let's look now at how you'll build the armrest.

Building the Frame

Making the Base and Top

You'll always start with the base—just as you would start with the foundation of a house. At Ron's shop they use 1/8- or 5/32 inch plywood panelboard. Some shops use Masonite. If you decide to use Masonite, be sure to use the untempered variety.

Tempered Masonite is extremely strong. Its strength is its problem. It's very hard to get a staple through it. Anything but the very shortest staple bends—and you'll be using 1/2 inch-long staples in this project. From your design, either measure out the base shape onto the panelboard or onto a piece of chipboard.

Chipboard works nicely because you can cut it out, take it to the door and be sure it looks right. If you don't like the way it looks, throw it away and start over. You've only lost pennies and seconds. If you make a mistake on the panelboard you may lose dollars and minutes. For experimenting, we always use chipboard.

When you've established a good pattern for your base (or because it was very simple, you went right to the panelboard) mark it and stack-cut 2 pieces. Stack-cutting is cutting two or more pieces at one time. By so doing, you're assured both pieces are identical. Usually two or three staples will hold the work together while you cut it out. Sand the edges smooth. Sand just enough to get rid of any splinters and make a smooth contour with no bumps or lumps. If your car has rear armrests, make their bases at this time. Now we'll make the tops—where your arm actually rests.

Notice in the photographs the wooden top of the armrest is considerably shorter than the base and is made from 1/2 inch plywood. You can also use Medium Density Fiberboard (MDF) but it's a bit expensive. Never use plain particleboard. Particleboard will not hold up to the use an armrest will get. Fiberboard is a very different product and will take a great deal of abuse.

The shape of the top is very important to the finished shape of the armrest. Study the shape and location of the top as shown in photos 12 and 13 on page 24. This is the standard shape Ron makes for all his armrests. Notice the length is about 1 inch shorter than the top of the base. We use a standard of 3 inches as a minimum width (4 inches is about the widest you would want to make a large armrest top). The armrest you're looking at on page 26, photo 25, has a top about as long as the base. In many cases the base will be far longer than the top. This can be seen on the '41 Willys armrest at the bottom of this page. Notice, though, the shape is still the same: it flares into the base just as the demo does.

This flare is important. The only place you wouldn't flare the top into the base is a case where the front of the armrest molds into the dash. Then the front would be the same as the portion of the dash into which it blended.

As with the base, stack-cut the top of the armrest so you have

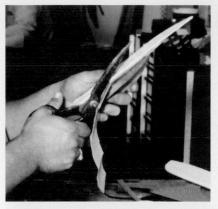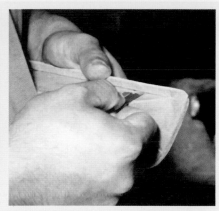

Photos 19 & 20. With scissors and razor blade, trim the excess chipboard.

Photo 21. Both layers of chipboard complete the finished shape of the armrest.

Photo 22. George uses the heel of his scissors to define the curve tightly around the bottom of the chipboard.

Photos 23 & 24. Let the chips fly! To smooth out the chipboard and flare it into the base and top, you must grind away excess chipboard. "Feather" the edges into the wood to make a smooth flowing design. Then, round all the edges. Carefully study the finished product to see how George makes the chipboard flow into the wood base by feathering the edges.

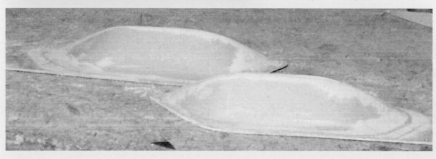

Photo 28. Good work, George! He got rid of those two wrinkles and is now rounding the edges of the foam. He again uses a sanding disk for this project.

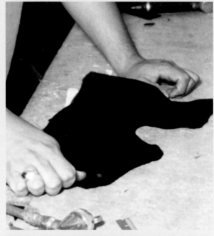

Photos 25 & 26. Cut out a piece of 1/4 inch closed-cell foam a bit bigger than the area it will cover. Don't forget to scuff up the foam surface. This removes the film created during the molding process and lets the cement get a good grip.

Photo 29. Leather is quite expensive. George goes through the scrap pile looking for a piece that will fit.

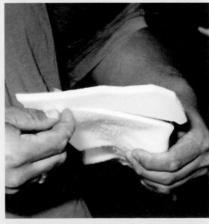

Photo 27. Trim away all excess foam. Note the two wrinkles George has formed in the base. He must get rid of these before the covering is finished.

Photo 30. By gluing one end of the leather to the bench, he can get a good pull across the length of the armrest. In so doing, the leather wraps tightly and smoothly around the armrest.

two identical (but mirror-imaged) pieces. Cutting two or more pieces at a time is a great timesaver—besides, it assures you that both sides will be identical. The next step is to glue and fasten the top to the base.

Gluing the Pieces

Gluing these two pieces together is pretty straightforward. One point, however, must be stressed. Before being upholstered, the armrest will be covered with closed-cell foam—the kind we would use under a vinyl top. We suggest you use 1/4 inch foam for your armrest construction. This will require the top of the armrest to be fixed to the base 1/4 inch below the top edge of the base. You will butt the foam at the top to the edge of the base. When you wrap a cover around this, the top edge of the base will give you a nice, straight, tight line.

Measure down from the top of the base 1/4 inch and draw a line the length of the base. Squeeze out a thin bead of yellow carpenter's glue just below this line. (Most of us use Elmer's [Aliphatic Resin] Carpenter's Wood Glue.) Press the top against this bead of glue and align it with the line you just drew—leaving a 1/4 inch lip above the top. Use your staple gun, loaded with 1/2 inch-long staples, and run a dozen or so through the base and into the top. When the glue dries (in about an hour) the joint will be strong enough to allow you to continue working. The glue reaches maximum strength overnight.

Shaping

Now we want to develop the beautiful teardrop shape you see in the photos of the finished product. This is done with that miracle product, chipboard. I don't know how they managed in the days before chipboard. Well, actually, I do. Back in the '40s my father would have carved the armrest out of wood. He would have bandsawed the rough shape and finished it on a sander. Besides the work involved, think how hard it would have been to make two exactly the same. Our eternal thanks to the inventor of chipboard!

The exposed edge of the top must be sanded to an angle that would follow a straight edge laid from the edge of the top to the bottom of the base.

Check the drawing on page 28 for a clear description of this angle. Although this angle is not critical, use your best craftsmanship to get it as close as possible. The more accurate it is, the greater gluing surface you will have. Of course, the more surface you have bonded, the stronger the finished product will be. Any kind of small, high-speed disk sander will work. We also use the popular 1 inch, three-pulley belt-sander, but the disk sander works the best. When you have a "fair" edge, you're ready to fill in with chipboard.

On page 28 is a drawing of the shape you'll cut from a scrap of chipboard. Cut two for each armrest. This semicircle shape with the slashed edges allows you to form the chipboard around the top and base. Lay the two semicircle pieces out on the bench and give each a thin coat of contact spray adhesive. This is rubber cement, not the carpenter's wood glue. Apply a similar thin coat to the beveled edge of the top and to the inside of the base piece. Select one of the chipboard pieces. Align the straight edge of the chipboard with the top of the beveled edge of the top-piece, centering the chipboard. Bring the bottom of the chipboard piece into contact with the bottom edge of the base. Working from the center out, press the chipboard down onto the base, contacting about 1 inch of surface all the way around.

As you work around (from the center) press the top edge of the chipboard onto the edge of the plywood. You won't be able to

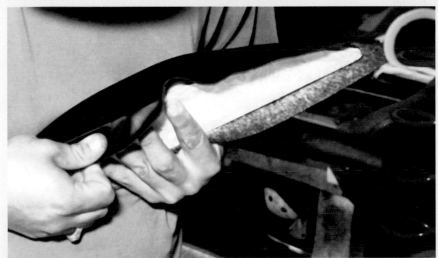
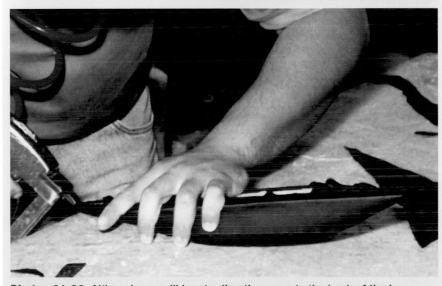

Photos 31-33. Although you will be stapling the cover to the back of the base, the project will go faster if you use cement. Working it dry, you can lift it off with little problem. Then, when it looks just right, you can staple it in place.

Photo 34. Be sure to trim away any excess materials. The base must fit tightly to the door panel when installed.

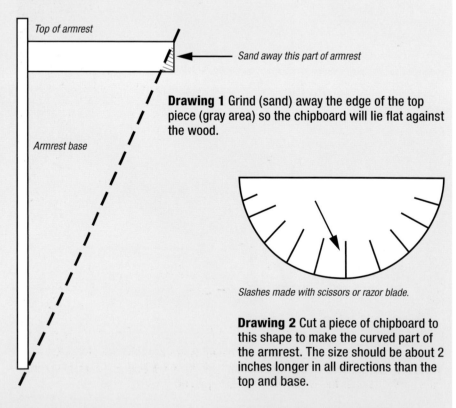

Photos 35 & 36. Here's the finished product. Notice how smooth everything looks. George has done a great job.

Top of armrest

Sand away this part of armrest →

Drawing 1 Grind (sand) away the edge of the top piece (gray area) so the chipboard will lie flat against the wood.

Armrest base

Slashes made with scissors or razor blade.

Drawing 2 Cut a piece of chipboard to this shape to make the curved part of the armrest. The size should be about 2 inches longer in all directions than the top and base.

keep both the chipboard edge and the plywood edge aligned. The front and rear of the chipboard will work their way above the top piece. Later, this "selvage edge" will be trimmed away. All edges should now be cemented all the way around.

Go back, and with a blunt instrument, such as the heel of your scissors, press down on the edge of the chipboard where it contacts the base and crisply define that edge. Finally, with scissors and a razor blade, trim away all the selvage chipboard. The last step in this section is to glue on the second layer of chipboard.

You've already coated the remaining piece of chipboard with contact cement so spray a coat onto the piece you just attached to the armrest frame (base and top). Wrap the second piece of chipboard over the first just as before, define the bottom edge with your scissors and trim away the excess. Make sure everything is well sealed and all the edges are flush. The last thing to do in the construction phase is to bevel the edges of the chipboard by sanding them with the disk sander.

Beveling the Edges

We want all of the edges of the armrest to be rounded and flow smoothly over the frame. Using a disk sander with a 2-1/2 to 3 inch 80-grit disk, begin sanding the chipboard around the edges. The idea is to thin out the edges—especially on the flat areas—so the chipboard flows from two thicknesses to nearly nothing out at the ends and along the bottom. Then, you'll round over the edges along the top of the frame and along the edges of the base. When you finish, everything should flow out smoothly, all edges rounded with no bumps or lumps.

This requires a bit of practice and something of an artistic touch. You're actually sculpting the piece, changing it from a hard-edged block to a supple, smooth form around which you'll wrap leather, vinyl, or fabric. Compare your work to George's as seen in photo 24, page 25.

Covering in Closed-Cell Foam

Closed-cell foam, which from now on, in this section, we'll refer to simply as foam, is molded with a very thin "skin" over it. This skin holds cement quite nicely. However, it tends to peel away from the body of the foam quite easily. Therefore, it will be necessary to break it away from the body of the foam before you apply cement.

In the shop, as Ron and the crew work, they save the old sanding disks that have become too dull to use on wood or metal. These are then used to abrade the skin described above. Most of the molding skin is removed during this operation. What little remains is not enough to cause a separation problem.

Cut out a piece of foam, lay it on the bench, and with a piece of 80-grit sandpaper (or used disk) lightly go over the entire surface of the foam. You'll see scratches developing in the surface. You want the entire surface to show these scratches. Wherever there are scratches, the molding skin has been removed. This is an important step. Omit it and the foam will surely pull away from the armrest frame. When you've completely sanded one side of the foam, you're ready to apply cement.

Apply a thin coat of contact spray adhesive to the sanded side and a thin coat to the armrest top and front (not on the back). Allow the cement to dry. You'll know the cement is dry when it no longer feels sticky to your touch. An even better test is to try pressing a piece of Kraft paper onto the surface. Lunch-bag brown paper works great. If the piece of paper releases easily, the cement is dry.

Photo 37. This is our armrest with the cutout for a finger pull. The light stripe behind the armrest is a separate piece and not part of the armrest.

Photo 38. Although much larger than the armrest just demonstrated, it begins the same way. Here, though, we're demonstrating the cutout for the finger pull. We have two half-moon shapes aligned together. This will become our pull.

Photo 39. To fill in the pull, cut a 4 inch circle (larger if needed), make slashes in the chipboard down to the wood. Then, bend each tab over and cement down. Once again, feather the edges with the disk grinder.

Photo 40. For this armrest, George has covered the finger-pull area with foam. Compare this to the Willys armrest that has been left unfoamed.

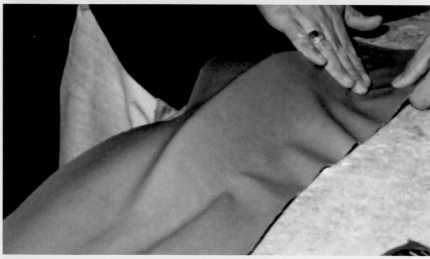

Photo 41. This is another demonstration of covering the armrest. George began by cementing one end of the vinyl to the bench then stretching the material tightly over the armrest. He works the wrinkles down and out to the edge—where they disappear.

Photo 42. This is our final example. To achieve such a graceful arc, it's necessary to curve the top to follow the base.

Lay the foam, centered over the armrest, and begin working it smoothly over the surface. You are molding the foam to the surface of the armrest. Because you're working with compound curves, the foam will try to wrinkle. Don't let this happen. Stretching the foam will usually eliminate any wrinkling. Having let the cement dry well, you can pull the foam up after placing it, if you haven't pressed it down too hard. Continue working the foam onto the armrest until it completely covers in one smooth flowing piece. Now, press it (the foam) tightly to the wood and chipboard. This is an important step. Having let the cement dry, a little pressure will be necessary to achieve a good grip. With a razor blade, trim away all the excess material. Be sure the foam butts up to the 1/4 inch lip you made where the top piece fastens to the base. Now, sand everything again. Remove the molding skin as you did before. Sand all the edges round. There may be tiny, unavoidable wrinkles in some areas. Sand these flush with the rest of the surface. When you've sanded everything out you're ready to cover it. For our demonstration, we'll be using black leather as the upholstery material.

Upholstering the Armrest

Once again, apply cement to the full surface of the armrest and to the back of your upholstery material. If you're using vinyl or fabric, the stretch of these materials must be with the length of the armrest you're covering. As usual, be sure to cover everything with a light coat and let it dry well. Now, here comes one of those tricks you bought the book to learn.

Set the armrest face up on the bench. Center your material over it. Glue one end of the material to the bench (see photo 41). Now you can stretch the devil out of your material as you lay it over the armrest. This stretching action causes the material to curve and wrap smoothly around the armrest with no wrinkling. Bring the end you're holding while stretching into solid contact with the armrest and press it tightly onto the armrest. Lift everything off the bench and work the remaining areas smooth and flat. In two or three minutes you should have the material covering the armrest, looking as if it had been sprayed on.[1] If you get the stretch of the material going around the armrest instead of along the length, you'll be wrestling with it for half an hour. So be certain the stretch is along the length.

Turn the armrest over and spray a layer of cement to the back—about 1 to 2 inches wide all the way around the edge. When this is dry, pull and wrap the material around the base and anchor it to the cement. Be sure you pull the material tight. Check, however, to be sure you're not pulling dents into the edges by pulling too tight. When everything is cemented in place, go around the edges (on the back) with 1/8 inch staples and lock everything in place. Take particular care with the corners. This is where it will come loose the easiest. Trim away the excess material and you have a finished armrest.

Added Details

Making a Finger Pull

Not every armrest will be as simple as that which we just demonstrated. A more complex design will include an indent which will allow you to fit your fingers into it and pull the door closed. Most of us have this feature on the family bus. To demonstrate this feature, we've selected the armrest for a 1957 Ford coupe. Follow George Torres

Photos 43 & 45. Frank first cuts a top, just as we did in the first two examples. Then, he cuts the ends into 3/4 inch slices. After numbering them, to keep them in order, he glues and staples them in place. When you do this, be sure to keep your 1/4 inch allowance between the edge of the base and the top.

Photo 45. Here's a shot of the finished top attached to the base. Note the delicate "S" shape of the curve.

[1] As a passing historical note, this is the same way canvas-covered canoes were made. The canoe frame was anchored to a frame in the middle of the floor. One end of the canvas was clamped tight and the other end clamped into a winch. By winding the winch, the canvas was stretched and wrapped around the canoe.

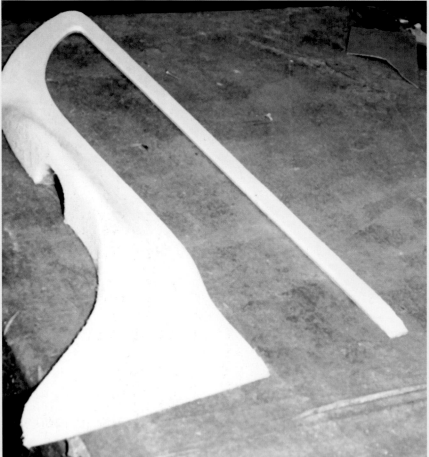

Photos 46 & 47. These two photos show a continuation of the process. First, chipboard is applied, trimmed and feathered. Finally, it's covered in foam—all as before.

as he develops this type of armrest. (See page 29 photos 38 and 39.)

The project begins by cutting a half-moon shape into the base that will fall directly into the center of the top piece. This should be about 3 to 3-1/2 inches wide and about 2 inches deep. Then, a corresponding half-moon is cut, in the center edge of the top piece. The top and base are glued together as before, with the two half-moon cutouts aligned. The resulting frame is sanded, shaped with chipboard, and sanded again. But what about the cutout for the finger pull?

This is filled in as follows: Cut a full circle about 4 inches wide from a scrap of chipboard. Cement the back side of this, and an area in the armrest frame about 2 inches wide all around the cutout. Without creasing the chipboard, press the circle into the cut out creating a nice smooth U-shape. With your scissors or a razor blade, make slashes in the edges of the overhanging chipboard, about 3/4 inch wide, right down to the wood. Bend these over like tabs and press them tight into the cement.

Once more, sand these tabs to feather them out into the wood of the frame. You can now return to the process of foaming and covering the finished armrest. Follow the photographs on pages 29 to 32 to watch George make the Willys armrest.

Making a Curved Top Piece

When the shop got to the '41 Willys, the armrest became the design feature (as discussed in the beginning of this chapter). Upon careful examination of the finished product you will note that the top of the armrest flows with the curve of the base in a very shallow "S" curve. We'll watch as Frank shows how he arrived at this shape.

Having peeked ahead, I'm sure you have discovered just how simple it is to get this curve. After cutting out the top, just as before, Frank now slices the first and last 4 inches or so into 3/4 inch pieces.

These are numbered 1 through 12 (in our example—you may have more or less). This makes sure none of the many pieces gets out of order. Now, when he glues and staples the top to the base, the pieces will all conform to the curve. Pretty darn slick! The rest of the armrest is finished as before. Nothing more changes. Two layers of chipboard create the rest of the shape, a little foam pads it out and leather makes the finished upholstered surface.

Tuck That Tail

If you have been in the trade for any time, one of the things that probably drives you crazy (as it has us) is finishing the trim around an extremely tight radius. Usually we bunch it up and drive in a few very short staples, then try to trim it flat. Here's a great new trick Ron developed to finish that radius and attach such a small end to the panel at the same time.

Instead of trying to wrap the material around the end of a sharp panel, let the material simply hang loose. Drill a 1/8 inch hole in the door panel, just below where the added panel will go. Thread the end you made through this hole and staple it to the back of the main panel. This finishes the radius and firmly affixes the end of the add-on panel to the body panel. Neat, huh?

Summary

By now, making an armrest should be far less mysterious than before. By applying the techniques above, you can make any kind or shape of armrest your brain can imagine. Your challenge now is to carry these techniques further. Can you use other products to create interesting shapes? Should the top always be just large enough to support your elbow? What might happen if it ran the full width of the door? The excitement of custom upholstery work is developing new approaches to old problems.

Tuck That Tail

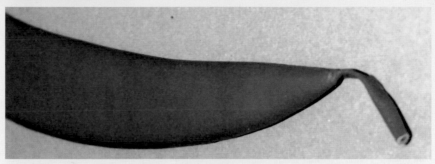

This neat trick is being done on the front panel of a '32 panel delivery. The panel you see in the photo will be inset into the door panel. Notice the little "tail" sticking out from where it would normally be wrapped around the panel to give a finished end. If you've ever tried to finish such a panel you know how difficult it is to get all that material underneath and fastened down. Try it this way next time. Roll the last bit of material into a tail, cementing it together.

Drill a 1/8 or 3/16 inch hole exactly where the end of the decorative panel will fall on the door panel. Fix the decorative panel to the door panel in the usual way and pass the tail through the hole. Pull it tight and staple it to the back.

The finished panel gives no clue to what has been done. Notice the extremely thin decorative panel above its larger partner. In reality this panel was less than 3/4 inch wide.

We thought you might like to see the whole panel. Another eye-grabber.

4 • Fabricating and Upholstering Door Panels

Photo 1. To get a perfect fit, Juanito must first fasten the door panel to the door. He does this in the "best-fit" position. When it fits the best it will, all around, he'll drive in a screw into the door on each side of the door panel to hold it in place. He can then mark it for trimming, remove it, work on it, then replace it exactly.

Photo 2. No matter how accurate you make the pattern, there's going to be a little bit of refining needed. Here, the panel overlaps the garnish molding, not a big problem but one that must be rectified.

In the previous chapters you learned how to make a pattern—and then used that skill to build an armrest. We'll now take those skills further by learning how to build a door panel (using your pattern) and then hang the armrest upon it. It might be helpful to go back to Chapter 2 and review how to make a pattern for a door panel and we'll pick it up from there.

Fitting the Door Panel

You have made a pattern of the door, stapled it to a piece of panelboard or Masonite and cut it out. You must now be sure it fits and the door can close. Closing the door with the door panel attached is the one place where a trimmer is most likely to go astray. He or she makes the panel, covers it, attaches it to the door and now the door won't close! The panel is too big. To prevent this, trim the door panel first—rather than going back, removing the cover and trimming it to fit.

In our illustrations we demonstrate with two door panels; one from the 1957 Ford Coupe we introduced earlier and the other is the '41 Willys. After Juanito made the pattern for the Willys, he transferred it to the panelboard and cut out the door panel.

Place the rough-cut panel on the door in the "best-fit" position. Drill a hole on each side of the door panel and drive in screws into the door to hold it in place. In this position you can see where there is overhang. In the photographs the panel bumps into the garnish molding. Not seen is the ill fit along the hinge side. It will be very easy to see where the fit is off. All that needs to be done is to mark the area to be trimmed then sand away the excess. Using screws to hold the panel allows you to take the panel off a number of times and always get it back in the right place.

When all the obvious poor-fitting places are adjusted, close the door with you inside the cab. This way you can see how the panel fits within the door frame. If the panel touches the frame anywhere, you'll have to trim to allow for the thickness of the covering material. For leather and vinyl, figure about 3/32 inch. Fabric is thinner by about half—maybe 1/16 inch. Pay special attention to the area where the door meets the rocker (floor-pan edge). This is where most of the problems will be.

Sometimes a very serious problem arises in the rocker area. There will be little or no room for the thickness of the panelboard and the covering. Remember, in this area you'll not have just the thickness of the covering material, but the padding beneath. Additionally, as in the case of the Ford, you may have a piece of carpeting here. To solve this problem you may have to eliminate the padding at the bottom of the panel to let the door close. We've even sanded down the thickness of the panelboard to get a door closed. If you think there'll be a problem, temporarily cement a piece of padding and material along the bottom of the panel to see if you have room. When you have the door panel neatly fitted within the door frame with just the right allowance for covering materials, you're ready to attach the panel to the door with clips.

Attaching the Panel

The easiest way to fix the panel to the door is with Auveco door panel clips. If you've never used these clips, they come in two shank sizes: short, 5/8 inch, and long, 3/4 inch. This accommodates the difference in thickness

Photo 3. Juanito gets busy with the sander and takes off a little bit where it hit the garnish. He'll also sand down other areas where the panel was too big.

Photo 4. Here's the finished rough panel on the passenger side. Note the Auveco clips holding it in place. You also see a cutout for the door handle. It's interesting to note that it falls right in the middle of the armrest. Is this a mistake or a design problem? We'll see in a later photo.

Photo 5. This is a finished rough panel for the Ford. It too is held to the door with Auveco clips.

Photos 6-8. George has padded the door panel with 1/4 inch closed-cell foam. Now he locates the two main design features and marks their position with a pen. In the first photo he's locating the pad discussed in the body copy. In the second, he places the armrest in the location the customer asked for. The last photo shows his markings. Now, he'll cut away the foam so the panel and armrest can be inserted.

between fiberglass and stamped sheetmetal. The short clip is Auveco part number 808 and the long shank is number 1202.

Fasten the door panel back to the door with its two screws. Every 5 or 6 inches, drill a 1/8 inch hole through the panel and door. Follow up with the Auveco clips and snap them in. The flat part of the clip rests on the top of the panel while the shoulders of the clip keep it from pulling out of the door. You can, however, pop out the clip by prying the panel up with a screwdriver. After you get three or four clips out you can simply pull the panel from the door with your hand. To replace the panel, start the clips into their holes, then push them in with your thumb. If you need more pressure than your thumb can create, give it a gentle smack with the heel of your hand. When the padding is laid over the tops of the clips, they'll not show through.

Padding the Panel

In Chapter 1 we discussed the three basic designs used in rod interiors: the "retro" look, the "hard" look and the "soft" look. In this chapter we demonstrate the hard and soft look and discuss the retro look. The hard look incorporates closed-cell foam as its padding while the soft look gets that way from using polyester (Dacron) padding.

We start our demonstration with a hard-look panel for the '57 Ford. Look at photo 29 on page 42 to see the finished panel. Notice the area above the armrest. It stands above (proud of) the rest of the panel. Below this is the armrest with a thin line of trim. This trim is a light piece of fabric in the same yellow shade as the paint of the car. Below the armrest are two very attractive grooves that flow from the front kick-panel, across the door panel and terminate at the rear quarter-panel. You see this effect in the two companion photos. Let's follow George as he pads this panel, then carves the design into it according to the customer's wishes.

To make the center panel that stands proud of the basic panel, George cuts a piece of panelboard in the desired shape. He covers this center panel with a piece of 1/4 inch, closed-cell foam. This is the same foam used under vinyl tops. Ron buys this foam in 1/4 and 1/8 inch thickness. Unlike open-cell foam (polyfoam), closed-cell foam can be carved, sanded and hold its shape when cemented. George will then carve the grooves into the foam and cover the panel. We describe this technique below.[1]

George lays the small panel on top of the door panel in the desired position. He traces around this panel with a ballpoint pen. Next, he places the armrest where he wants it and traces around that. Using a yardstick, he lays out the pattern for the grooves he'll cut along the bottom. These are located according to the design the customer presented. Now George is ready to cut out these areas. To do this, he uses a single-edge razor blade. You can use a razor blade, an X-ACTO® knife, or craft knife—as long as it's as sharp as the razor blade.

With the razor blade, George begins cutting the foam. He's careful to make the edges 90 degrees to the panelboard. This is because a piece will be set-in here. Grooves are cut in a "V" shape with each side of the "V" 45 degrees to the panel. This, when covered in fabric, leather or vinyl, gives a beautiful, chiseled effect.

Notice the interesting shop-made tool George uses to remove the selvage of the groove. This screwdriver is bent to a 90-degree angle with the tip sharpened just enough to clear the groove of unwanted foam. The drawing on page 39 shows how the point is

Photo 9. George continues to develop the door-panel design. Here, he's laying out for the grooves he'll cut next. Notice the customer's drawing at left.

Photo 10. The grooves are made by cutting about 1/8 to 3/16 inch on each side of the line, making a "V" cut of 45 degrees. If you have trouble "eyeballing" such a close cut, lay out the groove with a piece of 1/4 inch masking tape. You can then make an exact 1/4 inch groove by cutting along each side of the tape.

Photos 11 & 12. To remove the strip of foam after cutting the side, George uses this tool he made. He heated and bent an old screwdriver and tapered the blade until it fit into the groove. He uses this to remove the foam and clean away the hard cement all in one motion.

[1] You'll notice in the photos that both the armrest and the center panel have been made and covered. The center panel, like the armrest, is also a focus of the design. As we've discussed, the armrest is made first so it may become part of the design. The center panel has been made first for the same reason.

Photo 13. We must continue to stress sanding away the "skin" of the foam. If you omit this step, the material will adhere to the skin but the skin will pull away, leaving an area "flapping in the breeze." George uses an old sanding disk for this operation.

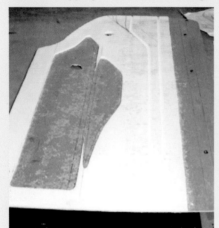

Photo 14. Here's the finished foaming, or padding, step with all the cutouts.

Photo 15. "Thin" and "dry" are the two key words here. A heavy coat of cement will eat into the foam. The cement must be quite dry so the fabric can be pulled away in case you accidentally get a wrinkle or crease.

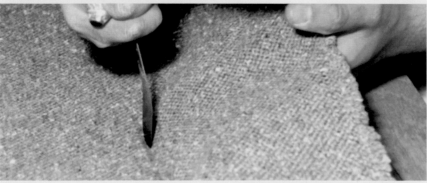

Photos 16 & 17. George is working the material from the bottom of the panel to the top. He uses his bent knife to force the fabric into the groove and further define it (the groove).

ground. As before, George scuffs the foam to remove the bonding skin which will allow the cement to adhere. Now he can turn his attention to covering the panel.

Upholstering (or Covering) the Panel

There's a bit of technique to covering a panel, getting the material into the concave areas, and leaving a good, crisp edge. Begin, as always, by spraying a thin layer of cement over both the foam and the back of the fabric. The secret is to let the cement dry. Let it dry until it is no longer tacky to the touch. Depending on the temperature and the weather this could be as little as two or three minutes to as long as 10 or 12 minutes. This will let you place the material gently over the foam and, when necessary, lift it up again without it bonding. Later, when you feel you have the material just where you want it, some heavy pressure on the surface will attach it fast to the foam and panelboard beneath. Now comes the tricky part.

In the past we always suggested you work from the center out. If you're an experienced trimmer, you've worked this way since you learned the trade. For this exercise, however, you must learn a new technique: You'll start from the bottom (or top) working your way up or down. This lets the material drape into the grooves without stretching. Again, this gives the nice, sculpted edge we want here.

In the photographs, you see George working up from the bottom of the panel. As he approaches the grooves, he smoothes the material into them, without stretching it. If you stretch the material, or attempt to pull it tight, it will crush the foam, ruining the very straight edge you made with your razor blade. In his hand you can see what appears to be a bent putty knife.

He uses this to define the edges of the grooves. Also, it creates that pressure we discussed above, which adheres the material to the panel. Here you see what the finished face of the panel looks like. It was in this same manner that George made the top, or inserted panel. Instead of working from the top to the bottom, he worked from one side to the other.

To attach the edges to the back of the panel, spray a little cement, wrap the edges around the panel and press them down. Finally, trim around the clips and any other place the material bunches up.

Attaching the Armrest

The armrest (and in the case of the Ford, the top panel) is cemented and stapled to the main door panel. If you worry about getting cement on the fabric, mask off around the area you're going to cement. As always, cement both sides—the armrest back and the door panel front. Allow the cement to dry then carefully place the armrest in its location. Turn the panel over and run in a couple of dozen staples. Be careful to select the correct length of staple to avoid coming out through the armrest. This may seem to be a weak arrangement for attaching an armrest, but in all the years Ron and I have been doing this, we've never had an armrest fall off.

Adding a Carpet Bottom Edge

Often, the customer will want a strip of carpet along the bottom of the door panel. Sometimes this is just for appearance, other times it will be to make the door panel "original." We'll be adding carpet to the door panel at the customer's request.

Photo 18. The finished front of the door panel. It looks as if it were carved by a machine. The edges are crisp and well defined. This is the result of very careful work: cutting was accurate, and the laying on of material was done with care. If you follow the directions, your project should look just as good.

Photo 19. To fasten the armrest to the door panel, spray a medium coat of cement on the panel and the back of the armrest. When the two have dried, bring them together, then drive lots of staples in from the back. Be sure the staples do not penetrate the material of the armrest or can be felt through the material.

Photo 20. To begin making the carpet strip for the bottom of the panel, George fits a piece of chipboard into the space to be covered. Note that he's cemented two pieces together to get the full length.

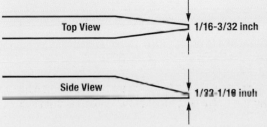

Top View   1/16-3/32 inch

Side View   1/32-1/16 inch

Drawings 1 & 2 If you want to make a groove cleaning tool like George uses, just copy what you see here. Use an old screwdriver. Heat the shank and bend it to a 90-degree angle—then grind the tip to the dimensions shown.

Photos 21 & 22. Cement both the chipboard and the back of the carpet. Contact the two pieces and trim away the excess. Be careful not to trim away any of the chipboard. Likewise, be sure the nap of the carpet faces down.

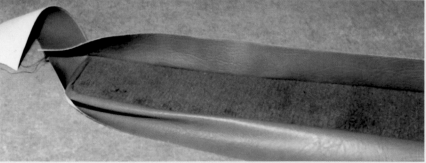

Photo 23 & 24. The carpet must be bound on all sides. Begin at the front edge, work your way around the bottom and finish at the rear end. Be sure to lock your stitch at each end. Cut the binding (trim material) flush with the top edge of the carpet. Lay the top binding in place with about 2 inches of overhang. This overhang will be wrapped around the panel to give a good-looking, finished edge. Sew the top binding in place.

The difficult part of making a carpet strip is to get the top edge straight and free of bumps and waves. To do this, we first apply the carpet to a piece of chipboard. George lays out a piece of chipboard along the bottom edge of the panel and trims it to an exact fit. Next, he selects a piece of carpet that will fit the chipboard base—making sure the nap, or lay, of the carpet is facing down. He'll also make sure there is enough carpet so the nap on all of the door panel carpet pieces is facing down.

With the carpet cemented to the chipboard and trimmed to fit, the next step will be to sew binding to all four sides. Cut two, 2 inch-wide strips of vinyl, leather or fabric—one long enough to go around both ends and the bottom and one long enough to go across the top with 2 or 3 inches of excess. These are then sewn to the edge of the carpet through the carpet and chipboard with about 3/8 inch seam allowance.

Turn the finished product over, spray cement on the back of the trim and to the chipboard just along the top edge. When dry, wrap the trim over the edge of the carpet and press it into the cemented edge of the chipboard. Now you have a very smooth, straight top edge of the carpet. Just what we wanted.

George can now cement the whole assembly to the bottom of the door panel. He'll finish by wrapping the trim pieces around the panel and cementing them in place. The finished appearance is one of razor straight edges. The photo shows the finished door panel. It looks as if it had been chiseled from a single piece. We think you can see why the customer was truly pleased with the results.

Adding the Soft Look

We turn our attention now to the Willys. The door panel for this car was made exactly like the Ford, except for the ruffled (or pleated) center insert. Frank has a real knack for custom interiors. The photos, starting with photo 32, show the start of the door panel. We pick it up after the outside has been covered. It's the center we're interested in.

Frank begins by making a pattern for the shape he wants the soft or ruffled area to be. In our Willys, this will be the area inside of the armrest. From his pattern, Frank marks and cuts a piece of panelboard from the same material the door panel has been cut. He cements and staples this into place, after making sure it fits within the area he wants.

At this point we introduce a new material, polyester. Often, this product is referred to as Dacron and has been for so long, as to make the two synonymous. We'll refer to it as polyester. You may know it also by one of its trade names—Fiberfill.

Polyester comes in two styles: one has a very thin, heat-sealed bonding on it. This is referred to as bonded polyester. Without this bonding we simply call it plain polyester or just polyester. The plain polyester is what you find as pillow filling, doll stuffing and sometimes as a wraparound for polyfoam chairs or sofa cushions. In the trim shop we generally use bonded polyester. For our Willys job, Frank has selected a scrap of bonded polyester to be the padding beneath his pleats.

He cements a piece of bonded polyester to the piece of panelboard he just installed and trims it flush around the edges. Next, he selects a piece of leather twice to three times as long as the length he wishes to cover. He carefully sprays cement around the outside edges of the leather, being careful not to get any in the center. Then he sprays another

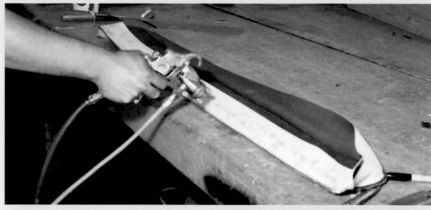

Photos 25 - 27. Complete the carpet trim by cementing the back of the top binding to the back of the chipboard. Trim away all but about 1/2 inch of excess binding. You now have a very sharp, warp-free, top edge of the carpet trim.

Photo 28. George cements the trim to the panel. To finish it off, he'll wrap the binding around the panelboard and cement it to the back. The two "tails" of the top binding will be wrapped around the panelboard and stapled to the back.

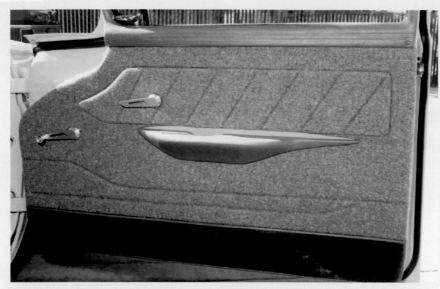

Photo 29. The finished panel is flawless. With care, the panel will remain so for the life of the car.

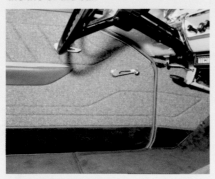 

Photos 30 & 31. Note how the groove(s) in the bottom of the panel flow from the front kick panel, across the bottom of the door panel and into the rear quarter. This takes a bit of pre-planning but is well worth the final results. Notice also the clever way the seat belt exits between the body of the panel and the carpet trim. These little touches create show winners.

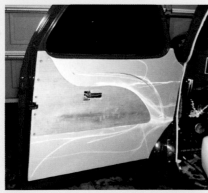 

Photo 32. We turn our attention now to the Willys. Observe all the chalk marks on the chipboard. These were possible design combinations Ron and the customer sketched out as they contemplated the design of the door panel. If you jump forward a bit and see where the armrest ended up, you'll see it covers over the door handle. Ron and the customer elected to move the door handle rather than change the design.

Photo 33. The door panel has been removed, the door handle dropped down a few inches and the first layer of upholstery (leather) affixed to the panel over closed-cell foam—just as on the Ford.

Photo 34. Frank has finished the armrest and laid it into position. Now he can mark around the inside of the armrest to develop the area he will pleat. Pay special attention to the details of this armrest. It incorporates the whole door panel. Is this not the focal point of the door-panel design?

Photo 35. Having created a pattern for the center area of the armrest, Frank cuts another piece of panelboard for an insert. This is cemented and stapled to the main panel.

Photo 36. Over the centerpiece, Frank cements a layer of polyester (Dacron) to be the padding. This gives a much softer touch, or feel, to the finished project than the use of polyfoam. As Frank does, so must you: accurately trim the polyester around the edge of the panel. Any bumps or lumps will "telegraph" through the leather.

bead around the outside of the panelboard and polyester center. Both leather and polyester centers must not be cemented—only the outside edges.

With the same "bent putty knife" that George used to anchor the grooves in the Ford, Frank begins to seal the edges of the leather to the base of the door panel. Here, the taste of the trimmer and the desires of the customer must work together. How much pleating is enough? Our Willys customer wanted about 100 percent. That means if the area to be pleated is 20 inches long, the material covering that dimension will be 40 inches. Frank "squishes" the material together so that for every inch, he uses 2 inches of material, sealing it as he works from the center out to the ends. Notice how nicely it stands above the rest of the panel. This is the result of the panelboard beneath the polyester.

When the leather is firmly attached to the panel, Frank trims away the excess and further seals the edges of the leather to the panel. This makes for a flat surface on which the armrest will sit. The finished results are shown on this page.

The Retro Look

The fabrication of the retro look, or as it was once called, pleats-and-rolls (in some areas, tuck-and-roll) must be delayed until we get to the section on making pleats. However, we can cover fastening a pleated cover to a panelboard door panel. Pleats are very thick. Therefore, you'll not use any padding other than that in the pleats. There are only two tricks to learn about applying the cover.

The first trick is to be assured that the seams forming each individual pleat are individually cemented to the panelboard. Make a centerline with pen or pencil. This will be the line on

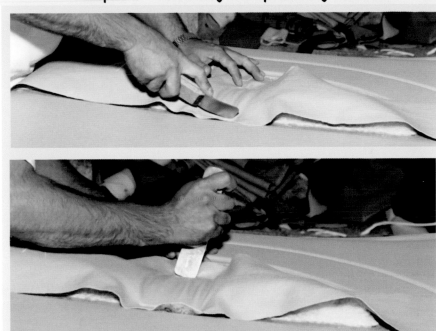

Photos 37 & 38. Work the pleats into the fabric from the center both ways. The customer wants 100 percent fullness in these pleats. This means Frank had to gather twice as much fabric into the pleats as the length of the panel would suggest. As George did when he defined the grooves in the Ford panel, Frank now defines the edge of the panel with his bent knife.

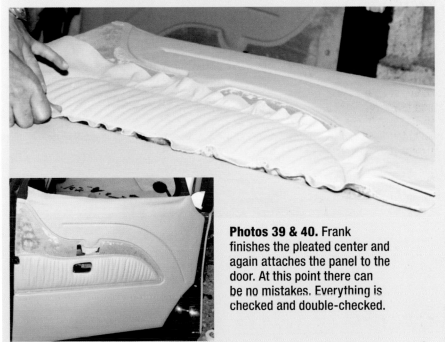

Photos 39 & 40. Frank finishes the pleated center and again attaches the panel to the door. At this point there can be no mistakes. Everything is checked and double-checked.

Photo 41. Hooray! The finished panel—up-close and personal. The door handle is from an indecipherable vintage Volkswagen. It has been dyed to exactly match the color of the leather. (It was originally black.) If you're interested in the dying process, turn to page 184 and watch how "The Vinyl Lady" performs her magic.

Custom door panels for big-rig tractors. Note speaker pod in left photo, light in photo at right.

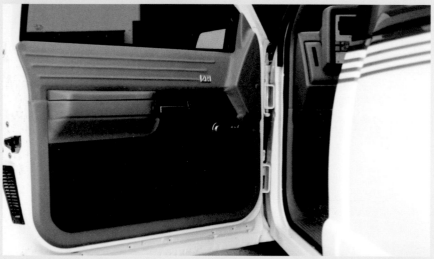

Chevrolet-GMC 1989-95 pickup with sculpted cloth and leather applied over stock plastic door covers.

Chevrolet-GMC 1956-59 truck. Under dash cover. Door panels with custom armrest.

which the center pleat seam will fall. After cementing the back of the pleats and the panelboard, spray an extra portion of cement along each seam of each pleat. Now carefully lay the center seam over the centerline and rub down tight. Very gently stretch out the pleats until they fall correctly on the panel. Never allow the center of a pleat to fall at the edge of the panel. There must always be full, even, pleats on the panel. You may end on a seam, or better, omit the seam that falls along the edge of the panel and simply wrap the material around the panel, cementing it on the other side.

Likewise, trim the pleat material along the bottom of the panel. There should be no pleat material (polyfoam or cotton) wrapped around the bottom edge of the panel.

Flames

While we were doing the photography at Ron's shop, a beautiful little coupe he did last year came back for new heel pads. Ron created a very exciting interior for this car using an ingenious application of pattern-making. We wanted to show you how this was done so we quickly re-created what Ron did, albeit a bit after the fact.

By looking at the photos you can see the flames of the paint job have been incorporated into the door panels. Although we don't show it here, they also appear as ghost flames in the headliner. To transfer the flames from the exterior to the interior, Ron used clear vinyl as his pattern material. He taped a sheet of this material to the car and, using a grease pencil (China marker), outlined the flames. The flames were then cut from the sheet of vinyl and became the patterns for the door, quarter and kick panels. The photos show the success of the effort.

Summary

We hope you've learned some exciting new tricks to try. You've learned the advantage of using closed-cell foam over open-celled polyfoam. It can be shaped, sanded and sculpted to meet any need. You now know how those fancy designs have been incorporated to give today's high-tech, "hard" look that goes so well with our advancing automotive technologies.

We hope you don't get side-tracked changing your working order on the sculpted door panel where you must now work from the bottom up, top down or side-to-side. This is a lot different than working from the center out—but it prevents a lot of problems.

Finally, we discussed the "soft" look, a wonderful counterpoint to the "hard" look, and it takes a bit of the edge off. The part to remember here is to at least double the length (100 percent) of the material you're going to pleat with. Sometimes you'll even want 150-200 percent. It will be up to you and your customer or your own artistic temperament.

Mike Rhine is serving as the model in this demonstration. Usually Mike is in the office making sure the business is running smoothly. Today, he's pretending to be a trimmer. In so doing he has taped a large piece of clear vinyl, normally used for the rear curtain on a convertible and for side curtains on a roadster top. Now it's being ingeniously used to trace the flames on the exterior of the coupe.

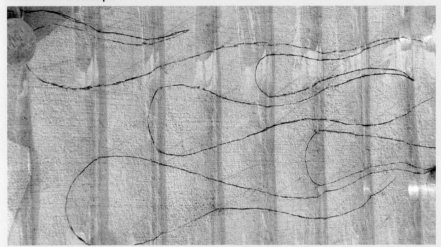

Here's what the finished tracing looks like. The pleated effect in the vinyl is the result of having been rolled up, left on the shelf for a year with bunches of other materials on top of it. Had we time, we would have set the material out in the sun to soften up. Unfortunately, the car had to leave and we wanted to photograph this trick for you.

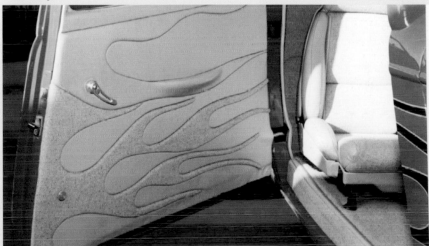

This is the finished door panel. The flames were cut out of the vinyl and transferred over. Even the armrest is incorporated into the flames. This is a consistent attention-getter at every show and rod run.

Specialty Panels • 5

Photos 1 & 2. We fabricate the back panel just as we did the door panel. Juanito made a giant pattern, then used it to shape the panel for the rear of the Willys.

In the world of custom auto upholstery, the trimmer is called upon to cover every conceivable area of the vehicle. Beyond seats, headliner and carpet, the rest is usually some kind of panel: door panel, quarter panel, kick panel, luggage panel, and even a panel we'll call a modesty panel. Some panels are flat and fairly straightforward. Many, however, are curved. Not only are they curved in one direction, but often in two. When something is curved in two directions at once, we call it a compound curve. The ultimate compound curve, of course, is the sphere. We see spheres upholstered all the time—we simply call them baseballs.

In this chapter we'll discuss fabricating panels with compound curves. The most frequent use of these curved panels is to hide the "plumbing" found under the instrument panel. This includes all the wiring, cables, hoses, heater and air conditioning. For lack of a standard name for these panels, we call them modesty panels. This name actually comes from the panel placed across the front of a secretary's desk to preserve her modesty while wearing a skirt. Such is the history lesson for the day.

Other uses of the compound curved panel include luggage panels, consoles and rear quarters that mold into the seat or form one large armrest. Then there are panels yet to be built that we haven't even thought about. For an interesting example of a curved panel, turn to the section of the book on dune-buggy upholstery. Essentially, the seats you see there are curved panels.

Although the first panel we examine in this chapter is not curved, it's still a specialty panel. We've included it for three reasons. First, you've been exposed to part of it in the earlier chapters. Second it's fairly complicated in its construction. Finally, it's an excellent example of incorporating a pocket into a panel. Pockets in panels are a frequent request and you should be able to make one. So, our Willys rear panel is a great place to start.

Building a Panel with a Pocket

Let's begin the process, as always, by making a pattern of the area you wish to panel. Our first illustration is similar to the illustration in Chapter 2, only the pattern has been further refined and is ready to cut. Juanito cuts the panel out of a piece of panelboard and Frank prepares it for covering. In photos 5 & 6 you'll see a black strip across the top of the panel. This is a piece of half-round rubber door sealer. Another Auveco product, it comes in 3/8, 1/2, and 5/8 inch. This is a good product to become familiar with.

In this project, Frank uses the 3/8 inch material to give a rounded edge to the top of the panel. This gives a very smooth finish over an otherwise fairly rough piece of board. It's also used on the face of panels, such as door panels, to give a raised design. When combined with the grooves cut in the closed-cell foam, as we discussed in the previous chapter, it creates a very interesting effect. You'll find dozens of uses for this product.

After Frank cements the half-round to the top of his panel, the next step is to bevel the foam around all the openings. This will make a smooth transition between the leather covering and the components. The foam is then sanded, a thin, even, coat of cement is applied to the foam and leather and they're allowed to dry.

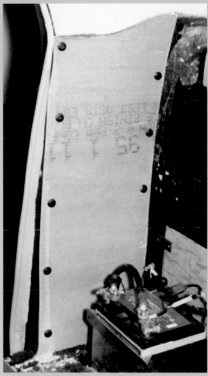

Photos 3 & 4. Here's another panel. This one incorporates plastic clips (Ford product) to retain it. This could be considered a rear quarter panel.

Photos 5 & 6. Frank applies a soft-rubber, half-round piece of weatherstrip to the top of the panel. When the leather is wrapped around this, it will give a very smooth appearance to the top of the panel. It also hides the rough edge of the panelboard. The panelboard is 1/8 inch thick and the foam is 1/4 inch. Together, this is 3/8 inch so no trimming is necessary.

Photo 7. Start the covering process in the middle and work from the center out. In the photo, there is so much cement on the bench that the leather sticks to it. This can be seen above Frank's left hand.

Photo 8. The finished panel really looks nice. The darker panel in the foreground will become the back of the pocket.

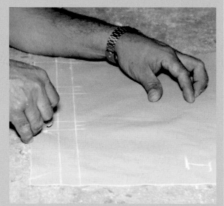

Photo 9. Here's half the layout for the pocket. The top is at the right. Frank has started to cut out around the outside. The extension lines at the left will be cut away. Two of these pieces will be made and sewn together in the center. For a discussion of all the lines, read the text.

Photo 10. Frank is using a razor blade to cut slots for the elastic to pass through. This will form the pleats when the project is sewn.

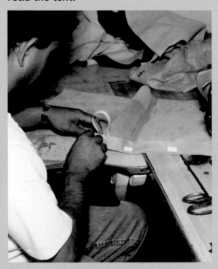

Photo 11. The elastic passes through the slots Frank just cut with the razor blade. The first seam has already been made.

Photo 12. This also shows the path of the elastic and the final seam to make the placket through which the elastic tape must pass.

Working from the center both ways, Frank fixes the leather to the foam. As you do this, remember not to press the two pieces together with a lot of force. Gentle pressure will allow you to lift the material up without tearing the foam. When everything is wrinkle-free, then you can apply pressure to bond the union. With the correct amount of pressure applied, you'll not be able to pull the leather from the foam without tearing it.

In the finished piece note two different situations: the openings for the CD player and FM receiver have the material wrapped around the hole and cemented on the back while the speaker openings have simply been cut out—leaving about 2 inches of leather as selvage. When the speaker grills are snapped in place over the leather, there'll be no gaps or "holidays" to be seen. Use this trick anytime there's a fascia or reveal molding. It makes an excellent finish. In the right corner of the panel, you see a second panel of a different shade. This will be the backing for the pleated pocket.

Making the Pocket

There are several ways to make a pleated pocket. The one we describe here is the most difficult because it's very tailored. To start, determine the number of pleats you'll have in the pocket.

In our demonstration, Frank has decided that five pleats will look best. This is an arbitrary decision and is based only on his trimming experience. The number of pleats must then be evenly divided across the width of the finished pocket. Here is an example: If the panel is 30 inches wide, five pleats must be spaced every five inches. If the panel were 33 inches wide, the pleats would be spaced every 5-1/2 inches. Let's stay with the 30 inch panel and see how much material we will need to make a finished pocket.

We'll need at least 30 inches of material as a minimum for the panel. Now we add 2 inches for each pleat: $2 \times 5 = 10$. So, we add 10 inches, bringing our panel piece to 40 inches. We must have something to wrap around the panelboard and affix to the back so we add 2 inches more to each side. Our finished width is now 44 inches. This is how wide we will cut the material. If we wanted the finished pocket to be 14 inches tall, we would add 2 inches for the pleat containing the elastic and 2 inches to wrap around the base of the pocket board, making our piece 18 inches tall. We would then cut a piece of material 18 × 44 inches. Let's assume this is the size of our Willys back-panel pocket.

In the actual development of the pocket, Frank did not have a piece of leather 44 inches wide. He did, however, have two pieces in excess of 22 inches. Therefore, he made the pocket with a center seam (two pieces sewn together). In photo 9 on page 48 Frank has laid out the material to accommodate spacing for 2-1/2 pleats. (When he develops the other half of the pocket—with spacing for 2-1/2 pleats, he'll have a total spacing for the desired 5 pleats.) The top of the material is at the top right of the photo.

The first horizontal line represents where Frank will cut. The second line will be the line on which the material will be folded under. The third line is the seam line—forming a placket for the elastic. Each of the vertical lines (at the top) represents where he will make a razor cut for the elastic to pass through. In photo 10 you see Frank making this cut with a razor blade.

At the bottom of photo 9 are two horizontal lines. The one at the bottom is the cutting line and the one above will be the line on which he will sew the bottom of the pleat. The two sets of three vertical lines indicate where Frank

Photo 13. Flip the pocket over and sew the bottom of the pleat. Take care to follow the layout marks so all pleats are the same size.

Photo 14. This is the finished part of the sewing. The elastic lies in a straight line while the pleats stand above it. This allows the pocket to be opened, then the elastic pulls it back into place. The pleats in the bottom take up the excess material created by the pleats at the top.

Photo 15. Frank checks for tension on the elastic and how the pocket will fit on the panel.

Photo 16. One edge of the pocket has now been stapled to the backing board. The elastic passes through a pre-cut slot in the main panel. When the elastic is properly located, Frank will cement the pocket backing board to the main panel. You can see the carefully made cutout to accommodate it.

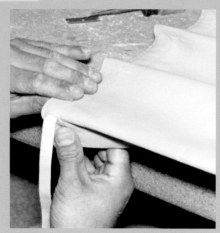

Photo 17. This is the exit area of the elastic. Frank will pull it snug then staple it to the panel. Don't make the elastic too tight. It will overstretch when the pocket is opened and tear away from the panel.

Photo 18. The project is finished by stapling the two sides to the big panel. Be careful stapling the bottom of the pleats to be sure they retain their correct shape and position.

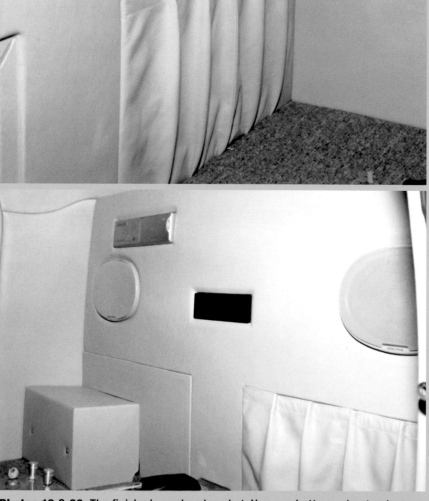

Photos 19 & 20. The finished panel and pocket. You can better understand now how the elastic works within the pocket. Notice also, the two speaker grills. These two grills have been vinyl-dyed to match the leather.

will fold the material together to make the pleat. Let's watch as he puts it all together.

Frank made a decision to make each pleat 1 inch tall. He therefore made his pleat lines 2 inches apart. He then cut a slit about 7/8 inch long to accommodate 3/4 inch elastic. Each line then has a 7/8 inch slit in it, centered between the fold line and the edge of the material. This can be seen in photo 10. Here, Frank folded the material along line number two and sewed a seam as close to the edge of the fold as possible. In photo 11 he's threading the elastic through the slits in the edge. For another look at how the elastic is threaded through, look at the drawing on page 55.

Leaving a little elastic at each end, Frank now sews the second seam that forms the placket through which the elastic passes. Finishing the top of the pocket, Frank turns to the bottom.

Each pleat is folded, as shown in the drawing on page 55 and is sewn in place along the previous laid out line. The fabrication of the pocket is now finished and it can be fastened to the panel. Before it's attached to the main panel, it must be fastened to its own backing panel. Because our demonstration panel has only one finished edge (the others are part of the main panel) it is the one to which we've stapled the pocket. This can be seen in the photo of the finished job at left.

To finish the ends of the elastic, Frank cuts a small hole in the main panel and passes the elastic through. Note photo 16. He'll staple this to the back of the panel. Next, he cements the pocket panel to the main panel, stretches the elastic until it just starts to snug up and anchors the remaining end. He finishes by stapling the bottom and side to the main panel. The finished product is seen at left.

This type of panel can be placed anywhere. Some of the

most frequent locations are on the kick panel, door panel and rear quarter panels. Gaining in popularity is placing one on the outside back of the driver's and passenger's seats. We've even seen them on sun visors. Maybe you'll find a completely different application.

Fabricating Panels with Compound Curves

Making curved panels is lots of fun. You can let your imagination take over and make all kinds of interesting things. We will, however, be a bit serious and again use our Willys as an example. Here, we make a panel to cover everything under the instrument panel and, as stated before, we call it a modesty panel.

Reviewing the Basics

There are few rules in making curved panels—that's what makes it fun. You'll have to think of ways to fasten the panel to the vehicle. We use Velcro, Auveco fasteners, snaps, screws and just about anything that comes to mind. Of course, the panel can be covered in anything you want.

Before we get to our Willys modesty panel, let's talk a bit about the generalities of curved panels. Any skills you have picked up in making patterns can now be applied to making curved panels. Like pattern making, panel making is just the process of cementing a bunch of pieces of stiff material together until you get something resembling the shape you want.

Then, you grind it all down smooth, cover it with closed-cell foam and upholster it. That's so easy we don't even need to finish the chapter! Well, you won't settle for that, so let's get a bit more specific.

Photo 21. This looks more like a plate of black spaghetti than the underside of an instrument panel. It's the result of "shoehorning" an air conditioner into an area meant only for a very small heater (an optional luxury in 1941). Our little Willys would never win a prize looking like this, but we can fix that.

Photo 22. Just two pieces of chipboard make it look better already. This is the beginning of fabricating a panel to cover all the ugly "spaghetti."

Photos 23-25. By cementing piece after piece onto the main panel, we build up a solid, substantial panel that form-fits the area we want to cover. Study how the various pieces are placed to get a good, fairly smooth surface. In this condition it looks terrible—but we're just getting started.

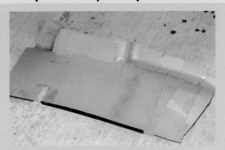

Photo 26. Here's the same view, only we've removed the panel from the car. Notice it holds its shape very well. Opposing stresses, combined with cement, keep the shape.

Photo 27. This is another modesty panel shaped around a steering column. It has been constructed on two pieces of waterboard. Can you count the layers of chipboard? I see five on the right side. This gives it sufficient body to begin grinding it to shape.

Photos 28 & 29. The panel is sanded down to give it a good, smooth surface. Much of the material has been sanded away. That's why it's so important to use several layers of chipboard. Can you see how nicely it has been feathered where the chipboard has been cemented to the waterboard?

Photos 30 & 31. The panel has been foamed and covered in these two photographs. If you didn't know better, you might think the panel had been formed out of a sheet of aluminum.

Photo 32. The Willys panel has also been sanded down. Now it's beginning to look like a custom fabrication. Look carefully at the forming around the A/C vent. Juanito has been able to incorporate very small details here.

Photos 33 & 34. Here's our panel with foam. Look carefully at the left edge. Juanito has mounted a 1 x 1 inch piece of pine here. This will be a mounting point for the panel that will cover the steering column. You can also see the Velcro on the bottom of the panel.

The materials we use consist of plywood, panelboard, chipboard, waterboard and various scrap pieces of wood—mostly pine and fir. Chipboard is by far the most frequently used material with waterboard running a close second. Velcro, screws and hidden fasteners are the main source of fastening materials. Closed-cell foam is used 90 percent of the time while the other 10 percent is devoted to thicker pieces of foam such as 1 inch polyfoam. In the seat building chapter we'll demonstrate what is essentially a compound-curved panel. Here, we'll use 10 inches of polyfoam. You'll learn all the little tricks and ideas, then put them to work in new and interesting ways. Let's take these tricks and materials and make a modesty panel for the Willys.

In our demonstration, Juanito comes back as chief panel-maker. Patterns and panels are Juanito's specialty. He begins with two pieces of chipboard cemented together to get the width he needs. About 1-1/2 to 2 inches has been folded under and the hook half of a Velcro strip has been cemented there. The carpet in the Willys will be looped Berber so the hook-half of the Velcro strip will fasten nicely. A very, very thin coat of cement holds the top of the chipboard to the instrument panel and to the A/C vent. (This is later washed off with silicone-and-wax remover from the paint shop.)

Forming

Look at the photos on page 51 to see how Juanito begins to build up the panel. As he cements and bends one piece of chipboard over another, the combination of stresses makes the whole piece retain its shape. Notice that many of the pieces are cut very small and glued over the tops of others to get the proper curve. Some pieces are slashed to bend them in two different directions.

We've also added another panel to our illustrations that has been developed as a one-piece modesty panel. (The Willys requires three pieces.) The dark panelboard beneath the chipboard is waterboard. This, because of its thickness and construction is a great material for long, (wide) flat, stretches. If you can accommodate the thickness, you can even use panelboard. You get to make all the decisions!

If you carefully study the photographs of the two panels you'll see a minimum of three layers of chipboard forming each curve. Anything less than three layers will not retain its shape well. Even if two layers looks good, add one more for safety. Of course, three is a minimum—four is even better. You'll be grinding away much of this material, so use it with abandon.

When the panel has achieved its desired shape, you must get rid of all the lumps and bumps, making it a smooth base for the foam that will follow. Again, you can use the 2- to 3 inch grinding disk chucked into your drill motor. At the shop, Ron's crew uses a high-speed air grinder—the kind used in body work. Because you're working with very soft cardboard (chipboard) and a coarse, high-speed abrasive wheel, you can take off a lot of material in the blink of an eye. Care must be taken not to get too aggressive with the shaping of your panel.

If you've never done this type of work, we suggest you make a practice piece to try out the technique. There's nothing to it, really. It's just too easy to take off more material than you want with a careless stroke.

Shaping

Start the shaping session by just hitting the high spots. Then, begin feathering the edges of the chipboard into the piece beneath it. For an excellent discussion on

Photo 35. The finished panel fixed to the instrument panel. There's no carpet yet but we must be sure it fits. The carpet will bump up to the panel, covering the edge that keeps it from sliding on the floor.

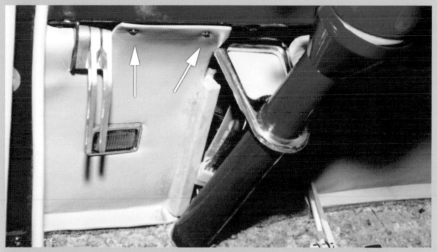

Photo 36. Using the same method as just described, we've made another panel for the left side of the steering column. We've also filled in the space between the steering column and the instrument panel. Note fasteners (arrows).

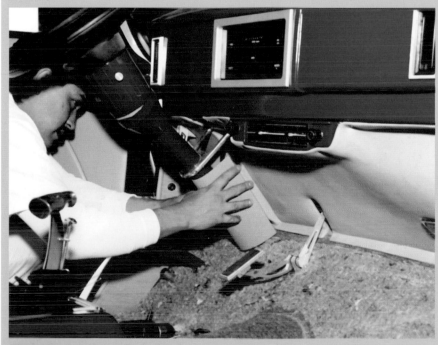

Photo 37. Juanito begins to develop a cover for the bottom half of the steering column. It will be fastened to the block of wood mounted earlier to the modesty panel.

Photo 38. The whole assembly is finished now. All that ugliness beneath the instrument panel is now hidden. We're building a good-looking car here.

Photo 39. Here's another curved panel. This is a rear quarter panel with a huge armrest fabricated to go over the wheel well. The flat part is made of 3/8 inch plywood with the curve made of waterboard.

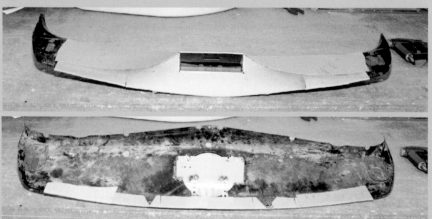

Photos 40 & 41. Here's another use of curved panels. We've reinforced a very rusted instrument panel and given it a new shape for the instruments. To have a new instrument panel custom-formed from aluminum or steel would take a federally guaranteed loan to finance. The shop knocked this out in a half-hour. Material? About a dollar.

"feathering," study that section in *Automotive Upholstery Handbook* by California Bill's Automotive Handbooks. Continue feathering the edges until they all blend into one another. Now, finalize the shape so it looks and feels smooth and flat.

If you've accidentally made a dip where one was not wanted, glue in another piece of chipboard, then level it out. This is just like using Bondo to fill a dent in a body panel. When your panel is just the way you want it, it's ready to be padded.

Padding the Panel

Padding a curved panel is not much different than padding a flat door panel. A few things should be brought to your attention. Most modesty panels, and many other curved panels, are positioned so the padding and covering materials are being pulled down by the force of gravity. In other words, the panel is "hung" from a support above it. Unless you're very careful with the cementing process, there is a good possibility that the foam and materials could pull away from the panel body.

To prevent such a disaster, it's necessary to sand not only the front of the closed cell foam with which you will cover the panel, but the back as well. This will ensure good adhesion to the panel as well as the fabric. There's little chance anything will separate after using this much caution. We should mention here, that this is the procedure we use for headliners as well. No one wants their headliner literally lying on their head!

As discussed in the door panel section, apply a medium coat of cement to both the panel and the foam. Allow them to dry until there is no tack left. If your fingers can't judge this, press a piece of brown paper bag (Kraft paper) onto the cemented surface. When the paper no longer sticks, the cement is just dry enough.

Bring foam and panel together and apply pressure to seal. Remember, if you apply little or no pressure, you can lift and adjust the foam without harm. It's only under firm pressure that true bonding is achieved. On inside, two-way (compound) curves, you're going to run into trouble.

You'll find that the foam bunches up in an area like this. You have more foam than you have space to put it in. Therefore, some will have to be cut away. With a razor blade or razor knife, make a slash in the foam from the center of the concave area out to an edge. Press one edge of the slit down, bonding it to the panel. The other edge will now "flop" over its bonded mate. Carefully trim the excess that's hanging over the previously bonded edge so you develop a new edge lying flush to the first. You will have simply cut out a large "V" in the foam, ridding yourself of the excess.

In some slightly concave areas you can force the foam into place. It won't, however, lie smoothly and there won't be enough material to cut away. In this case, you sand away the wrinkles. Just knock the tops off. Be careful not to sand away too much of the top surface. Now you're ready to cover this work of art.

Upholstering

Whenever possible, we like to cover a modesty panel with one piece of material with no seams. When using leather or fabric you'll find little problem making either of these two covering materials form into the compound curves. Just remember to work from the middle out to the edges. This gives the wrinkles—or excess—

some place to go. If you try to work from one edge to another, you'll get wrinkles and bunching. Remember: work from the center (middle) out.

Vinyl will sometimes present a problem similar to the foam. In a concave area it will want to bunch up. This can often be cured by trimming the excess material into a "V" discussed previously. Allow 1/2 inch seam allowance to sew what is now a dart, on the sewing machine. A flat-fell (or sometimes called a double French seam) works best for this. If either the concave or the convex area is too large to deal with in one piece, use two. Just remember to fit the two pieces before you do any cementing. Fit and sew—then cement. Finish your job by wrapping the excess material around the panel and cementing it to the back and installing it into the car.

Summary

Here's another great trick you've learned—a very simple way to make panels with compound curves. You begin with a base of chipboard, waterboard, plywood, or panelboard and build from there, cementing small pieces of chipboard to the base, shaping as you go. What should you remember? Right: no less than three layers of chipboard—preferably four or more.

To make it smooth you begin by feathering out the rough edges with a small disk sander. Then you finish shaping it to your desired configuration. Finish with closed-cell foam well sanded and bonded to the base.

Watch for tight concave and convex areas when you wrap the cover around it. Usually, a simple dart will solve any problems created when you use vinyl. Leather and fabric can be coaxed or stretched into some pretty tight areas. As a last resort, use two or more pieces of material to get a great fit.

How to Construct Pleats

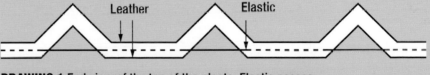

DRAWING 1 End view of the top of the pleats. Elastic passes straight through. Pleats act as hinges when the pocket is opened and closed. The elastic keeps it tight.

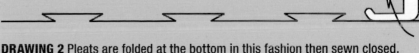

DRAWING 2 Pleats are folded at the bottom in this fashion then sewn closed.

Photo 1. This is the rebond material discussed in the body copy. It has been rolled up with the aluminum side out. The large roll next to it is 1/2 inch polyfoam.

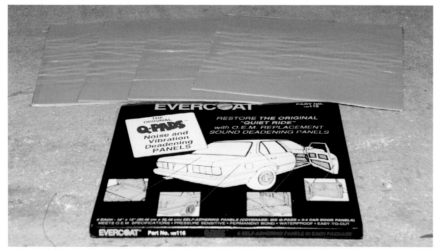

Photo 2. These "Q-Pads" really cut down on road noise, wind noise, vibration, rattles and heat. If you can't find them in your area, check the suppliers list.

Making an arbitrary decision, we decided to turn to the headliner as the next step in the trim process. Since the days of the carriage—and even the buggy, headliners have been an integral part of the interior package. In truth, they have changed little since their origin. From the earliest days, headliners were fastened to the inside of the vehicle by listings sewn to the fabric and suspended from bows or hoops (see Chapter 7). When metal-topped cars came on the scene the same fabrication method continued, only the listings were tacked to wooden bows—a part of the wooden frame of the vehicle top.

In the '30s metal bows replaced wooden frame members. Now the listings were sewn as loops and the bows passed through these loops. This worked well until the '60s when one-piece, fiberboard headliners were developed. These were covered with polyfoam then a layer of fabric cemented to it. This "sandwich" was snapped into place and stayed there by its own tension. For the last 25 years, this has remained the way headliners have been made.

If a trimmer needs to install a new headliner he generally buys one ready-made from an aftermarket manufacturer or from the OEM. He or she then installs it or snaps it in. Very few headliners are made from "scratch" anymore. In the next two chapters we're going to remedy this.

You'll watch Frank and Juanito make a one-piece leather headliner—with no seams—for the Willys we've been featuring and George Torres will make a three-panel headliner for a '34 panel delivery. You'll get to watch

George cut, fit and sew a stock headliner (although the fabric is far from stock) for our '57 Ford. Additionally, we cover everything that comes before: insulation, forming the panels on which the one-piece and three-piece headliner will fit, installing foam padding, plus making and installing windlace. There's a lot of work involved in this process, so we'll use two chapters to cover it all.

In this chapter we cover insulating the top for sound and heat absorption, making panels, foaming, carving designs and making windlace. In the next chapter we'll get to the covering materials, how they're installed and all the tricks to fitting the '57. If you've ever spent a whole week trying to fit a headliner, the next two chapters will turn your life around. You'll learn to love headliners!

Insulation

Over the last two-and-a-half decades, most headliner insulation has consisted of a 2 inch bat of fiberglass—the same material used in new home insulation. After a few years the fiberglass began to break up and fall down drivers' and passengers' necks. This lasted until the one-piece, molded-fiberboard headliner. Today, we can get away from all that with a couple of new materials.

Rebond

If you've had any experience with auto trim, you're familiar with rebond. This is a great recycled material. Manufacturers who make things from fabric sell their scraps to a company that grinds them up and forms them into a padding material that's 3/8 to 1/2 inch thick. For the trim trade, this material is cut into

Photo 3. This is the inside of the roof area in the Willys. There are two things to notice: the wooden bows and the rebond insulation. If we were going to install a regular headliner, we would sew in listings (as you'll see done in the next chapter) and tack them to these bows. Instead, we'll use them to retain our panelboard.

Photo 4. The fiberglass Willys body does not come wired for a domelight. Juanito had to make this support. It doesn't look like much but it will take a jackhammer to get it out.

Photo 5. Juanito makes the final adjustments after cutting out the panelboard for the top.

Photos 6 & 7. With the panelboard installed, the large gaps are filled with heavy waterboard. As with the panelboard, the waterboard is both cemented and stapled in place.

Photo 8. Piece by piece, Juanito fills between the waterboard and panelboard with chipboard. By cementing in small pieces at a time, he can develop the compound curved shape the job requires.

Photo 9. To smooth and level the edges of the chipboard, Juanito must grind it down. Note his use of safety glasses, respirator and kerchief to keep the dust from his lungs, eyes and shirt. The safety glasses and respirator are a must for good health.

Photos 10 & 11. Here we have the finished base. Note the cutout for the speakers over the windshield. These will be treated in a novel way when Frank installs the headliner.

Photo 12. This is the interior of the panel delivery. Just as with the Willys, the headliner will be supported by panelboard. In this case, however, the top and sides will be molded into what appears to be one piece. Again, chipboard forms the curves.

48 inch widths and used as padding under the carpet. In the custom trim business, we use it everywhere. However, one recent improvement has made this material 100 percent better.

A product Quality Heat Shield bonds to the rebond, a layer of plastic webbing and over that, a layer of aluminum. Plastic webbing gives the material much greater strength and the aluminum reflects heat. This wonder material should be in every trimmer's stockroom. If you can't buy it from your distributor, check the suppliers list in the back of the book and order it from ours.

Likewise, be sure all your wires have been run. It really makes a mess if you have to pull this insulation up or out. You have to get out your heaviest gasket scraper and go after the big lumps it leaves. Be sure everything is ready to be covered up before you start insulating.

To use this material, simply cut it to shape with a pair of scissors. Cement the reflective surface toward the heat source. If this is in the roof of the car, cement the reflective surface to the metal. This reflects the heat from the sun beating down on the roof. Using it for carpet padding, cement the aluminum surface toward the engine compartment or toward the ground, again, reflecting heat from those sources.

Be generous with your insulation. Cut it to fit tightly against whatever edge it abuts—another piece, against a roof bow, (as in our Willys) or a piece of metal. If you have room, use two layers. Be careful, however, that it doesn't make the padding beneath your headliner too thick. If your pad is too thick it may show through the headliner (or any other) material.

Closed-Cell Rubber Foam—with Lead

Leaded rubber is the really hot product for insulation. Its only drawback is its weight. Depending on the composition of this material it can weigh up to 2 pounds per square foot. It's available in many thicknesses. In the trim business, we use 3/8 and 1/2 inch thicknesses.

One product, Sound Mat by Sound Coat, consists of a layer of silvered Mylar, a layer of closed-cell[1] foam, a layer of lead and another layer of foam. Like the aluminum on the rebond padding, the silver mylar reflects heat. The first layer of rubber absorbs sound (and heat) while the layer of lead reflects or absorbs any sound that passes through the first layer of rubber. Finally, anything that escapes these first two layers is absorbed in the third. This is a very, very effective product. Unfortunately, its price reflects its quality.

Another product, a bit more affordable, (and heavier) is used in Ron's shop. It's called Q-Pads, a product of Evercoat. It comes in 12 X 12 inch pads, four to a package. This, too, is a rubber-and-lead compound. Unlike Sound Mat, however, it has no reflective mylar surface. It does have an adhesive backing, requiring no cement to fasten it to the body panels of the car. Like rebond, both products can be cut with scissors. (They can also be cut with a razor knife.) In using this material, just as with rebond,

[1] The cells of this closed-cell foam are much smaller, more densely packed and have much heavier walls than the closed-cell foam we've discussed in the previous chapters. It's also much less heat-sensitive than the material earlier described. Finally, it's dark gray in color compared to the stark white of the closed-cell foam we use for armrest and door-panel padding.

the tighter the fit, the better the quality of insulation for both heat and sound.

If you decide to use one of the rubber compounds in the roof area of the vehicle, there are several precautions you must use to ensure the weight of the pad does not pull it down from the roof of the car. The first step is to clean the surface on which you will bond the rubber of all rust, dirt, old cement, tar (the original sound deadener) fiberglass, and any other foreign matter with a solvent.

You can then go after the surface with a sanding disk. Eighty-grit sandpaper works best. It removes very little metal or fiberglass but really gets after rust, dirt and other debris. Follow the sanding or grinding operation with another wash of solvent. The surface should now be clean enough to hold tightly to any adhesive. Perform the following on a cool top only. If the car was out in the sun, pull it into the shade and let it cool off for an hour or so. If you live where things really get hot, you may want to let the car cool overnight.

If you're using a self-sticking pad, cut the rubber to fit before removing the protective sheet from the adhesive. When you have a good fit (and the roof has cooled off) remove the protective sheet and place the pad in position. Try to place the piece in the correct location the first time, so you won't have to remove it to adjust its position. When it's correctly located, press it hard to the surface. You are forcing the adhesive into the pores of the metal or fiberglass. When you finish the job, let the car sit in the shade (or inside) for 24 hours, keeping it out of the sun until the adhesive sets.

To cement this material with your regular contact cement, begin by cleaning the surface as described above. Remember: the cleaner the surface the better the bond. Using any good solvent,

Photo 13. This photo demonstrates how to make a very tight compound curve. Cut a piece of chipboard about 8 inches in diameter. Then, make slashes around the edges about 1 inch apart, cement the back of it and force it into the corner—then grind away the edges as usual.

Photo 14. George comes back to do some touchup grinding Ron wanted. He should still be wearing his safety equipment.

Photo 15. Frank begins the installation process of the foam in the Willys top. Look at the bottom of the photo. Here you can just see the knee pads Frank wears when he does this type of work. This really saves wear and tear on the old knees.

Photo 16. Frank has pulled out the last wrinkle and is beginning a rough trim around the windshield. You can see many of the marks where he has knocked down the tops of the wrinkles.

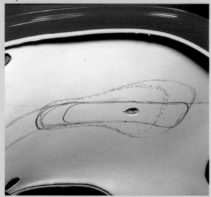

Photo 17. We see at least three, maybe four different designs Frank has tried out for the center of the headliner—the raised section we refer to in the body copy.

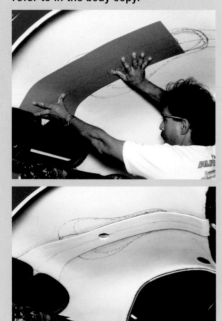

Photos 18 & 19. Everybody settles on a stripe. Frank begins by developing a pattern from chipboard. You can see his finished product. Notice the centerline to help keep things even on both sides and well centered in the vehicle.

wipe the surface of the rubber on which you'll spray the cement. It, too, should be clean and free of any material that would prevent adhesion. When the surface is clean and cool, you can begin the cementing process.

Begin by spraying a medium coat of cement to both the rubber and the top. Now let the cement dry for at least 20 minutes. If you have the time, let it dry for an hour. Drying time is important. Give the cement time for the carrier (solvent) to evaporate. This hardens the rubber cement and bonds it tightly to the two surfaces.

When the first coat of cement is dry, spray a light second coat. As soon as the second coat is dry to the touch (use the Kraft-paper test) contact the rubber to the metal and press tightly. Allow to dry 8 to 12 hours before taking the car out into the hot sun. Carefully following these directions will keep the heaviest leaded rubber in place over your or your customer's head.

Making and Shaping Panels

We opened this chapter with a very brief discussion of headliner history. We discussed using bows and listings to hold the headliner up. Well, hot rodders, street rodders and custom car nuts seldom follow the historical method. We are about bend the rules like they did to create an entirely different look.

Our Willys and '34 panel delivery will not have headliners with bows and listings. The Willys will have a single, one-piece leather headliner with no fitting seams. The panel delivery will have a novel three-piece headliner, incorporating side panels and headliner into what appears to be one piece. Let's start with the Willys.

Making a Headliner Panel

Study the photograph of the finished Willys headliner, photo 41, page 76. It appears as if, perhaps, a fiberglass inner liner was covered and then fastened into place. Not quite. It's all made from panelboard and chipboard—something like the modesty panel we built in the last chapter.

When the Willys came to the shop, it had wooden bows installed in the roof of the car. Instead of using them to retain listings, we used them to support a big piece of panelboard. Juanito made a pattern of the inside top of the roof and transferred this to panelboard. He then cut it out and test-fit it a few times. When the fit was right, he cemented it in place and drove staples through, anchoring them into the top bows. This gave a base to work the sides and edges.

In the front, Juanito stapled in a large piece of waterboard. This was stapled first to the wood frame around the windshield then to the panelboard and first bow. There are wood frame members around the windshield, doors, rear window (backlite), and at the radius of the quarters. In a similar fashion he installed a piece of waterboard between the rear window and the rear bow. Finally, he cemented in small pieces of chipboard to shape the compound curves in the quarters, around the doors and across the top of the windshield.

Note the cutouts for the two tweeters just above the windshield on the driver and passenger sides, page 58, photo 11.

The last step, like shaping the modesty panel, was to grind down the edges of the chipboard, giving a smooth base over which to lay foam and leather. And, as with the modesty panel, the multi-layers of chipboard provide excellent strength and shape. Turn your attention now to the panel delivery. It incorporates the same techniques.

Incorporating Headliner and Side Panels

The novel arrangement in the panel delivery begins with the installation of side panels from the roof line to the floor. These panels are permanently installed by screwing them into the interior stamped-steel frame members. Then, as with the Willys, chipboard pieces are used to shape the curve between the top and sides. Notice in the photos that chipboard forms all the curve between panels and doors. This method works beautifully in the compound, concave area in the upper rear quarters next to the rear door. As always, the chipboard is ground to shape. What was once an area for a headliner and side panels has now become one large surface to cover. In the next chapter we'll see how this is done.

By now, you understand how many fun and interesting things you can do with the chipboard and panelboard technique. Think of some other areas where this application might work: in the trunk; shaping a complex console; making flares around protruding objects like speakers or lights. The list is endless.

Applying Foam

If you started reading the book here, go back to Chapter 3 or 4 and read up on how you bond 1/4 inch closed-cell foam to a panel. This is important information and must not be skipped. In this section we'll discuss how you make the foam form into a concave shape

When looking at the Willys headliner area, you can imagine the inside top of the car as a very large bowl. If you were to get out a cereal bowl and try to line it with a piece of paper, you would find it couldn't be done without wrinkling the paper.

Photos 20 & 21. These two photos illustrate a very deft touch in feathering the edges of the foam. In the top is the cutout for the domelight and the photo at the bottom shows the foam feathered right up to the windlace.

Photo 22. An inside view of the panel delivery. The two stripes you see along the top are pieces of masking tape George laid out to roughly define where he wants the foam to stop. The sides of the headliner (and side panels) will be of fabric. The taper you see here will be made of vinyl.

Photo 23. George lays this piece of foam into the truck just as Frank did in the Willys.

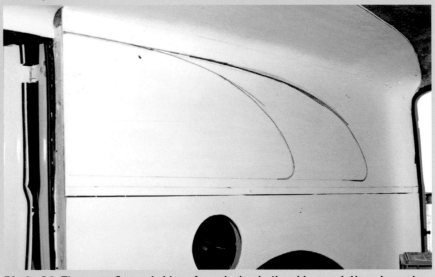

Photo 24. These are George's ideas for a design in the side panel. He only made a couple of false starts before he came up with this idea, pleasing both the customer and the boss.

Photo 25. George refines the design with 1/4 inch masking tape. He'll use this to guide his razor while he cuts a "V" into the foam.

Quarter inch foam can be just about as hard to shape as our paper-and-bowl example. However, it can be done—and without wrinkles. As we described earlier, begin by scuff-sanding the surface of the foam to which you will apply the cement.

Don't skimp when you cut the foam. Leave at least 1 foot of material all around. This will give you a little leeway when you start. Mark a centerline on the headliner panel and on the foam. Make it dark enough so you can see it after cement has been applied. Draw one centerline from front-to-rear and another from side-to-side on both panelboard and foam.

Bring the cemented foam into the car, align the "crosshairs" (the intersection of the two centerlines) and gently press the foam into place, covering an area of about 1 square foot. Now you're ready to form the foam into a wrinkle-free bowl shape.

Working from the center out, gently wipe the foam onto the panelboard with your hand in ever-widening circles. This will work fine until you begin to approach the tighter curves. As the foam tries to wrinkle, pull in the direction of the wrinkle. This serves two purposes. First, by stretching the foam, some of the wrinkles disappear through the tension. Second, this same stretching action makes the remaining wrinkles much smaller.

You have been applying very little pressure to the foam as you perform this operation. Therefore, you can lift the foam away from the panelboard if the wrinkles are too large, and try again with more stretch, or a little tug right or left. The object is to get out as many wrinkles as possible while those that remain are as small as possible. When the foam is well placed, any wrinkles remaining are tiny, tiny—press the foam tightly to the panelboard. Now you're ready to get rid of any remaining wrinkles. You'll need some 80-grit sandpaper for this.

In the area where the wrinkles have formed, spray a very light coat of cement. Allow this to dry for several minutes, more if you have the time. Twenty minutes is not too long. With your 80-grit sandpaper, very carefully and gently begin sanding down the tops of the wrinkles. The cement will have hardened the surface of the foam just a bit—enough to make the tops of the wrinkles pull off. Of course, if you start scrubbing with the sandpaper, you'll cut right through the foam and down to the board. Therefore, the sanding operation must be delicate and gentle.

Take off as little as you can with each brush of the sandpaper. Take your time. Use your hand to feel the surface. It's much better than your eye to "see" any remaining wrinkles. Finally, stop when the wrinkles are gone! It's everyone's tendency to give it just a bit more. Sometimes, that "bit more" is too much and you create a hollow. So be careful. Stop when the job is done.

Feathering the Edges

We've discussed feathering in the last chapter. There, we were feathering the edge of a panel. Now you must learn to feather the edges of foam. The two principles are the same, only the materials are different. Because the foam you're using is 1/4 inch thick, pulling fabric, vinyl, or leather over this will give you a bumpy edge. To prevent the associated bumps and lumps, we eliminate the possibility by feathering all the edges. Note the photos of the Willys foam on page 61. Here, Frank has feathered the edge of the foam next to the windlace and around the domelight.

Using your 80-grit sandpaper, begin feathering a minimum of 1 inch away from the edge. Depending on the area you're feathering, you may want to start 2 to 3 inches from the edge.

Photo 26. This is the finished foam job. You can begin to see how the final headliner may look. Don't peek into the next chapter to see how beautiful it finished!

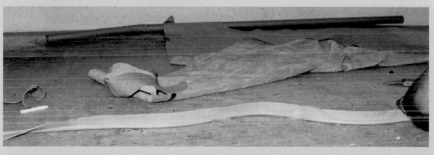

Photos 27-29. Frank cuts his windlace strip from the largest part of the hide. This makes it possible to form a piece of windlace with no joints or unions in the material. He cements only the leather and seals the edges with the rubber core inside.

Photos 30 & 31. George forms his vinyl windlace just like Frank did the leather. In the photo he's using the handle of his scissors to crease the material tightly against the rubber core. Notice how tightly it seals to the core. It almost looks molded.

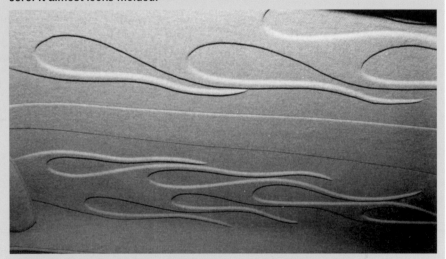

Photo 32. Custom hard-look "flamed" headliner in 1955-57 Chevrolet. The same idea can be applied to most 1928-95 cars.

How to Make a Dart

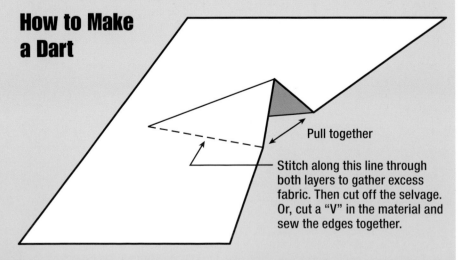

Pull together

Stitch along this line through both layers to gather excess fabric. Then cut off the selvage. Or, cut a "V" in the material and sew the edges together.

As always, work gently, taking off as little as possible with each stroke. Keep your edges straight and level. If you started the feather 2 inches from the edge, maintain that same 2 inches across the entire area or job. If your feather wanders from 1 inch to 2 inches back and forth, it will be noticeable when the material is cemented over it. Be careful!

Incorporating Designs

Our two examples, the Willys and the Ford, incorporate two different styles of foam design. The Ford has a design carved into the existing foam and the Willys has an extra piece of foam applied over the base to give a raised effect.

Carving

Looking first at the panel delivery, you can see the sketches George has made on the foam to develop an idea for his design. Finally, when the design was developed to everyone's satisfaction, (George, Ron and the customer) George outlined it with 1/4 inch masking tape—just as he did with the door panels. Then, again as with the door panels, he used the edges of the tape to guide his razor cut. Holding the razor blade at a 45-degree angle, he cut a very even "V" groove the full length of the masking tape design.

This is a very simple process but requires some skill to develop a smooth even cut. If this is your first attempt, we'd suggest you make a practice panel to develop your skills before committing to a real job.

Layering Foam

On page 60 you can see some of Frank's ideas for a design he sketched into the Willys top. To us it looks a bit like a guitar.

The customer felt the same and eventually the wide "stripe" effect was developed to the pleasure of all involved. Frank began the process by developing a chipboard pattern. This was carefully cut and fit using a centerline on which the chipboard was folded. This allowed Frank to make both sides of the stripe exactly the same.

He also had centerlines on both the headliner foam and the stripe. This made it possible for him to cement the stripe to the headliner foam with no worries about getting it off-center. Always work with centerlines. It doesn't make any difference whether you're doing custom work or regular aftermarket upholstery. Without centerlines and square corners you'll wind up off-center or "cockeyed." The more you plan ahead, the better the finished job.

Windlace

The name windlace goes back to the coachwork days also. It was originally a real lace material, draped around the doors and side curtains to help keep the wind from blowing in through the cracks. It was changed with the advent of the automobile from lace to a fabric or leather-covered rubber "tube" (first a rubber hose—then a solid-rubber core— actually, a foam-rubber core). This stayed with us until the '60s when good weather stripping finally was able to keep most of the wind from whistling in our doors. For those vehicles from the 'teens to the '60s, we must make new windlace when we trim the interior.

We watch both Frank and George make windlace. Frank for the Willys and George for the '57 Ford. The rubber core is purchased in rolls of either 3/8 or 1/2 inch diameter. Almost all of the vehicles you'll do will use the 1/2 inch material. Only occasionally will you find a need for the 3/8 inch. Both men make

the windlace in the same manner.

It is considered bad form to have a union (two pieces of material joined together) anywhere along a piece of windlace. Therefore, to get all the way around the door of the Willys, Frank had to cut his material from the center of a hide. George is using vinyl so he had only to cut up the roll to get all the length he needed.

Both men cut their materials 2 to 2-1/2 inches wide and as long as needed to go around a door frame. They next applied a medium layer of cement to the backside of the leather or vinyl. No cement is applied to the rubber core. Note how they lay the material out the full length of the bench. This helps keep the finished windlace from curling. The material is wrapped around the core, the edges aligned, and then closed. Finally, with their creasing tool they seal the leather or vinyl tightly against the core.

Some of you will have had experience making windlace. That experience, however, will probably have included sewing the material around the core as if you were making a giant piece of welt. Try this new technique, which eliminates sewing. We find it makes the edge of the windlace much "crisper" and it has less tendency to curl.

In the next chapter we'll watch Frank and George install these pieces of windlace and see a couple of neat tricks they use to keep it hung up there around the door frame.

Summary

In this chapter you've watched as two excellent trimmers have built up bases upon which to install different styles of headliners. You understand the types of insulation they use to keep down the heat and noise. You learned also how to cement the heavy rubber materials overhead and keep them from falling down.

More great tricks were developed to shape the inside tops and sides of the cars so custom headliners could be installed. This included using panelboard and chipboard much like the process used in making modesty panels. Chipboard can be used almost anywhere to make strong, curved surfaces.

Getting 1/4 inch closed-cell foam to lie smoothly on a compound, inside curve takes a little doing. The secret is to pull in the direction of the wrinkle. This is contrary to your experience and logic. Normally, you would pull the gathering out of the wrinkle by stretching it sideways. Unfortunately, that only puts the wrinkle somewhere else. This is a technique that's quickly learned and we think you'll really like it.

Try making your next piece of windlace the way Frank and George make theirs. It also helps eliminate wrinkles on tight, inside corners—and you have two of those corners on every door frame.

Photo 1. This is the vinyl strip referred to in the body copy. Two pieces are cemented together, one on top of the other. For added security, they've also been stapled together.

We're now ready to begin making, then installing, a custom headliner. By the way, please don't call it an overhead. Indeed, it is over head but that's the wrong terminology. In the trade it's always referred to as the headliner. This is a long chapter so we'll pass on the long introduction and get right to the details.

Windlace

In the previous chapter we discussed how custom windlace is made—cemented, not sewn. To cover the foam padding in a logical progression, we omitted the installation process. We'll pick up from there.

Because everything we do in the world of hot rod upholstery is made up as we go along, anything you can do to make the windlace stay up there around the door is just fine. Most every car that becomes a rod is over 30 years old. In 30 to 50 years, the material that once retained the windlace to the body has deteriorated and gone away. It becomes our job then, to either replace that material, or figure out some other way to hold the windlace up there. The '57 Ford presents some interesting solutions to the problem and is a good place to start.

Replacing Tacking-Strip

The material originally used to retain the windlace to the body was called tacking-strip. The very earliest tacking-strip was made of a tar-impregnated fiberboard. This worked pretty well when trimmers really did use tacks. This material fell out of favor after only a few years. When the tar got hot, it melted and stained the windlace and headliner. It was replaced by Kraft paper, twisted like a piece of rope, then stamped into a square shape in a press—3/8 to 5/8 inch square.

This material no longer stained the fabric, but it refused to hold a tack very well. The advent of the staple gun to replace hand-tacking solved the problem. Then, they stopped making windlace in the '60s and the whole thing became a moot point. For years, however, they continued to make the paper tacking strip. Unfortunately, by 1980 it became impossible to find and trimmers started developing their own solutions. The most popular solution was a strip of 1/4 × 5/8 inch vinyl. For many applications, we're still using it today. It can be purchased in 50- and 100-foot rolls from your local fabric house. If they don't have it, look in the suppliers list.

1957 Ford

Our Ford uses this material in part of the door channel. Because the original tacking strip was 1/2 inch thick, we had to use two layers of the vinyl material. It's held in place with contact cement and its own tension in the channel. In many cases, it's necessary to not only cement it in place but to run a few screws in to secure it.

We use #6 or #8 pan-head Phillips screws for this. The wide pan-head presents a large surface to press on the vinyl. Some trimmers use a countersunk head but we've seen the vinyl pull over this. Use the pan-head screws where feasible.

Fifties Fords used a really poor-quality, metal retaining-clamp to hold the windlace over the top of the door. It could only be used once and then it broke. Through the early '60s you could still buy them from the dealership.

Photos 2 & 3. This is a great trick to replace tacking-strip in all early to late fifties Fords. Even if you have the weatherstrip retainers, throw them away. Then, hammer down the two horizontal wings (arrows). Over the edge, lay a strip of 1/2 inch wood quarter-round and use the top wing to hold it in place. Finish by driving a couple of screws into the ends.

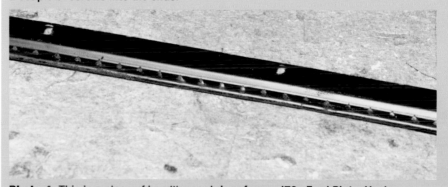

Photo 4. This is a piece of headliner retainer from a '70s Ford Pinto. You're looking at the back side of the strip. You can see the serrations that hold the headliner in place.

Photos 5 & 6. To form the retainer to the door, make cuts about 1 inch apart along the edge. This allows you to bend it. Use aviation snips to make the cuts and wear heavy leather gloves when bending.

Photo 7. To finish tacking the weatherstrip to the car, here's yet another way. Cut a piece of plywood to fit in the groove. Use cement, screws or both to hold it in place. In this example, there was no backing for screws to bite into.

Now, the dealership no longer even knows what they are, much less inventories them. Our friend George has come up with a great solution.

There are three "wings" stamped into the sheet metal that originally held the windlace clips in place. George flattens the two horizontal wings and leaves the vertical wing in place. He cuts a piece of 1/2 inch quarter-round the same width as the door opening. He places it in the channel above the door, hammers the vertical "wing" down over it to hold it in place. He retains the ends with #6 sheet-metal screws. This becomes a very solid installation and one into which staples may be driven and expected to stay. I think this is a great trick.

With this solid base it is now easy to staple the windlace in place, all around the door. We like to finish by leaving about 1 inch of windlace lying on the floor of the car. This is then screwed to the floor pan. Carpet covers the end and its screw. By doing this, no one can kick the bottom of the windlace loose from its mooring when entering or exiting the car.

The Willys

Our Willys presents a whole different set of problems. Because it's a fiberglass replica, there is no "original" windlace mounting method. So Ron developed one. Remember, most of the top of this car is covered with panelboard. It is an easy step then to simply cement or staple the windlace in place. Wherever there was no panelboard, Ron used 1/2 inch plywood cut to shape. Not very original, but effective. The original part of the assembly is the way the headliner finishes off around the windlace.

Referring back to the early years, headliners originally finished off around the windlace with a product called "Hide-um."

This decorative binding allowed the trimmer to place a tack through the Hide-um in a groove. Then the groove closed together over the tack. Later, panels covered the tacks used to hold the headliner in place and were shaped to fit tightly against the windlace.

In the late '50s, and lasting through most of the '60s, most cars had what some trimmers called a tiger strip. This steel or aluminum stamping had one rolled edge with a row of sharp teeth-like protrusions behind the edge. The headliner rolled over this edge and was forced under it. The teeth-like projections kept the headliner from pulling out. Of course, the stamping was made to follow the contour of the windlace. Ron needed to find a supply of this material. Most of what he found was already shaped to fit a particular door. Then he stumbled on to the solution: Ford Pintos.

The Pinto has several long, straight retainers. Because they're straight, they can be curved to fit the trimmer's need. Look at photos 4, 5 and 6. Along the top edge Ron makes slashes about 1 inch apart using a pair of aviation snips. Then, with some serious hand work, he can bend this material to fit around most any door. Once shaped, he screws it in place. Note, however, how closely the screws are spaced. This, too, helps form it as well as retain it. Now it will just be a matter of forcing the edge of the headliner under the retainer to give a beautiful finished edge, flush with the windlace.

The Panel Delivery

The panel delivery used a combination of everything we've described—with the addition of one other trick. Along the door jamb in the area of the kick panel, Ron's crew decided to not only cement the windlace in place,

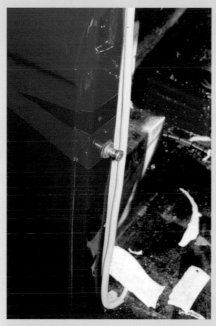

Photos 8 & 9. Sometimes, fiberglass bodies are not perfectly formed. Here, you can see the door jambs are not perfectly straight. To overcome this, Frank ran the windlace straight. With the door closed and inside the car, the door panel and windlace match.

Photo 10. Fasten the windlace to the car any way you can that looks straight and neat. On our panel delivery Ron used pop-rivets.

Photo 11. Note that George has installed rebond sound deadener between each of the bows. Never put up a headliner without some type of insulation.

Photo 12. This photo demonstrates how experience makes the job go faster. We advise you to attach the whole panel to the car before marking it. Here, George folds the material in half, holds it with his head and marks one end. From these marks he'll cut both ends together. The above demonstration saved him about five minutes. Saving five minutes per day, 12 times, saves an hour. As a beginner, however, take your time and do it right. Later you can develop speed.

Photos 13 & 14. This is the way we suggest you fit the headliner panels. Cement the material in place, mark for the seams and location. Add witness marks anywhere you think will aid in sewing, or installing.

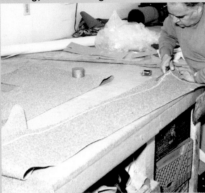

Photos 15 & 16. After marking one end for seaming, George cuts away the selvage. He then folds the material in half and uses the first end as a pattern for the other end. This assures both ends of the panel are identical.

Photo 17. Look at picture 14 and note the marks George made for the beginning of the listings. In this photo you can see he begins sewing his listing at that mark. Making any kind of mark is like writing a note to yourself. Use lots of them to ensure a good fit.

Photo 18. Insert the bows into the listing. Begin installing from the rear, working forward.

Photo 19. George has the headliner stretched out from the middle both ways and temporarily cemented in place in the front. Notice how few wrinkles there are at this point. This is the result of careful fitting.

but add pop-rivets. It's called a kick panel for a reason. It and its windlace take a lot of beating. If you can't drive in a few staples in this area, use screws or pop-rivets to really secure it in place.

Making and Installing a Headliner

Most of us with trim experience call one of the aftermarket headliner fabricators when we need a new headliner. If our customer has an idea for an unusual piece of material for his or her headliner, we pack up the material and send it to our aftermarket people. They slap their patterns down on it, cut it out, sew it up and send it back.

Interestingly, the fabricator made the pattern by buying an original headliner, cutting it apart and making patterns from the pieces. Very few were made from fitting to the car. Therefore, for many of us it's becoming a lost art. You, however, get a chance to relearn the mystical art, and so, become one of the few who can make a fitted headliner for any car in existence.

Preparation

Our '57 is the demo-dolly for this operation. We'll watch over George's shoulder while he puts it all together. Just to rub it in a little, George cut, fit, sewed and installed this headliner in a little over nine hours.

The car came to the shop with no backlite (rear window) or windshield. It also came with all the bows removed and unmarked. Save yourself a great deal of time and a big headache. Number the bows before you remove them. You'll also have a much nicer finished headliner if you remove the windshield and backlite.

George carefully fits each bow in place. He then anchors it to be sure it does not move while he's fitting. He does this with a little contact cement. Not too much or he'll have trouble later on. After installing the bows in their correct location, he begins the measuring and fitting operation.

Fitting

As with any upholstery or trimming operation there are two initial steps: finding the centerline and squaring the material. George begins with a centerline in the front and one in the rear. You can make centerlines at each bow if you wish. It's not necessary, however, as you'll be making witness marks along each piece to get them to line up. Additionally, you'll be locating and matching centers of each piece you fit.

George measures the largest width between each bow and adds about 2 inches to each side. This will give him plenty of room for adjustment. Notice at the backlite he measures and cuts from the last bow all the way to the luggage panel. This lets the panel be one piece all the way along the edge of the backlight. The fitting operation begins in the front and works to the back.

The trick to the whole business is to spray a thin, narrow layer of cement on the bow and on the material. Now you can stick it up there, hold it in place, stretch to remove the wrinkles, then mark along each bow with chalk.

George folds the front piece in half, nicks the edge with his scissors to mark the center, then makes a centerline across the width of the material. In the photo you see George with the material folded over on itself at the centerline and he's fitting along the first bow. George has been fitting these headliners for many years. He can fit one half and make the other side from the fitted side. If this is your first attempt, or even first few attempts, get the panel up there fully spread out so you can see there'll be no wrinkles.

Photo 20. Following the anchoring of the front, George cements the rear in place. In the quickie shops they peel the rubber back from around the backlite and cement the headliner selvage behind it. It never looks right and is seldom smooth. As a custom upholsterer, always remove the front windshield and backlite.

Photo 21. The headliner is completely installed and ready for glass.

Photo 22. The finished headliner ready to leave the shop. The job is flawless.

Photo 23. George has applied the fabric to the top and sides of the truck. Always begin with a centerline on both the fabric and foam. This will allow you to match the two together, resulting in a straight application. Omit this step and you may wind up with the material at an angle.

Photos 24 & 25. Just like he did with the door panel, George installs trim pieces to the headliner and side panels with cement and staples.

Photos 26 & 27. The panel delivery truck begins to take shape. This is certainly a far different look than the original upholstery.

Photo 28. To make the center piece, George had to cement three pieces of chipboard together. Note the penciled centerline.

Photo 29. We're ready now to foam the center panel. Look carefully and see the areas where the edges of the chipboard have been ground down. By doing this, the sharp edges will not show through the finished product.

Photo 30. George has the panel all ready for covering. The domelight holes have been cut and the surface of the foam scuffed to help the cement attach.

Photo 30a. The finished panel cemented in place. We suggest you spray a medium coat of cement on both surfaces to be bonded and allowed to dry. When thoroughly dried (at least an hour) spray a second thin coat, let dry for about five minutes, then clamp the two together.

In the photos you can see George works out each panel, one at a time, gluing and fitting, then making his witness marks. Note that he also makes a fitting mark at the edge of each door frame and along the window frame. This will be important when he trims the selvage at the bench. When all the pieces are fitted and numbered, George gathers them all up and heads for the bench.

Trimming

To begin, George lays out the front piece on the bench and begins to trim away the selvage, leaving a 1/2 inch seam allowance. However, he only trims one half of the piece. He then folds it at the centerline. He checks to see if the other half of the panel fitting lines matches the half he just trimmed. Now he cuts the second side to match the first.

In this manner, George is assured that both sides of the panel are identical. If one side is narrower than the other, it can be corrected at this stage. Likewise, if it's larger it can also be corrected. Sometimes it's necessary to trim a little off the first side and add a little to the other side to get that equal fit. It's more important to have both ends of the panel the same than it is to worry much about 1/4 to 1/2 inch. This material will stretch to make up for such a small amount.

Earlier we said that it was important to mark around the edge of the door and window frame. This serves two purposes. First, it gives you lines to match when you start to sew. Second, if you fold the material so the marks come together, you have an exact center. Make a nick here with your scissors and you'll have a marked centerline. Again, fit each end of the panel so both are the same. Work all the panels the same. When each panel has been trimmed with a 1/2 inch seam allowance, both ends are the same,

and you've notched a centerline, you're ready to begin sewing.

Sewing

From here on it's pretty straightforward. George has a roll of 3 inch listing tape. If you don't do enough headliners to warrant buying rolls of listing tape, make your own from a very light muslin—about the weight of a bed sheet. Cut this material into 3 inch widths for as many bows as you have. If you want to be really fancy, cut the material on the bias (diagonal). This gives the material a two-way stretch and will often produce fewer wrinkles.

Fold the material in half and sew the ends to the vinyl or fabric. You are making a cloth "tube" or "tunnel" for the headliner bow to fit into.

Start the listings about 1-1/2 inches from the mark you made at the door and window frame. It's best if you don't have listing material in this area. When you wrap the material around the headliner retainers, you won't want that extra bulk the listing would provide. Sew it all together, matching all your marks.

You may have to stretch a bit here and there to get all the marks to line up. If any of the marks are too far apart to get them to line up correctly, you've done something wrong. Cut your work apart and go back and refit. You'll soon discover your error. Fix it now before you try to install it.

Installation

If you haven't done it already, insulate the top according to the directions in Chapter 6. Don't omit this step; it's so important to the sound-deadening quality of the finished job. With your insulation in, install the bows.

Begin with either the front or rear bow and run it into the

listing. Center it by eye for now. Then, one-by-one, insert the others; again, center them by eye. Smooth things out, bundle up the headliner and climb into the car.

Install the rear bow first. Always work from the rear to the front. All Ford products and most other marques have a little hook (or two) that anchor the bow to the top edge of the backlite frame. If these have been lost, make new ones with a piece of mechanic's wire or even garden wire. Be sure the ends don't poke through the headliner. In so doing, when you pull the headliner snug as you work forward, you won't roll the rear bow out of position. When all the bows are installed, center the headliner.

To do this, align the center marks in the front and rear panels with the centerlines you drew on the top. Temporarily cement them in place. Now begin working the wrinkles out. Smooth them out to the edges. Begin with the middle bow and trim back about 1/2 inch on the listing. You can cut anywhere along the listing except the seam line. Leave the seam intact. Give a little pull and bring some of the wrinkles out. Repeat this operation as many times as it takes to get the wrinkles out of one side of the seam. Then go to the other side and do it all again. You must repeat this operation along all the seams until there are no wrinkles anywhere in the headliner. From here on, the headliner is installed as you would any OEM or after-market unit.

For a full discussion and treatment on the installation of a headliner, refer to *Automotive Upholstery Handbook* by California Bill's Automotive Handbooks. Here, you'll get every detail of where to cut, how to pull, use of tools and everything else needed to install your first headliner or improve your existing technique.

The One-piece or Seamless Headliner

One of the "trick" things hot rodders like is one-piece headliners created with no seams. When you make this type of headliner, you can carve designs into the underlying foam, you can make built-up areas by adding foam and, in all ways, turn your imagination loose to create something exciting, unusual and creative. The first demonstration of this type of headliner begins with the panel delivery truck. Then we discuss and demonstrate with the Willys.

The Panel Delivery

Preparation

When we left the panel delivery, it had all its side and top pieces of panelboard installed. The chipboard curves had been made and a layer of 1/4 inch closed-cell foam had been cemented in place. George Torres had carved some attractive lines into the foam. Now, we're ready to begin covering.

As you can see in the photos, the panel delivery headliner is a three-piece arrangement. A large centerpiece is covered in leather (the length of a full hide) with two side pieces covering one-third of the top and halfway down the sides of the sides. The rest of the sides are made in two pieces to accommodate the limit of 54 inch-wide fabric. This is well demonstrated if you look at photo 22 on page 61 and then photo 30a on page 72. The piece we're interested in is the one that makes up part of the headliner.

George wants the fabric to lie straight along the length of the vehicle. Therefore, he marks a centerline the length of the section he plans to cover and a corresponding centerline along the back of the fabric. By matching

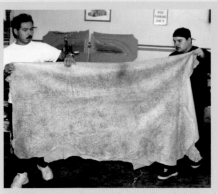

Photo 31. Frank and George together must bring the cemented hide into the car. Notice that it's folded along the centerline.

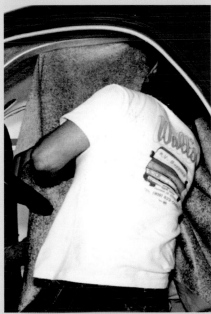

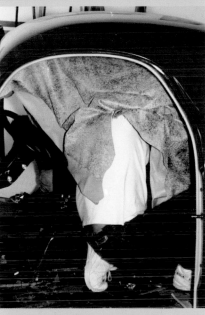

Photos 32 & 33. Frank begins the installation by matching the centerlines. After smoothing the center, he starts working on the driver's side.

Photo 34. We pick the job up after the driver's side is finished. The center is firmly attached but the edge is not yet defined.

Photo 35. With his bent knife, Frank works the leather around the edge of the center piece and makes it tight.

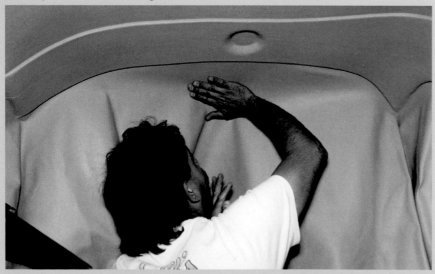

Photo 36. He begins working the leather out from the center in each direction. You can see the indent for the domelight just behind his right hand.

these two centerlines the material will lie straight and even.

Installation

George sprays a medium coat of cement on both the fabric and foam. He allows this to dry until it passes the touch-test described earlier. When both pieces are dry he matches the centerlines and sweeps his hand over the material, gently tacking it in place. As described before, if you apply very little pressure at this stage the material can be pulled away from the foam with no ill effects. Now George begins to work from the centerline both ways, sweeping the material onto the foam with no wrinkles.

If he finds a wrinkle developing, he'll pull the fabric away, adjust for the excess fabric that was making the wrinkle, then smooth the material into place once again. Finally, as you saw him do in the door-panel section, he'll use his bent putty knife to work the fabric into the previously cut grooves in the foam. This gives the design effect we call the "hard" look.

The third section of the "one-piece" headliner is the leather centerpiece. To make this, George began earlier by making a pattern. Because of the length, he cemented three pieces of chipboard together. Next, he drew a centerline the full length of the three pieces. Using his eye, he sketched in a curved line that suited his design idea. Finally, this line was refined and the selvage cut away. The quickest and easiest way to refine a curved line is to bend a yardstick along it. While you hold the yardstick bent, have a helper mark the corrected line with a pencil or pen.

To make both sides the same, George folded the halves along the centerline, then used the formed edge as a pattern to mark the opposite side. This is the same thing George did when he was making both ends of the '57 headliner pieces the same. The resulting pattern, with identically formed sides, could now be used for two solutions. The first was to develop the lines on the top panelboard to which George would bring the foam, and the second to make a centerpiece to be covered in leather.

For the panel delivery truck, Ron, George and the customer decided the centerpiece should be built up from chipboard padded with 1/4 inch foam. Had they wanted the design to stand more proud of the side pieces, it could have been made from panelboard or even plywood.

George cemented three more pieces of chipboard together to make the base for his centerpiece. This time, however, he ground the edges of the chipboard at the glue seam to prevent lumps from "telegraphing" through the foam and leather at these unions. He finished the panel by cementing a layer of 1/4 inch foam over the chipboard and covering this with leather. The finished product stood proud of the rest of the headliner by the thickness of the leather, chipboard and the edge of the headliner fabric upon which the panel was cemented. This was about 3/16 inch.

Installing the Willys Headliner

The Willys headliner presented a bigger problem than the panel delivery. The Willys headliner is, indeed, a two-way, concave area to be covered with no fitting seams. Although a daunting task, it's not impossible. The secret lies in the stretching.

Frank begins with a whole hide! Rather than worry about how much to allow for selvage, he simply uses a full hide. Whatever he trims off, if the pieces are big enough, he'll use for other things. He doesn't want to come up short,

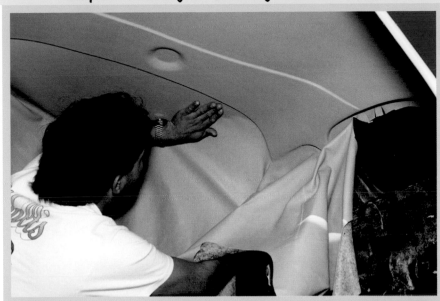

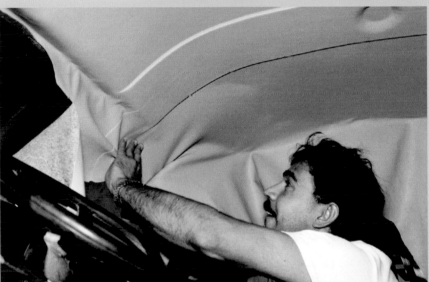

Photos 37-39. From the center he works toward the back; then, from the center he works toward the front. You can see his right hand beneath the leather holding it away from the foam while his left hand presses the leather tight. He is also using his right hand to pull on the material.

Photo 40. The last step is to trim around the windlace then force the selvage edge under the retainer strip.

Photo 41. A beautiful job. It looks like the leather was "sprayed" onto the base. Follow these directions carefully and even your first job should look this good.

though, after working all morning getting this thing in.

As always, both the leather and foam are cemented and allowed to dry. Also, as always, Frank begins in the middle and works both ways. There is only a two-way curve in the center of the headliner. This gives Frank a good base with an easy installation to begin the project. He starts by smoothly applying the leather to the raised-foam portion we saw in the last chapter. He carefully works the leather over the edge of this centerpiece and then defines the edge with his bent putty knife. He works one side of the car first, then works the other.

As stated above, the secret to making this inside curve is the way the leather is stretched. Think of the inside of the car as a giant bowl. You must work the leather not just from the center to the right or left, but from the center in every direction—360 degrees. After establishing the base, Frank gently pulls from the center out—first on one side, then the other, working as if in a bowl from the center to the edge—in our case, from the center towards the floor. He pulls with one hand and smooths with the other.

In the last chapter, as Frank installed the foam, he pulled in much the same manner. There, he had some small wrinkles that could be removed with sandpaper. The wrinkles that develop in the leather can't be sanded out. Therefore, he must pull each one out, not by pulling to the side, but pulling straight down. This forces the wrinkles together. There's enough give in the leather so it will absorb the smallest wrinkles. This works also with fabric but not very well with vinyl. Vinyl is so dense there's little room to absorb any wrinkles. When Frank sees a large wrinkle trying to develop, he lifts the leather, adjusts it a bit and works it down again, this time without the wrinkle.

Finally, all the wrinkles are stretched out, compressed, or fall away around the windows and door frame. Frank then finishes off around the doors by pushing the selvage edge of the leather under the tiger strips he installed earlier and cementing the loose ends around the windows.

Summary

This chapter has given you lots of new information. You watched as George fit a multi-piece headliner. The trick lay in cementing the fabric panels to the bows and fitting from there. Most trimmers we know either use the old headliner for a pattern or send away for a "ready-made" unit. Now you can make a headliner for any vehicle—even a Bugatti Royale or a Hispano-Suiza.

In the little truck and the Willys you watched as two fine craftsmen "molded" headliners inside the vehicle with no bows, no seams, but with a lot of pulling. Work slowly here. Don't rush. If you work slowly and carefully it will come out right the first time. If you work too fast you'll make mistakes and have to pull it out and start over, taking twice as much time as you would have otherwise.

Speaker FX

"I think he covered over the speakers with that headliner!"

Well, it may look like it but he didn't cover over them. Ron's shop has run into this problem before so Frank was ready for it. Let's follow the photos and see how the problem was solved.

1. Frank begins when the top is almost finished. He locates the speaker and chalks a circle around it.

2. By eye, he draws in a vertical and horizontal line within the circle.

3. This is a tool Ron made to solve the demonstrated problem. It's a circle of leather with 1/8 inch holes formed in concentric rings.

4. Frank places the pattern over the circle he recently drew, aligning the holes in the pattern with the vertical and horizontal lines he drew earlier.

5. With a pencil, he makes marks through the holes in the pattern onto the leather. He follows this by using a straight edge to be sure all the dots are in a straight line.

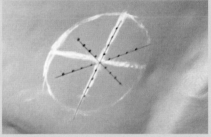

6. Here's what the finished marks look like. Frank elected to use a pattern a little differently designed than the original chalk line.

7. With the leather punch, Frank punches out each of the marks he made on the leather. For this job he selects the largest punch in the tool—about 1/8 inch.

8. The finished job is subtle, unobtrusive and very effective.

Front, Rear and Trunk

The interior of our car is about complete. Two major components remain to be completed. The car must have carpeting throughout, and then, freshly upholstered seats may be installed. In the next chapter we'll begin discussing seats. For now, however, we must concentrate our attention on carpeting. Let's start with a brief review of carpet fundamentals as a beginning.

Types of Pile

There are two main types of carpet: loop pile and cut pile. In the manufacture of carpeting, to get the height of the nap, the carpet-weaving machine "loops" the carpet threads about 3/16 to 1/2 inch above the backing. If this weave is left in place, we call it loop-pile carpet. An alternative to leaving the pile as it comes from the loom is to shave off the loop tops. When this is done, we call it cut-pile carpet. Because this is an added step in the manufacture, cut-pile is more expensive than loop-pile carpet.

When the factory makes a run of cut-pile, they weave the threads closer together to create a denser carpet. Because more thread is used at a greater expense to the manufacture, the price increases.

Thread Type

Carpet pile is woven from three distinct threads: rayon, nylon and wool. Rayon is the least expensive with nylon a close second. Wool, the material of choice for most hot rodders, is a very expensive third. Generally, wool is four times as

Photo 1. The safest way to cut carpet is to have a cutting diagram. If you find yourself short of carpet, as Juanito did, make your cutting diagram right on the carpet.

expensive as nylon. However, disregarding the touch and feel of real wool carpet, it will also last more than four times as long as nylon or rayon. Consequently, it's not only a luxury material, it's also cost-effective for the customer.

Backing

Backing, like pile, also comes in three (sometimes four) types or styles. The least expensive is a cotton-canvas material. Because cotton is so light, the manufacturer must reinforce this backing with a plastic-like material, sprayed on during the manufacturing process. This serves two purposes. First, it adds more body to the carpet and second, it holds the pile from pulling out or unraveling.

More expensive carpets are fabricated with a jute backing. Far more substantial than cotton, it almost entirely eliminates the possibility of pulling or unraveling a thread. Premium wool carpeting always has a double jute back.

On double jute-back carpeting, the pile is woven into one layer of jute, then another layer is bonded to the first. This style carpeting is almost indestructible.

Sometimes you'll find a carpet whose loops are held together with a plasticized backing with a nylon net imbedded into it. This is often the type of backing you'll find on Berber carpets (discussed later). One of the nice features of this type of carpet is the ability to remove the nylon netting on the back. In so doing, it allows you to hand-form the carpet around mild two-way (or compound) curves. Because you removed the supporting material from the back of the carpet, it must be cemented to the insulation to prevent it from unraveling.

These are the main types of carpet. Manufacturers, however, are always looking for ways to make better and

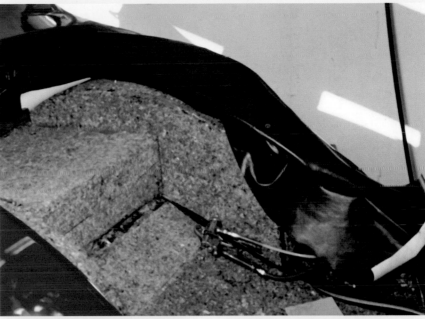

Photos 2-4. To get the most out of your carpet, make patterns of the area you wish to cover. Juanito had to make a pattern of the rear quarter panel in the trunk. He transferred the pattern to the carpet, saving many square inches over cutting the carpet first and fitting second.

Photo 5. Always start with the transmission tunnel. Cover this first, then fit around it.

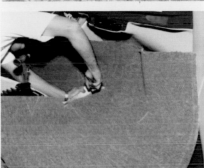

Photos 6 & 7. Here you see Frank fitting the carpet directly over the area he plans to cover. This is faster, and sometimes more accurate, than making a pattern first. However, it always uses more material.

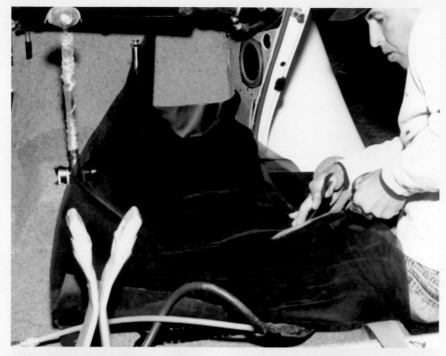

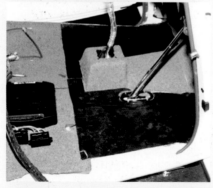

Photos 8-12. In this series we watch Ron use a "see-through" material for pattern making. Neither of us knows the name of this material as it was bought at auction for just this use. With the ability to see through the material, Ron can quickly chalk out the area he wishes to cover. He then transfers the pattern to panelboard. It would be impossible to fit the panelboard without a pattern.

Photo 13. For the panels in the rear, Ron can work directly with chipboard. Here, he has the advantage of starting with a square edge. This eliminates part of the fitting.

cheaper carpeting. During your career you'll see any number of combinations of the above and many that we've not described.

Remember that wool carpet is the premier product. Most customers will want cut-pile wool carpet. However, over the last few years a loop-pile wool carpet has gained in popularity. You should make yourself familiar with this product. It retains its name from home interior use—Berber carpet.

Berber carpet gets its name from the people who were the original weavers: the Berber nomads of the Middle East. These wanderers of the desert weave an extremely tight loop-pile carpet from the wool of their sheep. It's used for both the floor and sides of their tents, keeping out sand, sun, wind and occasional rain. For the home and auto industry, however, the Berbers do not weave the carpet. It's woven at regular carpet mills but retains the name Berber to denote its style and lineage.

You must choose carpet for yourself or your customer that fits the budget. However, keep the above information in mind as you make your selection. Always strive to get the best value for your dollar.

In the previous chapters we discussed insulating the car for noise-damping and heat control (keep it out in the summer and in during the winter). Always begin your carpet project by fully insulating the floor. Use as much insulation as practical and the best you can afford. We bring up insulation again because its presence—or lack of it—will change the fit of the carpet. In other words, insulate first, fit second.

We assume you have some experience with making automobile carpet. Therefore, we'll discuss the tricks we use and the problems we meet and overcome. If you're not sure of how a carpet goes together, reference, again, *Automotive Upholstery Handbook* by

California Bill's Automotive Handbooks. It takes you step-by-step through the basics.

We demonstrate again with the Willys and the '34 Ford. We'll also watch Ron do a few things to the '57.

Fitting

Good fitting is preceded by good planning. Decide first which sections will be carpeted and the order in which you'll carpet them. The usual procedure for the front of a car is to cover the transmission "hump" first. This is followed by the firewall then the passenger and driver areas. Sometimes the passenger and driver areas include the firewall with a seam joining the two together in the center of the transmission tunnel. These are design considerations and yours alone to make.

Often the rear floor is covered in one piece with darts sewn into the corners if the floor pan sets below the level of the driveshaft. This is common in all late (1948 on) model cars. Early models, such as the Willys and panel delivery, have a floor pan above the driveshaft, so one flat piece of carpet usually suffices.

The easiest way to plan your cutting is to measure, then draw a cutting diagram. This will always save material and often time. However, it does consume a bit of time making the diagram. The carpet material for the Willys is a home grade of loop-pile Berber as we discussed earlier. Unfortunately, only one piece was left and Ron's crew had to get everything out of that piece. To ensure they cut it correctly, Frank and Juanito laid the carpet out on the floor and drew the cutting diagram directly on it.

Usually, you'll measure an area to be covered as a square or rectangle; 15 × 34 or 21 × 22 inches. This is fine if you have plenty of material. If you're short,

Photo 14. The insulation for the trunk of the Willys has been laid. Note the areas around the wheel wells cut out for the selvage edge of the carpet. This is good prior planning.

Photo 15. In the progression of carpeting a trunk, begin with the quarter panel.

Photos 16 & 17. Follow with the outside of the wheel well. Juanito trims the outside material to match the edges of the insulation along the top of the wheel well, around the fuel tank area and down on the floor. Knowing he would do this, he cut the insulation to leave room.

Photos 18 & 19. The second step in the covering operation is to make the cover for the top of the wheel well. Notice the slashes Juanito made to fit around the back of the wheel well next to the quarter panel.

Photo 20. Here's the finished product. Both quarter panels and wheel wells have been carpet-covered, then the fuel tank between them. Juanito has only to make the carpet for the floor to finish the job.

however, make a pattern of the area to be covered. Then lay the pattern on the carpet, placing it at the most advantageous position, angle or location. This saves a great deal of material. Juanito made a pattern for the rear quarter panel in the trunk of the Willys. By its shape you can see how much waste there would have been had he cut a large rectangular piece and fit from that.

Another interesting demonstration is Ron's use of a loose-woven, netting type of material to make a pattern for the driver and passenger side in the panel delivery. He can see through this material and so follow lines beneath it without the need to fold the material back to see where he's marking. He simply lays the pattern material over the area to cover, draws the shape and cuts it right the first time. You can also use clear vinyl or shade cloth (screen) for this type of fitting.

There should always be a plan, if not on paper, at least in your mind about the sequence in which you will cover each area to be carpeted. This sequence will determine the size of many of your pieces—and in some ways, how the insulation will be installed. This is well demonstrated in the Willys' trunk. Follow along with the photos as we discuss the process.

Look carefully at photo 14 on page 81. You can see areas along the tops of the wheels, the bottoms of the wheel wells and other select areas where there is no insulation. You can see bare floor sticking out. This is to allow the selvage edge of the carpet to insert in the space. This edge becomes part of the insulation. Jump forward to photos 16 and 17. Here you can see the selvage edge of the carpet butting right up against the rebond insulation. The surface over the wheel well is now completely insulated and smooth enough to lay a top strip of carpet over the wheel well (photos 18, 19).

Covering the quarter panel, wheel wells and the centerpiece (over the gas tank) proceeded as follows (page 82):

1. Cover the quarter panels between the wheel well and the fender.

2. Cover the outside of the wheel well, leaving a selvage edge over the fuel tank and along the floor, and abutting the insulation at the top of the wheel well.

3. Cover the tops of the wheel wells, binding each side and leaving selvage along the floor.

4. Cover over the fuel tank, finishing the edges against the outsides of the wheel wells.

This is a fairly standard sequence for covering the inside of a trunk area. It makes the nicest appearance around the wheel wells of any system we've used. Feel free to use it as your own!

Cutting

In reality, cutting is cutting. You chop it out and sew it up. However, there are two schools of cutting carpet and you should understand both. Most trimmers mark the top (pile) side of the carpet with chalk and cut the piece with a pair of scissors. This is quick and effective and for thin carpet, works quite well. The other school marks the back and cuts with a razor blade.

The razor blade works very well on heavy carpet. First, by working from the back you can see the way the backing is woven. By following the weave of the backing as the line from which you square, your straight lines will automatically follow the weave both horizontally and vertically. This is a great help when the carpet is woven crookedly.

The second benefit to cutting from the back with a razor blade is you never cut the nap or pile at an angle. This is especially helpful on wool carpet. Sometimes, cutting with scissors leaves a ragged edge that can't be buried in the binding. Cut a piece

Photo 21. Ron uses the steamer to work the carpet into the curve of the floor pan in the '57 Ford.

Photo 22. This is the result. Using a little cleaning solvent, he'll wash the cement off the edge where the dart was cut and you'll never be able to see the seam.

Photo 23. When using stiff carpet (like the Berber in the Willys) use a matching vinyl for the binding. It will finish much nicer than off-the-shelf cloth binding. Juanito cuts his binding in 2 inch-wide strips.

Photo 24. The use of a second seam along the edge of the carpet and binding prevents the edge of the carpet telegraphing through the vinyl after it's wrapped tightly about the edge. It also helps the corners of the carpet to lie flat.

Photos 25 & 26. After sewing the binding, cement the back side in place. Don't omit this step. It makes for a much nicer finish than attempting to simply sew it in place. When cutting the corners of the binding to relieve tension, be careful not to cut so deeply into the binding that it shows on the top.

Photo 27. Finish the carpet binding by "sewing in the ditch" (an old quilting term) between the binding and the pile. Take it slow and easy here to prevent running up on the binding or pile.

Photo 28. Trim the selvage from the binding after you've sewn it down.

Photo 29. Not all of the '34 panels are made of panelboard. Here Ron makes one of chipboard. In this case he can use the pattern as his panel, saving one step in the process.

Photos 30 & 31. Ron covers the floor panels just as he would a door panel. From his pattern he makes a panel and covers it with foam. He carves his design, cements the fabric to the foam and refines the pattern with the bent knife.

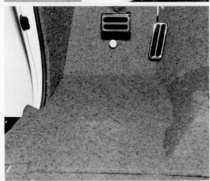

Photos 32 & 33. Here are the results of the pattern making and covered panels as carpet. A very interesting concept.

of carpet this way and see if you like it. (Ron cuts from the front with scissors, Don from the back with a razor blade.)

Sewing

Most of the sewing on a piece of carpet concerns itself with the binding. Occasionally, you'll have to sew in a few darts as in our example of the lowered floor pan on post-fifties cars. This is seen in the photo of the rear floor of the '57 Ford on page 83.

If the carpet is thin enough, it can be sewn together just as you would a piece of fabric. Unlike fabric, on carpet it's best to cement the selvage edges back against the body. This helps it to lie flatter on the floor. Cut-pile carpet, when dealing with a dart, can often be cut then butted together and cemented to the floor with no seam or binding. If you must have the carpet joined with binding, follow the drawing on page 91 to see how it's done.

Binding carpet for a custom job is more than just sewing a piece of cloth or vinyl binding to the edge. Follow Frank as he binds the carpet for the front of the Willys. See photos on page 83.

Juanito begins by cutting 2 inch strips of vinyl. Frank will use these for his binding. Laying the face of the vinyl against the pile of the carpet, Frank carefully sews in 1/2 inch from the edge around the entire length of the area to be bound. He's very careful to keep the edge of the carpet and the binding well aligned. He then goes back and sews an identical seam as close to the edge of the two pieces as possible.

Frank makes the second seam to flatten the edge. Without the second seam, the vinyl would be forced up by the pile. This vertical edge would then show through the vinyl after it was wrapped around the carpet. With only one seam, the bound edge looks

round. With the double seam the edge looks flat.

With the two seams complete, Frank coats the inside of the binding and the back of the carpet with a medium layer of cement. When the cement is dry Frank will wrap the binding tightly around the edge of the carpet. He clips the corners so everything will lay flat.

Frank now returns to the sewing machine and very carefully sews a seam in the groove ("ditch") between the binding and the pile. You should not be able to see this seam. It must not run up on the vinyl binding nor catch any of the pile. In fact, the pile must hide the thread. This seam prevents the binding from coming unglued from the back of the carpet. It also helps to keep the edge from rolling up. When everything is sewn in place, Frank trims the selvage of the binding from the back of the carpet.

Meanwhile, Ron has finished the '57 and has turned his attentions to the panel delivery. The "carpet" for this truck is not carpet at all. The customer has decided he wants the floor upholstered just like the rest of the car. Therefore, Ron will use the same tweed on the floor as you see on the side panels. Although this could be considered highly impractical, practicality is not the end result the customer is looking for—design consideration is more important. The vehicle will never be used for carrying cargo more damaging than a picnic basket. See photos 30 and 31.

Earlier, we saw him fit the floor panels using chipboard and netting. He's now cut out the plywood and prepares to cover it. This covering operation is done just like a door panel. In fact, in the photos you can see where Ron carved a design into the foam, just as George did on the side panels. The fabric is cemented to the foam, the carvings accented with the bent knife, and the edges cemented to the backs of the panels. The finished job gives the appearance the customer wanted: that of an upholstered driving compartment rather than a carpeted one.

Installation

In the world of OEM upholstery, we buy a carpet kit (usually molded to fit) from the local carpet distributor, take it out of the box and stick it in the car—sometimes without even removing the seat. In custom upholstery we can't do this. Each piece must be made separately and cemented in place. Cementing the carpet in place prevents wrinkles. It also gives a much nicer appearance. Finally, with a little coaxing, you can often force it into a compound curve.

Using Steam

One of the most important tools to a custom trimmer is the steamer. These come in many sizes and styles. The one used at Ron's shop and seen in the photographs is a 110-volt unit that can be moved from car-to-car on little wheels—much like a shop vacuum cleaner.

It's best to use distilled water in these units. This serves two purposes. First, it prevents build-up of mineral deposits in the jets and wand (the applicator). Second is a result of the first. With no deposit build-up, you won't get big globs of gray mineral deposits blasting out of the wand and onto your light-tan carpet. Here's a trick for those of you who have been using regular tap water in your steam machine: Run a gallon of white vinegar through your machine. This will dissolve most of the minerals.

Sometimes it takes a second gallon if the first doesn't do the job. Warning: don't perform the vinegar wash while you're working on carpet or fabric! Run the vinegar through when the unit is not in service.

Hot steam relaxes the weave of the material and the carpet backing. In this relaxed state, it's easy to force the carpet to lie flat, or even force it into an indented area. With enough steam you can often remove small wrinkles.

Apply a coat of cement to both the carpet and the insulation. From the front of the carpet, force steam into the nap and backing. Now, press the carpet into the area you wish to cover. Sometimes, you'll have to pull the carpet up and adjust it. If you don't press down too hard the first time the carpet will come up without tearing the insulation. Once the carpet is down, give it a bit more steam and force any small wrinkles into place, If you're working with a cut-pile carpet, brush the nap in one direction and allow to dry without touching it.

Other Fastening Methods

Sometimes, the customer will want to be able to remove certain parts of the carpet. We see this in the trunk of the Willys and the rear floor of the panel delivery. Let's look at the Willys first. See photos at right.

Here, the customer must have access to the sound system for adjustment and repairs. Once again, the job begins with making patterns. Notice in the photos that Juanito uses three pieces to make the cover: one over each wheel and one in the center.

After making a chipboard pattern, Juanito cuts panels from 1/2 inch plywood. He then cuts carpet to the exact size of the panel. Using the 2 inch vinyl he cut earlier, he binds all the edges of each piece. Again, the binding is sewn with double seams. Next, he cements the carpet to the panel, then wraps the binding around the edges of the wood and cements them to the back of the panel.

Photo 34. To make removable carpet panels, Juanito must again make a pattern. Here he'll make three of them.

Photo 35. After making the pattern, he'll use it to form a panel of plywood, then cover it with carpet. Here you see him stapling the Velcro in place. This prevents it from peeling off the vinyl.

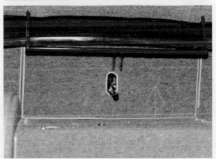

Photos 36 & 37. The finished product. The customer can remove the panels to service his sound system. Notice there are no visible fasteners.

Photos 38-40. Your most important tool for making carpet behave is the steamer. Steam relaxes the back and fibers, allowing you to shape and form what is otherwise a very stiff piece of material. Juanito uses it in the trunk, Frank on the transmission tunnel and Ron in the '57.

To hold the panels in place, you have your choice of several options. Juanito used Velcro on the Willys panels. If there is structural integrity to worry about, use screws. There may be occasions to use snaps or Lift-a-Dot™ fasteners. Mostly, however, Velcro will be the fastener of choice.

Let's jump over to the '34 now and see what Ron's doing in the rear. Here, we have a very simple but elegant installation. The whole back area of the '34 consists of four pieces of panelboard. As in the front, the panelboard is covered with foam, a pattern matching the front carved into it and everything covered in the same tweed. This is an interesting concept, very well executed. These panels stay in place with a force fit. They must be removed with some frequency so the customer didn't want to fool around with fasteners. See page 87, photos 41 and 42.

Finishing the Edges

Our last decision is what to do with the edges of the carpet that lie along the top of the rocker panel. Many cars, such as the '57, have aftermarket scuff panels that may be purchased. The carpet is trimmed and the scuff panels installed. In the panel delivery, scuff panels were custom-formed from aluminum by a local body shop. Ron then covered these in matching leather. What can you do, however, if there are no aftermarket products and your body shop can't weld aluminum? You check out how the Willys was finished.

Ron went to the local hardware store and bought two lengths of household carpet edge-protector. This is formed so one edge covers the carpet and the other edge tapers down to meet with a tile or hardwood floor. This is exactly what we have in any car. The edge of the carpet lies on the rocker (the rocker representing a tile or hardwood floor). See photos 43, 44.

The next step is to cut the aluminum edge-protectors to length. With this done Ron drilled screw holes along the length, being sure to place one in each end. Then, using a large bit, he countersunk each hole. It's safer to use a countersink bit because then there's no chance that the bit will dig in and make a much larger countersink than you wanted.

At the bench, Ron covered each of the edge-protectors with matching leather. Then, it was only a simple step to screw them in place using chromed, countersunk sheetmetal screws. Very slick.

Heel Pads and Gear-Shift Boots

If there is one secret to prize-winning custom upholstery, it is attention to detail. This attention to the details separates the greats from the "wannabes." We want you to be one of the greats. Therefore, you too must pay attention to the details. Two of the most important are heel pads and boots on everything that comes out of the floor. This includes the gear shift, emergency brake, and sometimes even the brake pedal.

Be generous with the heel pad. Any good shop will make the heel pad large enough to cover the whole surface of both the driver's and passenger's side of the floor. Fit the heel pad to conform to all the areas. Don't just cut out a square and call it good.

To make the pads for the Willys, Frank covered the backs with a product from the furniture end of the upholstery business. It's the dust cloth you find on the bottom of every piece of furniture. This material is called Cambric (pronounced came-brick). Don't confuse it with the top material called Cambria (cam-bree-ah). Without the Cambric backing,

the nylon in the back of the carpet would get hooked into the loops of the pile the heel pad was covering. This would soon begin to pull little threads and the carpet would look like it was covered in fuzz or had a terrible cat-hair problem.

To keep the pad from sliding, Frank sewed the hook-side of Velcro tape to the back. The hooks catch in the loops of the pile and the pad stays in place.

A second method of heel-pad building uses polyfoam on the carpet back. You can buy polyfoam in any thickness. Ron buys a special 1/8 inch-thick piece to use for heel-pad backing.

After the pad is cut to shape, cement a layer of 1/8 inch polyfoam to the back. Trim to fit; then sew on the binding as described above. This heel pad is guaranteed not to slip. When you can't use Velcro, this is a great way to go.

There is yet a third way. At the carpet stores selling home carpeting, they also sell a rubberized netting material used to keep throw rugs from sliding along wood floors. This can be cemented to the back of the heel pad and serves the same purpose as the polyfoam. Don uses this method because he feels it wears better than polyfoam.

Boots

Boots hide a lot of ugly mechanical unions and give everything a finished appearance. Every boot is a little different than the other, making it hard to demonstrate the actual making of them. Usually, they're made of two, three or four pieces in a pyramid shape. The gear shift boot for the Willys is made of four pieces fitted to the rubber cover that came as original equipment. The emergency brake boot is made from two pieces and is shaped a bit like a gooseneck.

The important lesson, or trick, to take away from this reading

Photos 41 & 42. All of the floor of the '34 is made of panels—all with carved designs. Custom upholstery work is based on new applications of old techniques.

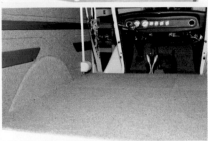

Photos 43 & 44. This is a really neat trick: make your scuff plates out of aluminum extrusion used to cover the edge of household carpet where it joins either a hardwood or tiled floor. Frank countersinks his holes before covering the extrusion with leather. Then he uses countersunk screws to hold it in place. The finished product looks like it was designed for the car.

Photos 45 & 46. Line the back of your heel pads with Cambric to prevent the back of the carpet from wearing on the pile of the carpet it must protect. Keep it from slipping with Velcro hooks when covering loop-pile carpet.

Photos 47 & 48. To cover a boot like this, fit it on all four sides, hem the top and cement the bottom of the leather to the bottom of the rubber boot. Each time you make a boot, make a pattern for it. It's very likely you'll be making another one sometime.

Photos 50 & 51. Here are two examples of anchoring the top of the boot with a wire tie (Ty-Wrap). Wire ties come in every length imaginable so it's easy to find one to solve your problem. Be sure to trim the end as close as possible to the anchor point. We like to try to tuck the anchor inside the hem so it can't be seen.

Photo 49. Ron's a fanatic about little details. After the car was finished he came back and made this boot for the brake pedal. Ron, is this overkill?

Photo 52. For an even more finished appearance, fasten the wire tie inside the boot. This is done by starting with the boot wrong side out. Pull it over the shaft and anchor it wherever you want it. Then turn the boot right side out over itself. Presto! The wire tie has disappeared.

is the way the boot is anchored tightly around the lever it covers. The secret is wire ties. Into each boot, where it fits around the lever, Ron sews in a plastic wire tie (Ty-Wrap).

These are available from any hardware store electrical department or from Radio Shack. They're used to clamp bundles of wires together. You see them used extensively in hot rods to keep the wiring neat and even.

Look at photo 51. Here, the wire tie has been sewn in exposed. The two ends have been joined and tightened. All that remains is to clip off the selvage. In the companion photograph, you cannot see the wire tie.

To do this, sew the tie in as you see in the other photos. Turn the boot wrong side out and slip the neck down over the lever. Now, tighten the tie and clip the selvage. Turn the boot right side out, over itself and the connection is completely covered. Most boots are finished with a nice chrome trim ring that comes as part of the shift unit or brake lever. In the case of the Willys transmission boot, it was cemented to the bottom of the interior rubber boot.

Trunk Lids

We finish the carpet section with a brief discussion of how we handle the trunk lid. The inside of the trunk lid is one of the ugliest parts of the car—second only to the inside of the hood. We'll leave the hood to the body shop. As trimmers, it's our responsibility to make the trunk look good.

What you see in the photos of the '57 is the standard way to finish the inside of a trunk lid. The areas between the ribs of the trunk are covered in carpet. For the '57, chipboard was covered with carpet and cemented in place. Notice that the carpet was wrapped around the edges of the chipboard. There is no binding here.

The carpet could have been cemented to the chipboard (or panelboard) with a sewn binding. However, notice that in the '57 there is no binding anywhere. This is part of the styling of the interior. The carpet must look like it was "sprayed" into the car.

The Willys presents an entirely different approach. Here, Frank and Juanito handled the trunk as if it were a door panel. First, a pattern was made from chipboard. The pattern was transferred to panelboard and covered in carpet. Look at the edge closest to the hinge mechanism, photos at right. Here, the panel has to curve. Remember our section on building curved panels? Here's another application of that process. After building the panel with its curved top, Auveco fasteners were installed, the panel covered, and snapped into place just like a door panel. Had the '57 customer wanted his trunk lid done this way, it could have easily been accomplished.

Summary

There's a lot of carpet in a car! Or, in the case of the panel delivery, a lot of upholstery. In this chapter you've learned a bit about how carpet is made. With this knowledge you have a better idea of how each type of carpet will perform while being fit.

Fitting carpet requires the insulation to be installed so the fitting makes allowances for the padding thickness. Good planning will help make the insulation and carpet fit better and save material.

When installing carpet, have a steam machine standing by, full of distilled water. The distilled water prevents mineral deposits from collecting, then discharging on the carpet.

Where there's no OEM product, finish the edge of the

Photos 53-55. Juanito makes the cover for the Willys trunk lid just like he did the door panels. There is a bit of addition, however. At the base of the panel where the hinge is joined, the panel curves. This is no problem for him as he makes the curved part from layers of chipboard just as he did when making the modesty panel. Note the Auveco snaps holding the panel to the trunk lid.

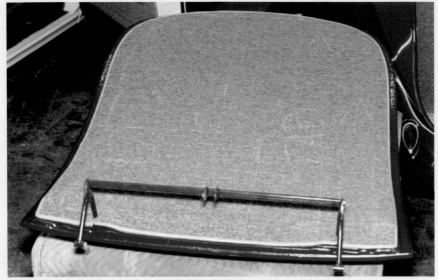

Photo 56. The finished job certainly passes our inspection. Of course, we'll erase all the extraneous chalk marks from the nap before the customer inspects it.

Photo 57. This is about the standard for carpeting trunk lids: make panels to go between the stiffeners and cover them with carpet. The '57 is a bit unusual, however. There is no binding here…

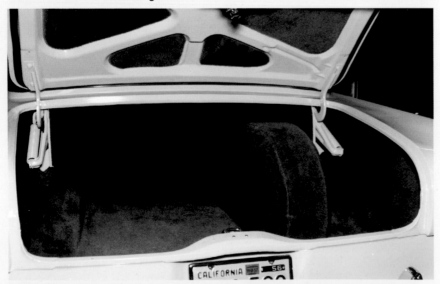

Photo 58. …or anywhere. It all looks molded. With a good piece of carpet and a steam machine you can do about anything!

carpet with edge trim from the hardware store.

The really trick way to fasten boots to the lever is with wire ties. Buy these at the hardware store or Radio Shack. Fit the boot using two, three or four pieces of material giving plenty of room at the bottom, narrowing at the top. If you want the wire tie to be hidden, turn the boot inside out, draw it over the lever, and tighten the tie. Then, turn the boot right side out over itself—hiding the wire tie inside.

You learned there was more than one way to finish the inside of a trunk lid. Using all the skills learned before, you can make a large panel to cover the whole area. It works just like making a big door panel.

To join two pieces of carpet edge-to-edge, follow this simple technique:

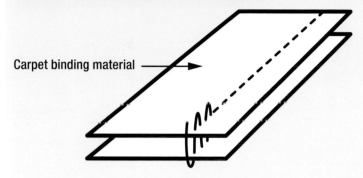

Carpet binding material ——→

1. Lay two lengths of carpet binding face-to-face, the length of the carpet you wish to bind. Stitch them together about 3/8 to 1/2 inch inboard of the finished edge of the binding.

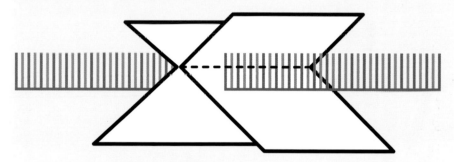

2. Crease the binding into a "V" shape along the seam line.

3. Insert the edge of the carpet into the "V" channel and bind as usual. When both edges of the carpet are sewn into their respective "Vs" you will have two pieces of carpet bound edge-to-edge with no gaps between them. Cement the binding to the back of the carpet.

To edge bind a carpet:

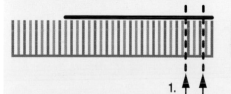

1.

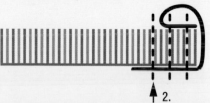

2.

1. Sew edge binding to top of carpet with 1/2 inch seam allowance. Then sew an identical seam as close to the two edges as possible.

2. Wrap binding around carpet, cement to back. Sew "in the ditch" to permanently fix binding to carpet.

We're now going to discuss how we build a hot rod seat. When we say build, that's what we mean. Not cover, but actually build a seat from scratch. Remember our discussion in the first chapter of how a car will often come to the shop with no interior of any kind? Well, that includes seats also.

This chapter is divided into three sections. The first covers building seats with bits of wood, panelboard and foam. Then, we'll watch Pete refashion the seats in our '57 Ford—starting with nothing but the old frame and springs. In the last section we'll follow Frank again, this time shaping a couple of junk seats to be used in the Willys. By the time we've covered all of this, you should be able to build or reshape any seat for any job.

Section One—Building a Seat from Scratch

The Frame

What we're about to describe here is just one way, of many, to fashion a seat from scratch. Ron and Frank use plywood, panelboard, waterboard and chipboard to make a base. On to this they add layers of polyfoam, shaped to fit the contour of the body. Let's follow as Ron builds a rear seat cushion for a two-door sedan.

By now you should know what the first step of our project is. Yes, it's making a pattern. Ron began by making a pattern of the driveshaft tunnel so the seat would sit squarely over this obstruction. The base of the seat is 1/2 inch plywood. To this, Ron added a 2 × 4 set on edge.

Photos 1 & 2. Two views of the seat Ron built for the back of the two-door sedan. A few pieces of wood and paneling turn into an excellent seat frame. The excellent fit was accomplished by making patterns, just as we've done for all our other projects.

This gives much of the height he needs under the passenger's knees. The rest he'll make up with foam.

To get a starting height under the passenger's knees, you have two options. The first is to measure an original seat if you have one, the second is a bit more difficult. Set a block of polyfoam not less than 2 inches thick in the area where the passenger will sit. Seat yourself on the foam and see how it feels. Check your headroom (space between the top of your head and the headliner). You need a minimum of 2 inches here also—and in this case, more is better. We like to have about 4 inches.

Adjust the foam under your "sit-upon" until you have a comfortable seat with sufficient headroom. Now, measure from about 4 inches behind your knees down to the floor. This is the height of your finished seat. Subtract the thickness of the foam you're sitting on from the measurement you just made. This is the height of the front edge of your seat frame. If you're sitting comfortably on 3 inches of foam and the distance from the floor to the back of your leg, 4 inches back from your knee, is 15 inches, the height of the seat frame should be 12 inches. These dimensions are made up for use as examples. Do not use them for determining your seat height. You must make your own.

In the photos you can see that Ron cut out a base for the seat from 1/2 inch plywood. The floor pan under the seat has a little rise so the seat base is angled back, but not enough to give the right height under the knee. Ron found the addition of a 2 × 4 was just enough to give him the height he needed. A wooden 2 × 4 is actually 1-1/2 × 3-1/2 inches. Setting the 2 × 4 on edge gave him an additional 3-1/2 inches of height. He glued and screwed the 2 × 4 to the plywood base, then glued and stapled the panelboard front piece to the face of the 2 × 4.

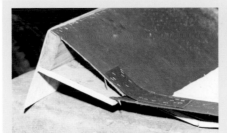

Photo 3. This edge view lets you see exactly how the frame is assembled. It begins with a plywood base and a 2 X 4 stretcher for strength. To this is added a piece of panelboard in front and a piece of waterboard over the top. Additional bits and pieces allow for the fit around the wheel wells.

Photos 4 & 5. Ron sits first on two pieces of foam to see how the seat feels. He then adds another layer of rubber to see how the finished seat will feel. This is part of the old axiom, "measure twice and cut once."

Photo 6. To support the passenger's spine, Ron builds up the back edge of the seat with a couple of layers of 1 inch foam. He bevels each one before adding the next.

Photo 7. After building up the back edge, Ron begins to add full sheets of 1 inch foam. These are trimmed even with the edges of the frame.

Photo 8. This is the seat fully foamed. Notice the bottom layer of foam is trimmed flush with the front edge. The second layer wraps over the first to give a rounded top edge.

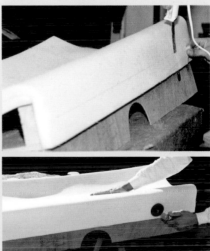

Photos 9 & 10. To keep from having a big lump under the front of the seat cover, Ron first tapers the edge of the foam with his foam saw. He finishes by sanding the cut edge smooth.

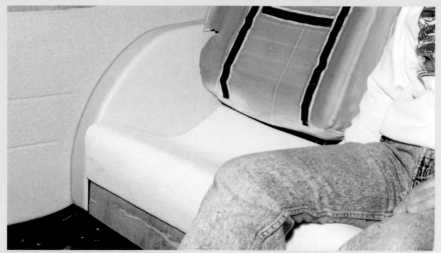

Photo 11. Ron tries the finished seat in the car. It looks good and feels good. Now he can start the upholstery.

Photo 12. This is the inside of the roadster without any upholstery. The customer wants a full rounded back in here, formed in one piece.

Photos 13 & 14. Although we've not seen Frank build this back from waterboard, the text has a full description of how it's done. Here, we see Frank building up the area of the seat for the lower back. He's used four layers of foam to build it this far. To get the shape he wants, he sands down the lumps in the foam with his sander.

Photos 15 & 16. Layer by layer Frank builds the back—from the bottom up. Notice that each piece gets larger to cover the one below. Each edge is tapered to prevent a lump in the layer above.

From the top of the 2 × 4 to the rear of the plywood, he formed the top of the seat from waterboard. This was glued and stapled in place. Together, this becomes a seat frame. A little padding, a little upholstery, and we'll have a seat.

Foaming the Frame

At Ron's shop, they use a medium-density, 1 inch, open-cell polyfoam for all seat building. Occasionally, they use a heavy-density foam for a base. When they do, however, they always finish with one or two layers of medium-density material. This combination gives good support, but with a soft feel. This is especially useful in building motorcycle seats. The hard foam takes up the road shock while the soft foam gives a feeling of comfort. Let's return again to Ron and the rear seat of the two-door sedan.

Now, with the seat frame built, he again layers foam beneath himself to be sure he has the right thickness and shape. When he's satisfied with how it feels and is assured there's enough headroom, he begins shaping.

Shaping develops the character of the seat—it makes the seat form to your body. Picture a side view of yourself sitting on a board. From the curve of your back, under the tail bone and up to the pelvic bones on which you sit forms a triangle with a half-moon shape where the longest leg (hypotenuse) lies. There must be something then, of this shape, to support the end of your spine. This is where Ron begins.

Under the tail-bone area Ron cements in a 1 inch piece of foam about 3 inches wide the full width of the seat. With his foam saw, he cuts away the front edge of the block, leaving a triangular shape. Over this, he adds a second layer of foam about 6 inches wide, and again, cuts it to form a triangle. Now he has support for the spine (above the tail bone).

He cements a full sheet of foam over his triangle pieces up to the edge of the seat, where he trims it flush. Finally, he adds another full sheet, but wraps this one around the edge of the frame and halfway down the front. Check photo 8, page 93 to see the results. Notice how the shape he's constructed looks just like the shape of the human body in a sitting position. Although the passenger only has 2 inches of foam beneath the pelvic bones, he or she will be completely comfortably because all areas of the body are well supported.

There is no need to sacrifice comfort for style in custom, hot rod upholstery. A customer who has a big investment in his or her car will want style, luxury and comfort. You can give it to them if you plan carefully and execute as we describe.

Shaping the Foam

Because foam has square edges, it's necessary to knock these down before you begin to upholster. Two tools will make the job go smoothly: a foam saw and a sanding disk in your drill motor or die grinder. With a very light touch you can sand polyfoam to any shape you want. In the photos you can see Ron bevel the foam with his foam knife, then smooth it out using a sanding disc in his die grinder. You've seen this before when George sanded the chipboard for the armrests. You'll see it again when Pete and Frank build their seats.

In photo 11 on page 94, Ron places the seat into the car and tests the finished product. Indeed, it sits well and he feels no need to change things.

Photo 17. As Frank builds up the seat, he puts it back in the car to be sure all parts are fitting together.

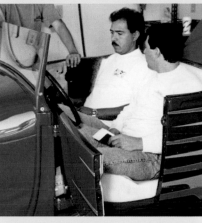

Photo 18. Frank and Ron have a "fitting session" while Juanito looks on. The object of the discussion is how the back feels. Is there sufficient lumbar support? How about the shoulders—is it comfortable there?

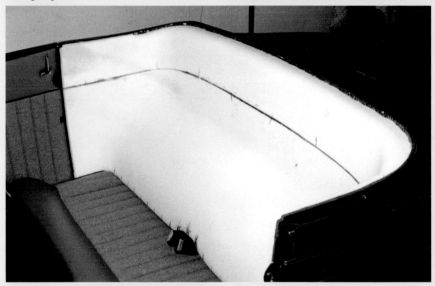

Photo 19. Here's the finished foam of the seat with lines drawn for the "tuck-and-roll" upholstery as you see in the cushion.

Photo 20. Although we haven't discussed these truck seats in the body copy, they deserve a mention here for the novel lumbar supports (arrows). Behind these supports are holes in the plywood, serving as speaker openings. The sound from the speakers will flow out the sides through vents in the seat covers.

Photos 21 & 22. This is how Frank sinks the crown of the cushion on the '57. By using wire ties threaded around the spring and its support, he can pull the top spring down as far as he wants. In this case, he brings the springs down until they're flat.

Photo 23. The springs must be covered with some type of material to prevent the springs from working through the padding. Frank is using vinyl for this seat. He could also use a light canvas.

Photo 24. If you don't have a foam saw to work with, almost anything will do. A serrated butcher knife works just fine. So does a hacksaw blade or straightedge razor.

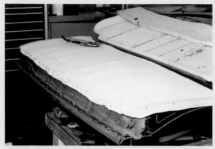

Photo 25. Notice how many hog-rings Frank uses on the vinyl cover. This keeps the vinyl from shifting. At this stage, Frank has also added the first layer of foam at the edge of the seat.

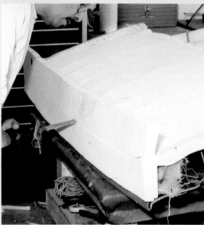

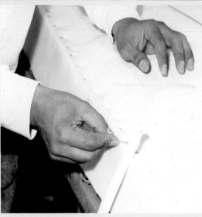

Photos 26-28. On the rear seat back, the foam does not wrap around the frame. The top of the back must be flat. Pete cements a piece to the top, then trims the excess with the saw. A final shaping of the edge, to get the right angle with the back, is accomplished with a razor blade.

Building a Seat Back

Earlier, we discussed building a seat cushion. Let's look for a minute at how we take these same materials and build the back of the seat, the part your back rests against. Our example is a beautiful roadster that Frank has been working on.

To form the back, Frank uses only waterboard. Again, he makes a pattern of the curve of the back inside the roadster. This he transfers to a large piece of waterboard. Next, he drills holes in both the board and the car body, just as he would if he were making a giant door panel. He inserts fasteners through the holes and into the body. This holds the back in place.

Left with this single piece of waterboard, it will want to spring back into its flat shape as soon as it's removed from the vehicle. To prevent this, and cause the back to keep its shape, Frank cements a second piece of waterboard over the first. He also drives in many staples to help hold everything together. Now, when he has to remove the seat back, it holds its shape.

Refer to photo 13 and count the layers of foam Frank uses for the back (lumbar) support. He uses four 1 inch layers—then follows with yet another partial piece that does not come all the way to the shoulder. He'll finish the back with two more layers of foam. Notice that Frank, like Ron, uses the foam saw and sanding disk to refine the shape of each layer.

Section Two—Reworking and Building on an Existing Frame

The '57 came into the shop with the original seats—and seat covers. Pete threw away everything but the seat frame. On these he will add support and new foam before beginning the upholstery. Let's watch and learn as he shows you his first really neat trick.

Dropping the Height of the Seat Cushion

On Fords and Chevrolets of the '50s, the seats were designed with an exceedingly high crown. When you sat in one of these seats, you had great vision but if you were over five foot ten, your head touched the headliner. This, coupled with the fact that most rod drivers like to sit a little lower in the car, has long presented a problem of how to lower the seat. At Ron's shop the problem has been solved.

It's really a very simple trick. You need not cut and weld any of the frame or do expensive tricks with the seat tracks. A handful of wire ties is all you need. To decrease the height of the seat cushion up to 2 inches, pass a wire tie around the no-sag (or zigzag) spring at about the third "zig" and anchor it to the reinforcement spring beneath. By tightening the wire tie, you can suck the top spring down as far as you want it to go. Repeat this step across the full length of the seat cushion. Just be sure to keep the depth even.

In the final photo of the '57 foam job you can see how flat the top of the seat looks. Now it's no longer a stock seat with a custom cover, but a whole custom seat. Use this trick as your own but don't forget where you learned it!

Foaming a Spring Seat

The foaming techniques described for the built-from-scratch seat we just discussed also hold true for foaming a spring unit. Because of the springs, however, you don't have to worry so much about building in support. This is the

Photo 29. Final shaping of the edge is done with the sander.

Photo 30. Pete lays out the lines for the center section and the end pieces. These are arbitrary decisions and they are arrived at with the combined efforts of the trimmer and customer.

Photo 31. Don't forget this step. Get some high-density foam under the edge of the seat. This helps prevent the edge from collapsing as people get in and out of the car.

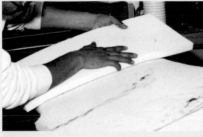

Photo 32 & 33. Pete cements a 1 inch piece of foam to the end of the seat, aligning one edge of the foam with the line he's drawn on the seat. The lines he's drawn match those on the cushion. This keeps all the seams aligned between the cushion and the back. Finishing off the foam at the edge of the seat, Pete hog-rings it in place.

Photo 34. Here's the back cushion with the ends and center attached to the foam. It now needs to be shaped.

Photos 35 & 36. A little work with the foam saw and Pete has the correct shape for the seat. In the photo on the top, he's trimming off some of the foam so the back will sit correctly on top of the cushion.

Photo 37. The final touches are put on the foam with a few passes of the sander.

Photo 38. The completed foamed seats sitting in the back of the Ford. They fit well, the centers and edges are aligned and there's just enough space to allow for upholstery.

Photo 39. Instead of wrapping a piece of vinyl around the outside back of the front back, Pete uses a piece of chipboard cemented to the frame.

Photo 40. As always, check each step in the build-up process. Pete is checking the back to be sure it aligns with the seat and can be pulled forward.

Photos 41 & 42. The foam that makes the ends of the split backs must be cut and sanded flat. Leave about 1 inch between the two backs to allow for the upholstery.

job the springs do. Sometimes, however, you or your customer may want some extra support in the small of the back. We call this the lumbar region—and the support there, lumbar support. Our '57 does not use this but had the customer wanted it, Pete would have padded out that area as Frank did on the roadster.

The design concept for the Ford seats will be modified buckets, but on a bench seat. This will require the sides and center of the seat to be taller than the area in which you sit. This is a common design and is used on most cars on the road today. We'll watch while Pete shapes the foam into this concept.

The job begins by placing a layer of vinyl or heavy canvas over the springs and hog-ringing it in place. This is standard practice on any seat to prevent the springs from wearing through the padding. To begin developing the tall sides of the seat, Pete cements a strip of foam to each end. He follows this by beveling the edge with the foam saw.

The second step, on the seat cushion only, not on the backs, is to reinforce the edge of the seat with additional padding beneath the edge-wire and springs. Three or four layers of foam will give this area additional support. Then, as driver and passenger slip in and out of the seat, this edge will not collapse.

After concerning himself with the edges of the seat, Pete lays out a full sheet of 1 inch foam over the vinyl-covered springs. On the cushion, this layer of foam is wrapped all the way around the front edge and hog-ringed to the springs. This gives a nicely rounded edge. The rear seat back cushion must have a flat top. To achieve this Pete stops the foam at the top edge-wire. He cuts the foam flush, then cements another piece along the top. Two of the applications or layers form the basic padding for the back.

The next step is to lay out the

area for the center rise and the addition of foam to the edges. Pete will also be making the upholstery for these seats so he makes the decision of where and how wide the extra pieces will be.

Notice in the photos that not only does Pete cement the side pieces to the seat, he also wraps them around the edge and rings them to the springs. The initial appearance is rough, but he'll soon sand them into a smooth, sculpted shape. Not only must you be an excellent craftsman, you must be something of an artist also! When both the sides and center have been foamed, Pete begins the shaping process.

As described before, Pete makes the big cuts with the foam saw—refines the cut with the sander. He must pay special attention to the side pieces that he has hog-ringed in place. These require a lot of care and patience. The edge must be rounded on top and squared off around the side. The foam should look like a finished seat. Take great care to make this happen. Don't expect the cover to hide any flaws. Pete shapes the seat exactly as he wants it, then makes the cover to fit perfectly.

The two front-seat backs require some special attention also. Look at photos 41 and 42. Notice how Pete has squared the edges of the backs. This allows them to fit together with about 1 inch space between them. Although the cushion edges are sanded flat, the edges of the back are severely flat.

The final step in foaming the Ford seats is to add a 1/2 inch layer of foam between the center and the edges along the backs of the front and rear seats. This will give the finished seat a stronger "bucket" look. Go ahead, you can peek at the next chapter and see what the finished job looks like!

This is also the way you'll build a seat if you purchase a seat of springs for the car from one of the aftermarket manufacturers such as Glide Engineering, Recaro, Cerullo or Tea's Design.

You now have a pretty good idea of how to use sheets of polyfoam to build the shape of a seat. Let's look now at how to modify an existing seat. It works much the same, but there are a few tricks you'll like.

Section Three– Reshaping an Existing Seat

Sometimes you'll have great luck and a "found" seat will only need some minor alterations to make it work just right. This was the case with the Willys. The customer found the style of seat he wanted (and one that fit) and brought it to the shop. Just a little work and Frank had it ready for a cover.

Those of you who are experienced trimmers may have noticed what seems to be an omission during the past discussion. About now you may be asking, "Where are the connections in the seats for listings?" Well, at Ron's shop they don't use listings in their seats. That's why they haven't been mentioned. The cover is completely cemented to the foam. This saves time and improves the appearance of the finished product. There are never any tell-tale puckers where the hog-ring is pulling on the listing.

For those of you who are novices or haven't read the *Automotive Upholstery Handbook*, listings in seats are like listings in headliners (as described in the previous chapter). They're cloth loops that have a wire passing through. The foam or padding in the seat is cut away to allow the listing and wire to reach the springs of the seat. The wire and listing are then hog-ringed to the springs, holding the cover to the seat. This has always been effective in holding the center of

Photo 43. Here's the front seat. It too is ready for a cover. Notice also how the foam on the back aligns with the foam on the seat. This is the result of good planning, measuring and careful checking as Pete fabricated the foam.

Photo 44. This is the seat selected for the Willys with the old cover removed. The Velcro once held the old cover in place.

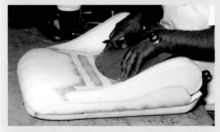

Photo 45. Frank has removed the Velcro and made a pattern for the soft center of the seat cover. The pattern was made from the seat, then used to mark its location.

Photo 46. Besides starting the build-up of the seat, notice that Frank has made lines on the seat where the seams will lie. The foam will be cut out to make channels for the selvage edge of the seams.

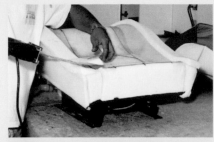

Photos 47 & 48. Frank tapers the edge of the top piece then wraps the entire "wing" with a 1/2 inch layer of foam.

Photo 49. After cementing polyfoam to the wings, they must be trimmed along the sides. Without this step the seat will become too wide and the crisp edge of the wing will be lost.

Photo 51. Here is the final cut. Notice that Frank has marked the top edge of the wing. This keeps the line straight and helps guide the saw.

Photos 52 & 53. Use a razor blade to cut grooves in the 1/2 inch foam. Frank cuts one edge perpendicular to the seat and bevels the other edge. Here, he easily pulls the piece out of the groove with his fingers.

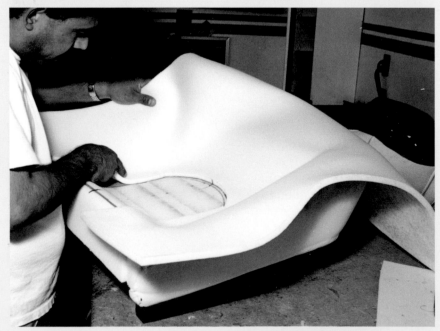

Photo 50. Using his pattern, Frank cuts a section out of polyfoam. He aligns the cutout with the line drawn earlier, then cements the piece to the seat.

a bucket seat. When we get to the installation of the seat cover in the next chapter, you'll see just how well the cementing process works. Let's follow Frank, through the photos, and see what he does.

Frank and the customer have worked up a design for the seat. It will be smooth leather everywhere except in the centers. Here, the material will be gathered to form what we call the "soft" look. This contrasts to the "hard" look described earlier wherein the foam beneath the covering is finely chiseled and sculpted. Frank begins by making a pattern that will fit properly in the center of the seat. Then, with the pattern, he marks the area where the gathered section will be and draws lines where he wants the seams to fall.

The customer wanted a dramatic recess in the bucket. Frank could have collapsed the springs but chose instead to build up the sides. He begins by adding a strip of 1 inch foam to the top edge of each seat, then beveling it with his foam saw. He then cements a 1/2 inch-thick piece over the entire "wing" of the seat, keeping the edge of the foam aligned with his previously drawn seam lines.

By feeling through the 1/2 inch foam, he finds the top edge of the wing, then draws a line with his marking pen showing exactly where that edge is. With the foam saw he cuts away the selvage foam on the side of the seat. Now, the seat wings are taller but the seat is the same width as before.

To smooth everything out, and to make an indent for the padded section of the cover, Frank applies a full layer of 1/2 inch foam to the seat, but with the padded area cut away. Again, he trims the sides to keep the width of the seat from increasing.

There will be a seam on each side of the cover, at the base of the wings, running the full length of the seat from front to back. This is where a listing would go if Frank were going to use one. Instead, he'll cement the cover to the seat. However, he does not want the selvage edges of the seams to telegraph back through the cover. To prevent this, he cuts grooves in the foam where the seams will be.

To cut the grooves, Frank uses a single-edge razor blade. Notice in the photos that one edge of the foam is perpendicular while the other edge is beveled away. The selvage will be turned to face the beveled edge. The result will be a smooth contour over both sides of the seam. Frank has finished the minor changes he and the customer want. In the next chapter we'll follow him as he fabricates a very complicated cover for this seat.

Summary

In this chapter we've discussed three areas of building up a seat for upholstery. In the first section you learned that a very comfortable seat can be built from scraps of wood, panelboard, and waterboard. You also learned how to measure for the correct height of the seat to support the passenger's legs.

Without springs to support you or your customer, we discussed the need to shape the foam according to the contour of the body in the sitting position. This requires support under the tail bone—the bottom of the spine. Without some kind of spinal support, the person riding in the seat would soon have a terrible backache.

In describing the Ford, you learned how to lower the height of the seat with wire ties—a really fun trick. We also covered how important it was to sand away excess foam carefully after cementing it in place. We want the foam to define the exact shape of the seat. Don't expect the seat cover to hide any flaws.

In adjusting the shape of an existing seat, work with layers of 1/2 inch foam. You can make finer adjustments this way. Don't forget to cut the foam away where the seam selvage will sit. Failure to do this will give you lumps beneath the seam.

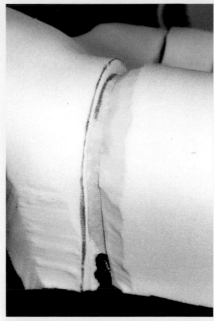

Photo 54. Close-up shot of the groove. You can see the perpendicular side and the beveled side. Turn the selvage toward the beveled side.

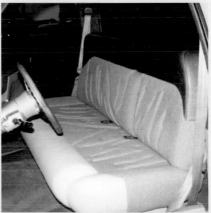

This 1989-95 Chevrolet-GMC pickup features a custom hard-look headliner, and a plastic overhead unit covered in leather. The hard-look seat foam was reworked and shaped, then covered with leather and tweed.

Photo 1. This is a trick to use when expanding a pattern with a crown. To add an inch to each side, offset the pattern from the centerline by 1 inch on each side. You must, of course, have a centerline on both your pattern and the piece you're working on.

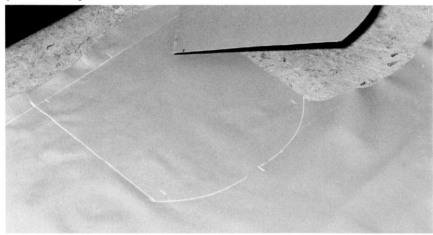

Photo 2. This 10 inch piece of material can now be gathered into an 8 inch opening with the finished crown the same as the crown on the pattern.

Here in Chapter 10 we cover the seats of our Willys demo car incorporating what Ron calls the "soft" look. This was defined for you in Chapter 1 and several examples were presented. Refer again to the '49 Mercury presented there. The seats are an excellent example of how appealing this look is in both style and comfort.

Our Willys will again be the demonstration car for this effort. Frank, our trimmer par excellence, will show you a couple of tricks to make this job a lot easier than it looks. Pay particular attention to the interesting way he fastens the elastic to the leather. This was even a new trick for Don.

Creating the "Soft" Look

Throughout this demonstration we're going to use the term "gathered." Gathered will be defined as causing the material to pucker, thereby forcing a large piece of material into a much smaller area. If we were talking in the shop we would refer to this as pleating the material. However, pleats have become synonymous with a style of upholstery called tuck-and-roll or pleat-and-roll. We'll use the term gathered to avoid confusion.

Forming the Gathered Centerpiece

In the previous chapter Frank made a pattern for the center of the Willys seat. This pattern was specifically made to develop the gathered center of the seat. In that chapter he used the chipboard pattern to locate the piece under discussion. He'll use it now to make the gathered piece. To gather material means to take 10 inches of material, stretch 8 inches of elastic over it, sew it down and let the elastic return to its original 8 inch length. Obviously, this will wrinkle up the material and we'll have that "soft" look. So here we go.

The pattern for the gathered piece was made to a finished size (the 8 inches described above.) Frank wants to cut a piece of leather 10 inches wide that he will force, with elastic, to become 8 inches wide. However, the piece is not square. It has a curve, or crown, to the top as seen in the photos. Here's how it's done.

Make a centerline on the pattern and notch the top and bottom. Make a mark 1 inch to both the right and left of the centerline. Now lay out lines on your material 10 inches wide with a mark in the center. Set your pattern on the material with its right side mark, on the centerline of the material. With chalk, scribe the left half of the pattern up to the centerline. (In the case of the Willys, it's the left half of the crown or arc.)

Shift the pattern so the mark to the left is over the centerline of the material and scribe the right half of the material. Now you have a 10 inch piece of material (with a crowned top) that can be gathered to fit in an 8 inch space. Frank demonstrates this in photos 1 through 9 for further clarification.

The next step is to make the padding that will go beneath the newly cut leather. This will be composed of 1/2 inch scrim-back polyfoam and a 2 inch-thick bat of polyester (Dacron). Using his pattern, Frank cuts this material to the exact, or finished size of the pattern. He then cements the polyester to the polyfoam. In the photos you see him doing this for all four pieces of the gathered sections: one each for the seat and back of both passenger and driver seats.

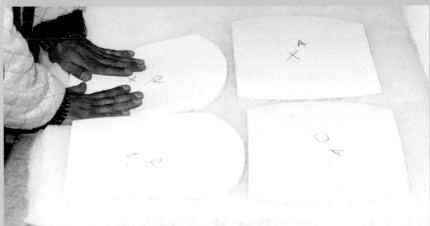

Photos 3 & 4. To pad the gathered piece, Frank uses both polyfoam and Dacron cemented together. The difference in piece sizes accommodates the seat cushion and back cushions.

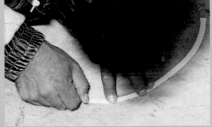

Photo 5. By cutting the elastic to the same size as the pattern, Frank is assured the stretch will be correct and the gathered material will return to its correct dimension.

Photos 6-8. Apply cement to both the elastic and leather. Stretch the elastic and carefully lay it on the leather. The cement will hold it in place. Give it a good rubbing to seal it tight. Now it can be sewn on the machine with assurance that the pull will be even across the width of the leather.

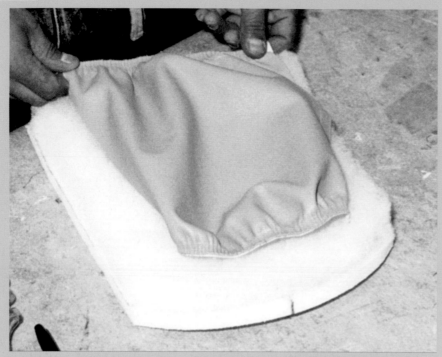

Photo 9. As always, Frank checks each step of his work before proceeding to the next. He's preparing to sew the now-gathered leather panel to the foam and Dacron sandwich.

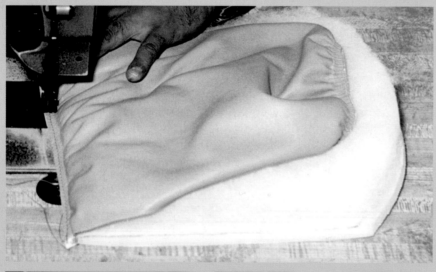

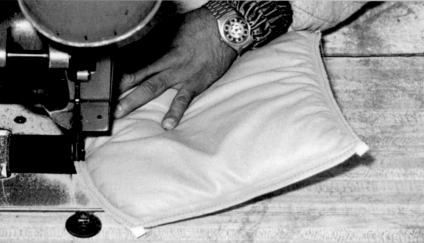

Photos 10 & 11. All four sides must be sewn to make this piece.

Now comes the fun trick we discussed earlier. Frank is going to apply elastic to the leather to cause it to gather. In Don's days at the sewing machine he put the material under the foot, grabbed one end of the elastic, stretched it out and sewed it down. The results were usually not wonderful. The elastic was either too tight or not tight enough. Often, it was tight in one area and loose in the other. Frank's way prevents this. He makes the cut length of the elastic the same size as the pattern, in this case, 8 inches long.

By making and using patterns, a lot of measuring and fitting can be omitted. Although for demonstration purposes we've used the numbers 8 and 10, the pattern could really be 7-7/8 inches or 8-1/4 inches. Adding and subtracting fractions can lead to errors if you're not a mathematical whiz. With his patterns Frank minimizes the possibility of mistakes.

The second step of the process is to cement the elastic to the leather. Because you can lift the elastic, if it's not stretched right, it can quickly and easily be adjusted until it "gathers" just the way you want it. The longer the elastic, the better this system works. To finish the elastic installation, Frank sews the elastic to the leather.

It's a simple step now to sew the gathered leather to the padding. Because we're using a scrim-back foam, the threads won't pull out. Frank stretches the gathered leather over the padding and sews it in place (all four sides)—with no worry about the elastic. Quick, easy and very effective.

Fitting

There are three principles or types of fitting. We've discussed one on several occasions and above: fitting from patterns. Another way to fit is to cut the old cover apart and use the pieces as patterns.

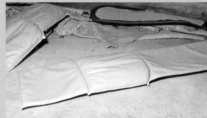

Photo 12. The finished piece. Sitting or leaning against this will be as comfortable as it looks.

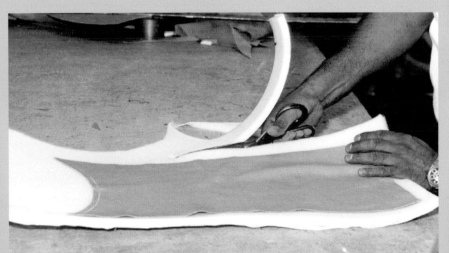

Photos 16-18. As with everything we do, even when sewing we start in the center and work out. Here Frank sews his gathered pad to the two center sections of the cover. Then, he sews the two outboard wings to the center. Notice that he's already fitted the wings. This shows Frank's faith in his own abilities. A less-experienced trimmer would have sewn straight panels here, then fit the whole piece to the seat.

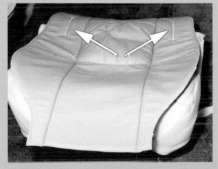

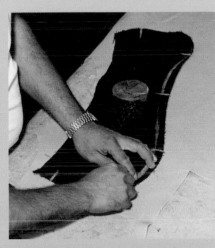

Photo 13. Frank has cut apart the old cover and is using it for a pattern. Note the witness marks he's made. Witness marks are essential to a good fit. You can't have too many.

Photos 14 & 15. In the past you may have cemented your material to the foam for a padded panel. This was like training wheels on a bicycle. It held things in place for you but it also opened a chance for creases. Learn now to sew the fitted panel to the scrim-back foam without the aid of cement. It's faster and the finished job will look better.

Photo 19. As accurate as Frank is, he continues to check his work at each step. The two lines (arrows) at the rear of the seat represent the cutouts for the legs of the back cushion. They'll fit through these slots and attach to the seat-cushion frame.

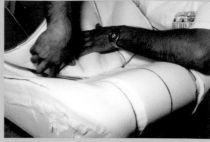

Photo 26. Beginning with the center, Frank is very careful to make sure his seams line up with the pattern lines and witness marks he made earlier on the seat-cushion foam.

Photos 20 & 21. These photos show how the bottom of the back cushion will be closed. Frank sews this loop to the outside back and one to the inside back. He'll pass a wire through each of the loops, then hog-ring the enclosed wires together.

Photo 27. This is the rear of the seat. Note the line drawn with a marking pen to witness where the finished seam will go. Frank is dead on.

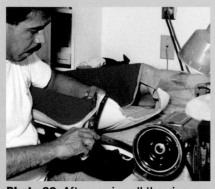

Photo 24. Here is the piece sewn into the slit made for the legs of the back cushion. It's a 4 inch strip sewn around the inside edge of the slit and lapped over itself on the inboard side of the seat.

Photo 22. After sewing all the pieces together, Frank trims away the selvage from the seams that lie on the outboard edge of the cushion. Here the seam has no groove to hide its bulk.

Photo 28. He now aligns the side seams with the foam. He has cut the foam on the area of the top facing perpendicular to the seat. The center section is beveled (see photo 26). By shaping the foam this way, the seam will stand erect next to the perpendicular side while the center body will roll smoothly over the beveled edge.

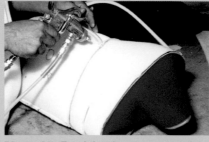

Photo 23. The bottom edge of the seat cushion is fitted and hemmed with a strip of vinyl. The finished bottom of the seat cushion must look just as nice as the top.

Photo 25. Frank begins the cementing process by spraying a medium heavy coat to all the seam areas he wants to be attached. He pays special attention to the gathered center.

Photo 29. Frank gives the cement a little time to dry. He then begins to peel the cover over the edges of the cushion.

The third way is to place the material over the section you wish to cover and mark around the area. All three ways are effective and should be used. Frank begins some of his fitting using pieces from the old cover.

In previous chapters we've also discussed using witness marks. If you plan to use the old cover for a pattern, be sure to make your witness marks before cutting the pieces apart. The mark should cross the seam leaving a witness mark on each side. With these suggestions let's watch Frank fit the Willys seat covers.

In photo 13 he fits one of the side panels from the old cover. Note two things here: the witness marks and the big piece of "pig iron" he uses to hold the pattern in place. Never depend on your ability to hold the pattern in place with one hand and mark with the other! In the second photo, Frank has fit one of the centerpieces and is cutting out foam for padding. We can tell he's used the pattern by the telltale crown at the end of the piece. Each section is carefully fit and cut out. These pieces must then be padded and sewn together.

Padding

In the custom trim business, everything is padded before assembling. This is true for everything—molded headliners, door panels, kick panels and all parts of the interior   seats included.

If, in the past, you've become used to cementing the material to the polyfoam, now is the time to give up that process. You must learn to sew the cloth, leather, or vinyl to the foam (1/2 inch scrim-back) without that crutch. Cementing the material to the foam can create creases when the face of the material is folded in on itself. In custom upholstery you can't have this. With a bit of practice you'll soon be able to sew without these "training wheels."

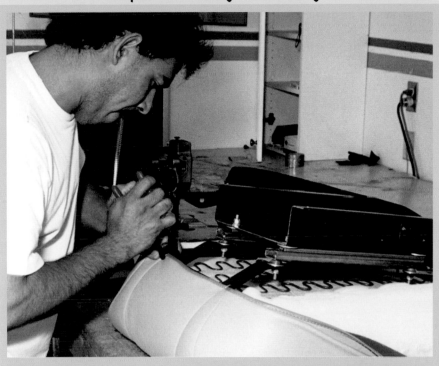

Photo 30. He anchors the front seams first with a hog-ring at the base of each.

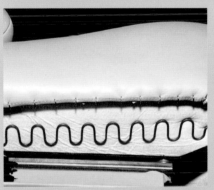

Photo 31. This is the finished bottom of the seat. It looks as neat as the top. Notice how many hog-rings Frank uses—far more than necessary to hold the cover on. But this way he has fewer pull marks in the leather.

Photo 33. Here's the back side of the finished cushion. You would never know there were no listings holding these deep rolls in place.

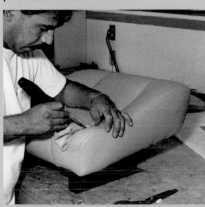

Photo 32. With a screwdriver, he forces the leather covers for the seat back logo into their holes. A few hog-rings secure them to the no-sag springs beneath.

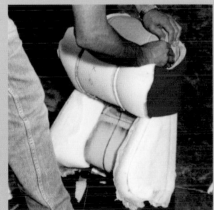

Photo 34. Getting the seat-back cover on is a real bear. Be careful with the use of silicone spray if you use it. Any silicone you get on the area where cement will be used will prevent the cement from adhering to the foam or cover. The best suggestion is brute force and work it on the floor for the extra leverage.

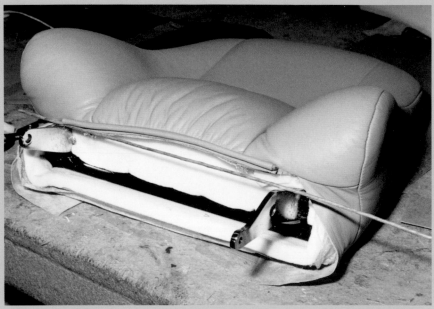

Photo 35. With the cover on, it now becomes time to close the bottom. As stated before, Frank will place wires in these loops. He uses a paper-wrapped wire-core welt specifically manufactured for use in listings. This is available through your local trim fabrics distributor.

Photo 36. The excess material of the stretcher (or tail) is folded under itself and the end hog-ringed to the foam. It's a nice solution to a tricky problem.

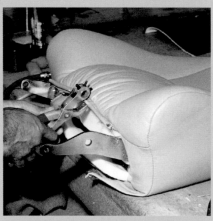

Photo 37. One of the nice touches Frank uses is to pre-punch holes in the leather before inserting the hog-rings. This prevents tearing the leather, creates few pulls and assures correct alignment.

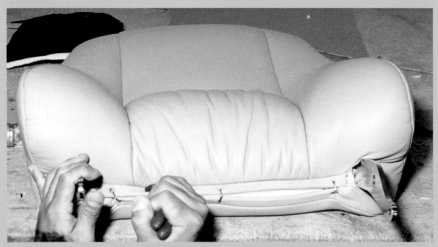

Photo 38. Watch as Frank hog-rings the front and back together.

Assembly

After sewing all of the pieces to foam, Frank assembles the tops of the cushion and back from the centers out. Study photo 19 and look at the chalk marks on the rear of the seat cushion. This is where the support legs of the back cushion will pass through to attach to the seat-cushion frame. Frank sews two seams here about 1/2 inch apart. He later cuts the material out from between these seams and sews in a 4 inch-wide piece of leather. This gives a finished appearance to this area when the leather is tucked into the channel through which the support legs pass. Making the seams before cutting the material makes the job neater and easier.

A second trick in the assembly is the listing Frank sews to the bottom of the gathered piece. He sews a similar listing to the bottom of the outside back. When the cover is over the back cushion, he'll pass individual wire-core welt through these two listings and hog-ring them together. You'll see this in the final assembly of the seats. The last part of the fitting and assembly portion (of the seat cushion) is to fit the bottom edge.

In regular upholstery you leave a couple of inches of material at the bottom of the facings. You wrap this around the frame somewhere and hog-ring it down. Not in custom upholstery! Place the cover over the cushion. Pull the sides down until all the wrinkles are gone—just as you would do if you were installing any cover. With clamps, trim pins or hog-rings, hold the cover in place.

Using either chalk or pencil, draw a line around the area where the cover will finally be hog-ringed in place. Remove the holding devices, take the cover off the seat and trim along the line you just drew.

After doing just this, at the machine, Frank sews a vinyl

binding around the bare edge. This trims and reinforces the edge at the same time. Now Frank is ready to put these covers on their respective frames.

Installing the Cover

Ron's crew never uses listings where they will be sat upon or leaned against. Why? A heavy passenger may bend the wire-core welt, damaging the shape of the cushion or back. Everything that comes in contact with the human body is cemented in place. Watch now as Frank does just that. The bottom of the gathered section and all of the seams will be tightly cemented in place. He applies a medium coat of cement to the gathered section, then a medium-heavy coat to all of the seams. A corresponding coat is applied to all areas of the cushion.

He then very carefully sets the gathered area onto the cemented surface of the cushion. He's extremely careful to align all seams over their respective grooves and assure that the cover is square on the seat and correctly located front-to-rear. He adjusts each seam to lie perpendicular to the groove he cut in the foam earlier.

The seam stands up straight, cemented to the straight side of the foam. The beveled side lies smoothly opposite it and presses against the cover. When the top of the cover is cemented in place, he rolls the sides over and prepares to hog ring it in place.

In photo 40 on this page you can see Frank's neat hog-ring job after the cover has been fit to the frame. A judge peering up under the seat will see a bottom finished as well as the top. Let's work on the back cushion.

The process begins by spraying a medium-heavy coat of cement to the seams. When the cement is dry, Frank works the top half of the back cushion cover. He carefully presses the seams

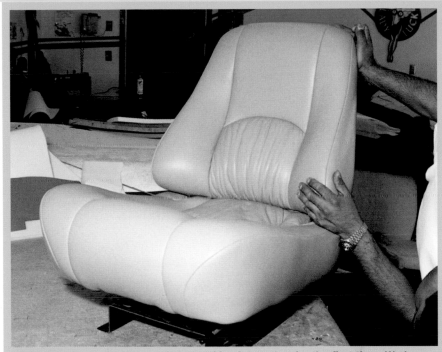

Photo 39. Here we see the cushion and back together for the first time. We have a nice-looking seat here.

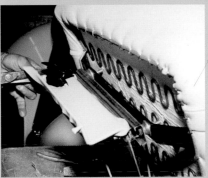

Photo 40. The final step is to cover the mounting platform of the seat. This can be seen from outside the car.

Photo 41. Here's the finished seat next to the original. There's been very little change in shape but a great change in design. We have no idea where these seats originated, but as you'll see, they look and fit great in the car.

Photo 42. We can all agree that the Willys came out looking like a little gem. The seats are a good fit. With backs that tilt forward, the owner can access the sound system behind the seats.

Photos 43 & 44. Pete begins laying out his pleats. After determining the size of the panel he'll need, based on the size of the seat area, he lays it out on the foam. To mark for the pleats, he lays the straight edge from one corner to the other on the diagonal.

Photo 45. Before he can cut the grooves (by hand) for the pleats, he must cement another piece of 3/16 inch scrim-back foam to the plain foam on which the pleat lines have been scribed. He can then cut grooves for the pleats going clear through the 1/2 inch foam. Why not just cut the grooves down to the scrim back on 1/2 inch foam? As accurate as Pete is, somewhere along the line he'd cut through the scrim and ruin his work. To answer the next question before you can ask it, they don't make 3/4 inch scrim-back foam.

into their corresponding grooves. He then sprays a coat of cement on the gathered section and its location on the seat. Now he can finish pulling the cover over.

The final step is to close the bottom of the cover in a neat and tidy fashion.

In the photo you can see how he folds the material over itself behind the support leg of the back. The corner is then hog-ringed to the foam. Remember the listings he sewed into the outside back and the gathered section? He now passes a piece of wire-core welt through these listings, then hog-rings the two wires together. First, however, he ensures he'll have a neat job.

Everywhere Frank will put a hog-ring, he punches a hole with the leather punch. This does two things: He can easily slip a ring into one of the holes and pull up or down on the material with his ring pliers. The second benefit is the neat appearance. There are no areas where the ring tears. No pull marks are visible on either the front or the outside back. The look is totally professional. No judge (or customer) will find fault with this type of workmanship.

The final step in crafting this seat is to cover the exposed areas of the seat track. There's no fitting here and Frank can make it all in one piece. As before, he cements both the material and the frame, then presses the material in place and trims away any excess.

This is how the "soft" look is achieved. It's a very comfortable look, and is comfortable to sit on. Now we'll watch Pete give a "hard" look to the '57 Ford.

The "Hard" Look

We've discussed the "hard" look throughout the book. By now you understand what we're talking about. The essence of the hard look in a seat cover is in the pleats. In the case of our '57, the pleats run on the diagonal rather than vertically. This sets the seats apart from your average pleated interior. Ron's approach to making pleats is a little different than you've seen in the past. Let's watch as Pete builds the first panel starting in photo 43, page 110.

Photo 46. Carefully cement the fabric to the foam without any stretching. This keeps the edges of the pleats crisp and even. Any pulling will round over or knock down the carefully cut sides of the grooves.

Making the Pleated Panel

The panel begins as a layout on 1/2 inch polyfoam. In this case, we don't use scrim-back foam—and you'll see why in a few paragraphs. Pete determines the size of the panel by the size of the area (on the seat) he wants to cover. He lays out the panel considering all of his seam allowances. The first step is to make a diagonal line from one corner of the panel to the other. Of course, he'll make a panel for the other side of the seat using opposite diagonal lines.

The customer wants 4 inch pleats so Pete makes lines 4 inches apart, working each way from the diagonal. Now comes the interesting part. Pete cements his panels to 3/16 inch scrim-back foam for an overall 11/16 inch thickness—just shy of 3/4 inch.

The second step will be to razor-cut 1/2 inch-deep grooves where the diagonal lines have been drawn. Had he used 1/2 inch scrim-back foam, his cuts would have gone all the way through to the delicate scrim. By adding another 1/8 to 3/16 inch, he's in less danger of cutting through to the back or having a loose seam.

Step three is to cement the cover to the foam.

In the past, to make this type of pleat, you marked the top of the fabric, laid it over the foam and sewed a seam. Three seams became two pleats. Quick and dirty but not pretty. Now try this. Run a light, narrow band of cement over each groove you've made in the polyfoam. Spray a very light coat of cement to the back of the material.

Fold the material in half along the diagonal. Lay it gently on top

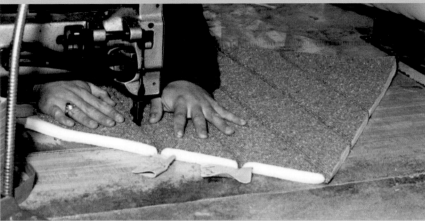

Photo 47. Finish the pleats by sewing down each "ditch."

Photo 48. As we did with the Willys seat, the centers are all sewn together first.

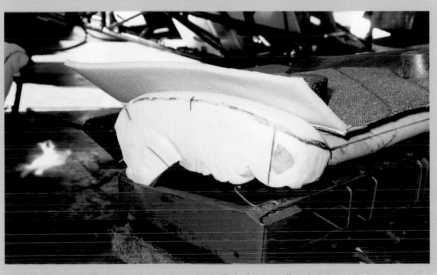

Photo 49. We took this shot to show how Pete has outlined the edges of the seat where his seams will be. Additionally, you can see his witness marks.

Photo 50. Don says he would have used trim pins here to hold the cover in place. However, these big hunks of steel do a very good job!

Photo 51. As Pete makes his marks on the cover, he keeps a close eye on the line below, previously drawn on the foam. The line on the cover must exactly duplicate the line on the foam. This close attention makes the perfect fitting cover.

Photo 52. Here it is, neatly drawn with witness marks in place.

Photos 53 & 54. Back at the machine Pete sews a seam 1/2 inch outboard of the chalk mark. He also allows for the thickness of the chalk line as he works. When the seam is finished he trims the selvage, taking care not to cut into the threads.

of the foam and carefully work the fold into the groove and seal it tightly with your bent knife. Working from the center each way, work the material into each of the grooves. The trick is not to break down the edge of the foam by stretching the material too tightly. Keep the material flat and smooth, flowing into and out of each groove. Look at the finished product in photo 66, page 115. Notice how crisp the pleat edges are. There are no gathers or crushed sides. Pete finishes the job by sewing a seam in each of the "ditches."

Working the pleats this way, whether diagonal or vertical, will result in a finished pleated panel that is exactly the same size as that with which you started. In the past, when sewing pleats from the top, or even when folding the material back on itself and sewing the pleat from the back of the material, the panel shrunk in the process. This required you to make a panel larger than needed and hoped it would shrink just the right amount. You can easily see how much more effective this new method can be.

Other Pleated Panels

Using the above-described method, you can make pleats of any size. This is also an excellent way to make pleats for the nostalgia rods incorporating pleat-and-roll upholstery. In the original covers, made before the invention of polyfoam, the pleats were hand-filled with a thin cotton material called coach wadding. This material was folded or rolled into the size needed and stuffed into the previously sewn pleat.

This same look can be achieved by the method described above using a thicker polyfoam. The trick is to work from the center out, flowing the material over each hand-formed pleat. Just remember not to stretch the material because this collapses the foam and gives you flat-looking pleats.

Making the Rear Cushion Cover

Let's review for a moment the fitting process for bench seats. Pete will make everything the exact size of the finished job (allowing for seams). This includes fitting along the bottom so the underside is as neatly finished as the top side. Witness marks are made on the foam of the seat—to be transferred to the cover as it's fitted. Like the pieces of the Willys seat, each piece of the Ford seat is backed with polyfoam, cut and sewn to fit. Keeping this in mind, let's watch Pete do his "thing."

The first step, as with the Willys, is to sew together all of the parts that make up the top of the cushion. This large panel is then fitted to the seat at the sides and edges. In the photos starting on page 111 you can see that Pete not only has witness marks, but he's also highlighted the edge of the seat with his marking pen. Notice also the iron weights he also uses to keep the cover from slipping as he fits.

In the following photos we see him transferring the lines and witness marks from the seat to the cover. This done, he takes the top to the machine and sews a seam 1/2 inch outside his chalk marks. He then makes nicks where there were originally chalked witness marks. He finishes by trimming away the selvage from the seam. Be sure to trim your selvage as close to the seam as possible without cutting the thread.

For the second step, Pete sews together all of the front and side facings. Notice in the photo that he's sewing a listing to the bottom of the facings. Like the closure on the Willys back cushion, Pete will pass a piece of wire through this listing and use it to hold the

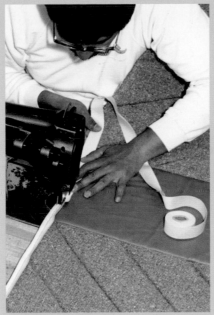

Photo 55. Pete will use a listing with a wire in it to anchor his cover to the frame. Because there's so much listing involved, he uses pre-cut muslin.

Photo 56. The facings have been fit independently of the top. After sewing around the edges, he adds the listing for the bottom.

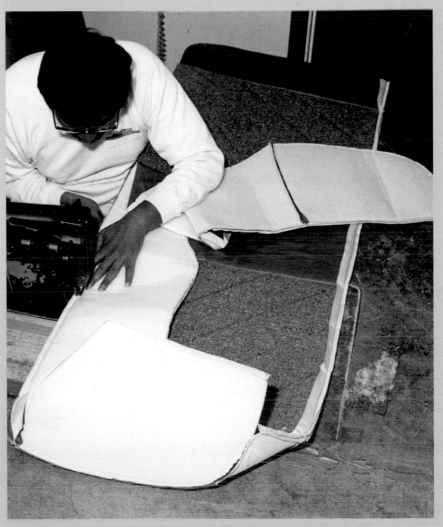

Photo 57. The final step is to sew the facings to the top. When this is completed, he can begin the installation.

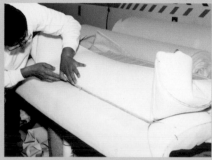

Photos 58 & 59. Although this is not the Ford seat, it demonstrates the same principles. Pete begins by outlining each pleat seam with cement. Then he covers the entire pleated panel area. He also applies a medium-heavy coat to the foam wherever a seam will fall. Aligning his witness marks, he very carefully brings the cover in contact with the cemented foam and seals it down.

Photo 60. With the top cemented in place, Pete can pull the cover over the frame and begin ringing it to the frame.

Photo 61. The next step is to fish the listing wire through the listing. Do this after the cover is on.

Photo 62. Pete anchors the rear edges of the cover temporarily. This pulls the majority of the wrinkles to the rear of the cover.

Photo 63. He begins now at the center and works his way around to the end. This keeps the wrinkles moving to a place where they can fall away.

Photos 64 & 65. Here's the ol' steam machine. Remember: it makes a good trimmer great! George is going to use it to get a few of the wrinkles out of the split back.

hog-rings securing the cover to the frame. In the final photo of this section he sews the facing to the top.

Pete is a very experienced trimmer and knows exactly what he's doing. He can start at one end of the seat and work his way all around the cover while keeping all of his witness marks aligned. If you feel this is beyond your abilities, start your seam in the middle of the cushion and work to the end. Turn the cushion over and sew the remaining facing to the top. This limits some of the slip during the sewing process.

Installing the Cover

The first two photos of the installation process are from a different seat—the rear back cushion of a '57 Chevrolet. Pete whizzed past us on the Ford before we had a chance to shoot the pictures. It does, however, show the same steps. Wherever there's a seam, Pete applies a layer of cement to both the cover and the seat.

Notice he starts in the pleated section by applying a coat of cement to each seam, then sprays a second coat over the entire panel. This ensures that the seam of each pleat will get a good coat of cement. After applying the cement and allowing it to dry for a bit, Pete sets the cover in place.

Note his concentration on getting the top seam in exactly the right place. Once down, the cover must sit exactly in the right place. If it's at all crooked, you'll have wrinkles that can't be removed. Unseen in the photographs is Pete using his bent knife to push each seam of the pleats into place. That's why it was so important to be sure the seams were well coated with cement.

When the top is well secured in place, Pete pulls the facings down over the seat. Now he can concentrate on fastening the bottom.

He begins by installing the wire into the listing. He pulls the back of the side facing into position and places a ring. He does this on both sides before turning the unit over to work on the bottom.

As all trimmers do, Pete begins hog-ringing the cover to the frame from the center, working out to each of the ends. This helps pull any small wrinkles out to the ends where they will drop off. Should he work from the ends to the middle, any wrinkles forming along the way would have nowhere to go except to the middle of the cover.

George Torres is helping Pete install the Ford covers and decides to use a little steam to help remove some very small wrinkles in the seam of the cover. Steam works several small miracles. First, it softens the vinyl and allows the polyfoam to push deeper into the material, helping to remove some of the wrinkles. Next, when used very carefully on the outside of the vinyl it will actually shrink it a bit. You must be careful, though, or you can melt or burn the vinyl.

On fabric, steam will shrink it, make the nap on velvet or mohair lie in one direction, and make stiff fabrics supple. It's a must-have machine. Photo 66 shows the finished rear cushion and back. Great job, Pete!

Front Cushion and Split Back

We started with the rear seat because it was the easiest. Now we must tackle the front seat with its split backs. Both are cut, fit and sewn much like the rear seat. There are simply more parts involved and a bit of difficulty in getting everything aligned. Let's look at some of these "difficult" things.

Refer to photos 67 and 68. In the first photo you can see the

Photo 66. Pete (and George) did a great job on the rear seat. The diagonal pleats give it a different look.

Photo 67. Study this photo carefully to see how Pete fit the back of the front cushion. It's made to fit the contours of the frame. Note also that all pieces are padded.

Photo 68. Here are those contours and the way the cover fits. Pete has even sewn in a dart (arrow) to make a smooth transition over the front of the frame. Because this area is hidden by reveal molding, no one will ever see the extra effort he put here. It could just as easily have been folded.

Photo 69. To be sure the pleats line up between the seat cushion and back cushion, Pete sets the back cushion in place and marks the location of the pleats.

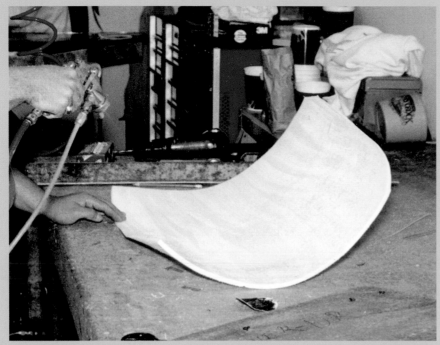

Photo 70. The outside back panel for the back cushion is made just like a door panel. George could even carve a design in it.

Photo 71. If you saw this photo in another chapter, you'd be sure it was a door panel.

Photo 72. It even snaps into place like a door panel.

Chevrolet-GMC 1967-72 truck with custom door panel combining vinyl and wool in sculpted look.

back of the front seat cushion. Note the cutouts on the stretcher (or tail) that allows it to fit around the dip in the seat frame. Check also that the edge of the stretcher has been closed with a seam but the listing is not yet applied.

Turn your attention to how Pete fit the corners. In a production shop this corner would be fit with a dart and considered good enough. This corner has been thoroughly fitted and pieced to allow the cover to lie correctly over the frame. Can you see the sewn dart in the front of the cover, beneath the plate that will eventually support the reveal molding? Even a discerning judge could not see into this area. Pete just wants it all to be right. You must learn to think like Pete.

Part of making everything align is to put the split backs onto the cushion and mark the location of the pleats. All of Ron's trimmers do this for any type of pleat alignment. The cushion is made first, then the back is made to match. This assures the trimmer that the pleats in the finished job will all be aligned.

The backs of the Ford are a lot easier than the backs of the Willys. These are fitted just like the cushions, installed the same way but finished off with a full panel. Watch George make these panels.

From the pattern he made earlier, George cuts a piece of panelboard. What he does next is exactly like making a door panel. He mounts the panel to the frame, drills holes through the panel and frame, and installs Auveco fasteners. After removing the panel he covers it with closed-cell foam and scuff-sands the surface. He cements the vinyl cover to the foam, wraps it around the edges and cements and staples the edges in place. Just a small door panel.

The finished seats are "letter-perfect."

Summary

We've now made two different types of seats: one incorporating the soft look and the other developed with the hard look. The soft look incorporates material that has been gathered into small folds. The hard look is based on very sculpted pleats and panels.

Ron's shop does not use listings to hold the cover to the top of the seat. Instead, they cement the cover in place. Where a seam will be cemented, they cut a groove in the foam to give the seam allowance a concave area to lie in. This prevents it from pushing up and making the seam sit above the surface of the cover.

One of the great tricks you learned in this chapter was cementing the elastic to the material rather than attempting to sew it together. This ensures that the gathers will be even.

Fitting the cover is the most important part of the construction operation. You learned there were three ways to fit a cover: using the old cover as a pattern, making your own pattern, and fitting the piece to the area of the seat you wish to cover. You also learned the importance of witness marks. Use them everywhere to make sure your cover is sewn the same way it was cut. You must now learn to pad out all pieces of your cover without cementing the material to the polyfoam. Lay it on the foam and sew it in place. This prevents creases in the face of the materials from the cement behind it.

Finally, we saw how both Pete and Frank pay close attention to detail. Even where it won't be seen, both men take great care and pain to make these areas as neat and finished as the face of the cover.

Photo 73. Well, here it is, ready for delivery. The customer has seen it and is crazy about it. It really is a fine job.

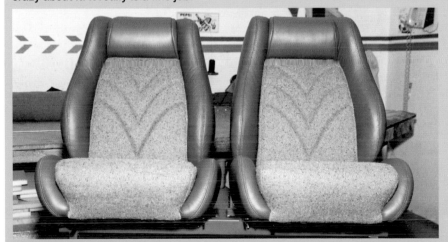

Photo 74. Though we didn't describe it to you, we thought you might like to see the finished seats for the panel delivery. Everything done to these seats has been described using the Willys and Ford as examples. There is one difference, however. Listings are used to secure the inserts (cushion and back) to the frame. The Willys and Ford had these parts cemented to the foam.

11 • The Convertible Top
Part One—The Top Well

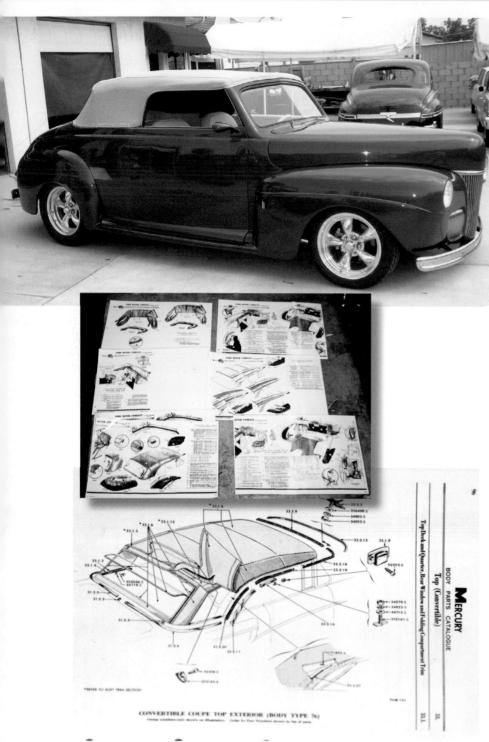

Of all the jobs in the trim business, we think fitting and making a convertible top from scratch is the hardest. If there is one mistake in the top, it's out there for everyone to see and critique. You seldom see a top (one that's used with some frequency) that has no wrinkles, no stretches, no scuffs from rubbing when it goes down, or any of the possible problems convertible tops face.

Flaws in the interior trim can only be seen from inside the car. A convertible top is like a paint job—it's all out there for everyone to see. Like a paint job, if there's a dip, it jumps out at the viewer. Unlike a paint job, however, you can't fill a dent in a top. In some cases, the top must come off, a new piece has to be made, and the top replaced. So, many trimmers turn away top business.

If you've ever turned away a top, it's unlikely you'll do it again after carefully studying the following three chapters. If you've never tried your hand at making a top from "scratch," we think you'll be extremely pleased with the results you can obtain using the tricks and tips we provide. Give yourself some extra time with the techniques that follow. They're a little more involved than what you may be used to doing. However, once you've made a top as we describe, you'll probably find you won't have to take it off and adjust it three or four times as you may have in the past. Our tricks should make it come out right the very first time.

We've not included any shortcuts in this section. You'll find your own shortcuts as you work with this technique. For now, we want you to concentrate on the accuracy of the fit. Speed will come later. Let's discuss what constitutes a top and its associated parts.

Photos 1 & 2. Make a serious effort to find a factory manual that shows how your top, well and boot are constructed. It will save more time than you invest chasing down these valuable aids. Usually, someone in a club devoted to the marque will have what you need. Usually, they'll not part with them but are often amenable to giving you photocopies. It can't be seen in these photos but these pictures are sealed in clear vinyl to prevent damage.

The Parts of a Convertible Top

The Top Well

We'll examine the convertible top and its parts in three sections or chapters. This, the first chapter, deals with the top well. The top well is that area between the back of the rear seat and the front of the trunk into which the top folds when it's put down. Usually this is trimmed out with vinyl, bow-drill (a cotton fabric), or sometimes with convertible-top material.

Our project car, a 1957 Mercury, will use the same vinyl as used on the seat covers and door panels. This presents an added problem for Frank, who's going to build this top. The customer purchased the material (original) without knowing how much to buy. Therefore, there is a finite amount of material with the likelihood of limited availability—at least in the same dye lot.

The Top

The top itself consists of three distinct parts: the pads, the rear curtain, and the cover, or top. When you purchase a kit top, these are the parts you receive. In the next chapter you'll see how all of these parts are fabricated and made into a good-looking finished unit.

Tops are generally made of either vinyl or fabric.[1] Vinyl top material is a two-layer material with vinyl on the outside and fabric on the inside. Fabric tops, or what we used to call canvas tops, are a three-layer material:

[1] In 1963, Don's then 18-year-old brother, also a trimmer, made a top for his 1960 Morgan roadster of all clear vinyl—one large window. His brother's friend attempted to cover a top on his '58 Rambler with 1/4-inch plywood. Both tops were lost to vandalism shortly after their fabrication.

Photos 3-7. This series of photographs follows Frank as he fits chipboard pieces to the back frame of the body. These will become both a pattern and support. As a pattern, it will define the rear edge of the top well. As a support, he'll temporarily cement the back of the well to this piece while he fits a pattern to it.

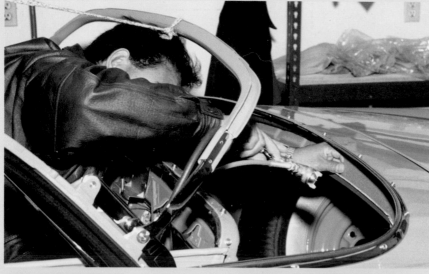

Photos 8 & 9. Frank has cemented the chipboard into place to use as a support. He applies a limited amount of cement because he'll want to remove it later.

Photo 10. To make the big pattern for the back piece (and later the front piece) of the well, Frank uses a leftover piece of inexpensive vinyl as pattern material. The cost of using this material is far less than ruining a piece of irreplaceable material. Although the vinyl for the Mercury is a reproduction piece, it retails for about $50 per yard as of this writing. Equally, being assured of finding the same dye lot would be nearly impossible. The savings of pattern making far outweigh the costs.

an outside layer of fabric (cotton and rayon or nylon), and a rubberized layer followed by another layer of cloth. There are, at this writing, two fabric top materials available: Haartz Cloth and Cambria.

Haartz Cloth is identified with a tiny herringbone pattern woven into the inside layer of the top. Cambria looks the same on both sides—but isn't. The outside layer is heavier and treated for resistance to ultraviolet rays. Close inspection of the weave on both sides shows a coarse weave for the outer layer and a finer weave for the inner side.

The Top Boot

When the top comes down, something has to cover all that ugly mechanism and folded material. This is the job of the top boot. The boot is usually made from the same vinyl as the interior but reinforced with top material and padded with polyfoam. It's not uncommon, however, to make the boot of the same material as the top.

Most boots are made to snap on and off and be folded away in the trunk. This is how our demonstration boot will be made. Each automobile has its own special fastening devices for the top boot. If the old boot is not available to see how it was fastened to the car, you'll have to look at the factory manual to see how it was originally constructed. It's through this manual that we move into the body of our chapter on the top well.

Fabricating the Top Well

The Factory Manual

Frank and Ron hit a bit of good fortune with the Mercury. The customer had a few pages from an original factory manual showing how the top, well and boot are all formed. Unfortunately, though, it gave no measurements.

It was the manual section on fasteners listing and showing every fastener used on the top. It even included the size and number of tacks to use and their specific locations. Although this information was of little use to the shop, the pictures were of infinite value.

If you tackle a top like our demonstration, spend time looking for some documentation on how the top was originally constructed. If you find it, the time spent looking for it will be made up 10-fold as you cut, fit and install. A few phone calls to friends in car clubs will usually get you the information about where you might find a manual, or at least some good photos. It saved Frank hours of time and much frustration having these diagrams. Another possibility is to contact some of the automotive manual and book suppliers who advertise in *Hemmings Motor News*.

There is one caveat that must be covered before we start our demonstration. Adjust the top frame before you attempt any upholstery work!

The windows must fit into their frames. Run them up and down. Do they seal front, rear and at the top? Does the rear quarter window track correctly? The side rails of the top frame should be perfectly straight and flat before the pads or cover are installed.

The frame should go up and down, fitting squarely into the well with no assistance on your part. Likewise, the height of the folded top in the well should be equal on both sides. Attempting to make these adjustments after you've started the top will result in frustration and probably require you to start over from the beginning.

Save yourself a big headache and be sure everything works and is in perfect alignment. You may

have to install new rubber seals on the frame before you can even start the adjusting process.

The Pattern

In this demonstration, we'll rely on making patterns to an even greater extent than in past chapters. It's so much cheaper to mess up a pattern of inexpensive vinyl or chipboard than it is to ruin $50/yard material—as Frank might have—had he worked without patterns.

The first pattern defines the body curve in the back of the top well area. This pattern serves three purposes. While Frank fits the back of the top well, he uses it as a base on which to cement the vinyl as he fits. Later it will be used to lay out the curve for both the back of the top well and then for the rear curtain. With so much riding on this one pattern, Frank takes his time and exercises a great deal of care in constructing it. In the photos you can see him piece it together around the entire curve of the back.

This is in the "well" where he removed the aluminum-reinforced tacking-strip. When finished, he lightly cements the pattern to the body ("well") of the car. In so doing, he'll be able to cement his other vinyl patterns to this surface. Then he'll have a solid platform on which to sketch his cutting and sewing lines.

Without exception, all American convertibles from the early sixties until today have this basic contour and top-installation technique. The top is carefully fitted to this rear contour along the base of the curtain— then stapled to a combination tacking-strip and clamp-down (an aluminum rail with a tacking-strip sealed into it). After being stapled to the strip, the top is secured to the back area with large lag screws through the aluminum-reinforced tacking-strip. Now Frank can make the second pattern.

Photo 11. Frank begins the pattern by cementing it to the previously installed chipboard. He has taken great care to locate the edge you see, directly in the center of the car. Thus, the edge of the pattern becomes a centerline.

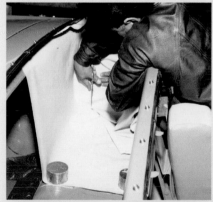

Photos 12 & 13. By placing a weight at the edge of the floor, Frank stretches the pattern material tight and locates the area where he'll seam the back to the floor piece. He then roughs out the area around the wheel well. The material goes all the way around the back and into the farthest front reaches of the well.

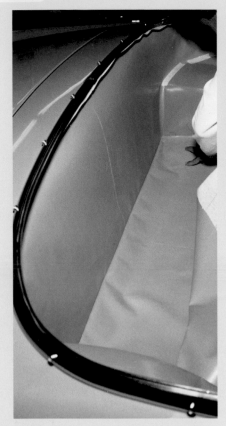

Photo 14. Frank has transferred the outline of the pattern to the vinyl he'll use for the well. The centerline seen in the photo has become a seam as has the bottom edge earlier defined by the big piece of "pig iron."

Photo 16. Frank now begins to fit a pattern for the front piece. It will be done the same as the back. the center edge becomes the centerline and two mirror-image pieces are cut from the pattern.

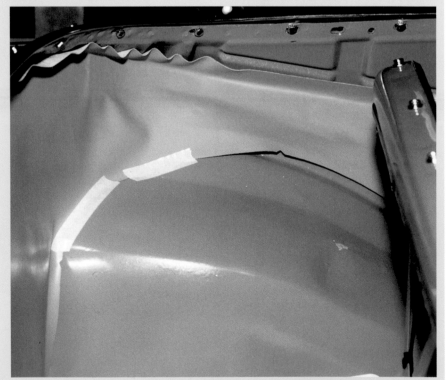

Photo 15. This demonstrates using masking tape to hold things in place while being marked. Feel free to use anything at hand to anchor your work.

The top well is too wide for a one-piece strip around the back, so it must be made in two sections. Cutting out a very large piece of an inexpensive vinyl, Frank cements the top to his chipboard pattern, places a weight at the break between the vertical and horizontal planes of the material, then rough-trims around the wheel well. Notice in the photo that the edge of the pattern material is directly in the center. The edge of the pattern becomes its own centerline.

At the bench Frank will refine the pattern, then transfer it to the vinyl to be used for the top well. One piece will be made from the pattern face-up and the other, face-down. Now the two pieces can be sewn together at the center to become one long piece. It will wrap around the back from the front of one wheel well to the front of the other.

A third piece is sewn to the bottom of the back piece to be the "floor" of the top well. For our Mercury, a wire-core welt is sewn into the break between the back and floor, and soon, between the front and floor. This gives a straight, tight line and an edge to anchor to the body.

To keep things straight and tight, Frank freely uses cement and tape to hold things while he marks for seams. This is one of his most important tricks. Yes, it takes time to do this. It's much quicker to grab a couple of clamps, hold things with your shoulder, and use the wrong hand to make the chalk lines.

Usually the job looks exactly like someone grabbed a couple of clamps, held the material with his or her shoulder, and used their left hand (assuming a right-handed trimmer) to mark the material. If every wrinkle is out of the material before you mark; if you use lots of witness marks; if you plan ahead; the job will come out perfectly.

The photos on this page show Frank making the pattern for the

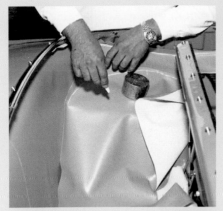

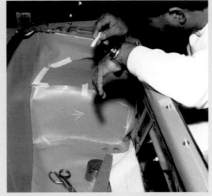

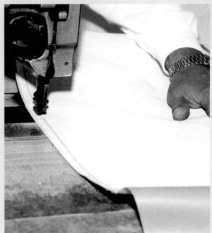

Photos 20 & 21. Fitting the side of the wheel well is no less effort. Note the arrow showing which way the material faces. When Frank transfers this chalked outline to the other side, the arrow will show which piece goes to the driver's side and which to the passenger's side.

Photos 17 & 18. Frank is fitting around the top of the wheel well. Look carefully at the photo and note all of the witness marks. These assure Frank that he has correctly sewn the pieces together and in place.

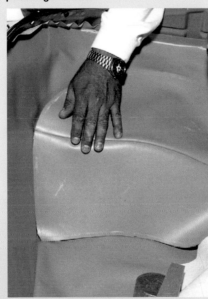

Photos 24 & 25. By allowing a 5/8- to 3/4 inch seam allowance in the bottom—front and back, Frank can sew in a pocket to retain a stiff wire-core welt. This gives the top well cover clean, straight edges along the bottom and also provides anchoring points.

Photo 22. The wheel well cover cut and sewn. It will be sewn into the top well after the front has been made and sewn in place.

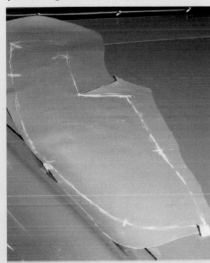

Photo 23. Frank has laid the back of the top well on the bench to give you a better view of its size and shape.

Photo 19. The finished piece for the top of the wheel well.

Photo 26. One of the anchoring points in the front. A sharp arrow-like stamping fastened to the frame, pierces the vinyl. With a hammer, it is wrapped around the wire-core welt inside the pocket.

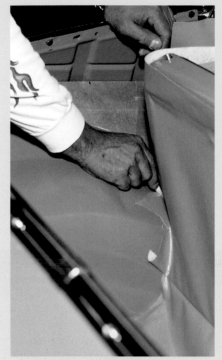

Photos 27 & 28. We watch as Frank fits the front of the top well around the edge of the wheel well and into the forward pocket where the top mechanism will fold.

Photos 29 & 30. Here are Frank's fitting marks. Rather than try to trim away the selvage while in the car, Frank prefers to do it at the bench. He can catch any mistakes here and straighten lines that were drawn crookedly.

Photo 31. To assure that both sides are the same, Frank fits only one side. He then folds the material in the middle and uses the previously fitted side as a pattern to mark the other. This is standard practice for trimmers (also furniture upholsterers). If this is not your habit yet, develop it. It saves time and promotes accuracy.

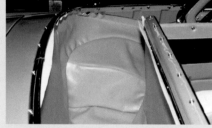

Photos 32 & 33. Now Frank can sew everything together. You see the results in the photo. Frank uses double seams throughout the sewing process. This ensures that when the selvage is folded over to lie in a particular position, both pieces of selvage will lie the same way.

Photos 34 & 35. Frank now uses his chipboard pattern to lay out the waterboard. Use tin snips to cut this material. You'll blister your fingers and get cramps in your arm trying to cut it with scissors.

front of the top well. Notice he has again cemented the pattern material to the framework at the seat back. Although we mentioned it much earlier in the book, perhaps it should be repeated here again. Using any good painter's silicone-wax-and-tar remover, will wash cement off any surface without disturbing the paint beneath. In fact, here's a tip that has nothing to do with trimming.

If you dribble a long, nasty, glob of cement down the side of someone's $5,000 paint job, leave it alone. Don't touch it. Allow the mess to dry hard, at least 24-hours; longer is better. Peel the dried cement from the paint and use the wax-and-tar remover to wash away any remainder.

A quick touch-up with a very non-aggressive rubbing compound (Meguiar's Show Car Glaze #7) will bring back the paint to its original luster. Never try to wipe wet cement off paint.

The wet cement immediately softens the top of the paint. Wiping it (the cement) causes deep scratches in the weakened paint. Allowing the cement to dry allows the paint to dry also. Then no harm is done.

Fitting and Sewing

Let's walk through with Frank as he fits and sews each of the pieces that will finish his top well around the wheel wells. He begins by fitting the top of the wheel well with the back and bottom of the top well cover in place. This allows him to make witness marks for the correct location. Next, he fits the side of the wheel well. Note the arrow pointing toward the front of the car (photo 21). At the bench he sews these two pieces together, then returns to the car to check the fit.

While at the bench, he transferred the marks from the tops and sides of the wheel well to another piece of vinyl for the opposite side. To do this, he laid the marked material face down on a fresh piece of vinyl. He then "slapped" the back side of the vinyl around the area of the chalk marks. This slapping, or patting action, transfers the chalk from the original piece to the new piece. Now, both sides will be marked identically.

The next step is to sew the vertical piece behind the seat frame to the floor piece of the top well cover. (The wheel well sections will be sewn in later.) As he does this, Frank will sew in a pocket for the wire-core welt that retains the floor of the cover to the floor of the well. This is done by simply sewing in a 5/8- to 3/4 inch pocket. When these pieces are sewn, Frank takes this part of the project back to the car for further fitting of the front piece.

He secures the bottom of the top well just as he would if the job were finished—again cementing the material to the frame in lieu of fasteners. He carefully fits around the top and front edges, then trims away the selvage at the bench. Trimming at the bench gives Frank the opportunity to straighten lines that might need help. Trying to trim the selvage while in the car could result in missing something.

In photo 31 we see Frank again, using one side of a finished end to fit the opposite side. As long as he continues to do this, both sides must be identical. He simply folds along the centerline and marks around the selvage edge. Now he can insert the wheel-well covers made earlier. The basic well is finished. Now he must finish the edges and attach any fastening devices.

Finishing the Edges

The chipboard pattern Frank made at the start of the project now comes into its second use. Frank will transfer the outline of the chipboard to a piece of very stiff waterboard. This will be used to back up the top edge of the top well. Behind this stiffened

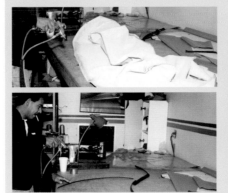

Photos 36 & 37. To fasten the waterboard to the vinyl, Frank begins by spraying a coat of cement to both pieces. We all wish, however, that Frank would not smoke while spraying highly volatile cement. A flash burn across the face would do little good for his mustache, much less eyebrows, eyelashes and possibly his eyes.

Photo 38. Frank has a line on both sides of the material along which he is matching the edge of the waterboard. By cementing the vinyl to the board with the board in the vertical position, he's assured the material will lie correctly when it's hung into the top well.

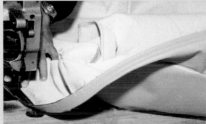

Photos 39 & 40. The waterboard is totally secured to the vinyl with two seams. Although this is a bit of overkill, it's good practice, assuring also a smooth lay of the material along the back side.

Photo 41. The next step in the finishing process is to make a chalk line along the edge of the vinyl where it folds over the waterboard. This gives Frank a "control line" to follow as he sews a piece of welt to the back side.

Photos 42 & 43. The welt is made first then sewn to the vinyl/waterboard sandwich. Note that Frank sews the welt about 1/2 inch in from his chalk line. This puts the finished edge above the retainer through which the welt will pass.

Photo 44. This is the finished welt sewn to the back of the top well cover.

Photo 45. The front is also attached with welt. In this case, however, the top of the cover is wrapped around a piece of welt cord, cemented in place, and then top-sewn for better definition of the welt cord beneath.

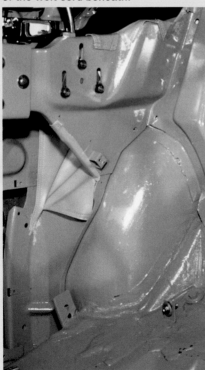

Photo 46. When fastening the top well in place (after the top is installed), the ends of the top well are cemented to the top of the wheel well and any convenient location. The quarter panels and seat cover this area.

edge, Frank will sew a piece of welt. When the top is finished and installed, a channel will be fastened to the tacking-strip of the rear curtain. The welt sewn to the back of the top well will slide through this channel and the top well will hang suspended from the waterboard. The front of the top well is likewise suspended from the rear seat frame, but without the waterboard stiffener. Let's watch as Frank finishes these two edges.

Frank removes his chipboard pattern and lays it out over the waterboard. Because it's so long, it must be made in three pieces. He then cuts out the pieces.[2] Both the back of the top well and the waterboard have witness marks so Frank can accurately locate things. The second step is to cement the waterboard strips to the inside edge of the cover. Notice in the photos that Frank takes infinite care and patience to get this accurately aligned. Remember: this is a two-way curve so the utmost care must be exercised in fitting the pieces together. With the pieces fitted, Frank now reinforces his union by sewing the waterboard to the vinyl with two seams.

The final step for the back edge will be to sew a piece of welt to the back of the waterboard and vinyl. Frank makes a chalk mark on the vinyl outlining the edge of the waterboard. When he sews the welt to the vinyl through the waterboard, he can follow this line. He then makes his welt piece and sews it as described. Notice that he sews it about 1/2 inch below the line. This will keep the edge above the retainer when the top well is attached. The last step is to sew the welt into the front.

When the top well was in the car for its final fitting, Frank chalked a line to locate where the edge of the vinyl would join the back of the rear seat frame. This line was transferred to the cloth side of the vinyl and a layer of cement was sprayed about 4 inches wide with the line in the center. A piece of welt cord was laid into the wet cement, with the short edge folded over and sealed down to capture the welt. To define that edge further, Frank ran it through the sewing machine as if to make a giant piece of welt.

The top well is finished and must sit on the bench until the top is installed. In this car, and other Ford products of the mid-fifties, the top well is always the last part to go in. For the trimmer, however, it should be the first part made. Trying to fit a top well after the top is attached is a job no one wants to do. It's dark, cramped, crowded and very uncomfortable trying to work beneath the finished top. Do yourself a big favor—make the top well first.

Summary

Although not very complicated, the top well consumes a lot of material and introduces a number of problems. Most of those are in the fitting. However, for an accomplished pattern maker, such problems are now simplified. Use any means at hand to make a pattern before you begin cutting into the material. Although we did not suggest it, if you're very concerned about your fitting job, sew the pattern together and see how it fits. If it doesn't fit, cut it apart, make adjustments and sew again. Eventually, you'll get the best-looking product you've ever made.

As you used anything at hand from which to make a pattern, use any and everything to hold your pattern (or material) in place as you fit. This includes cement, masking tape, duct tape, clamps, weights, trim-pins or even clothespins if it will help.

[2]If you've ever tried to cut waterboard with scissors, it's a terrible effort. Try using tin snips instead.

You watched Frank make his patterns then transfer them to the material he used for the well. You also found that the pattern for the back edge served several purposes: as a base to cement the material while it was being fit, a pattern to mark the rear edge of the cover and, finally, a pattern from which to make a stiff edge of waterboard.

Both the front and rear of the top well cover were held in place by a welt cord. The front material was wrapped around the cord, cemented and sewn. For the rear, Frank made a separate piece of welt, then sewed it to the waterboard-reinforced vinyl.

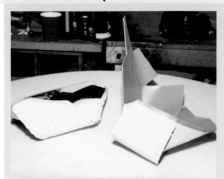

Photo 47. Although we did not describe these pockets in the text, they nevertheless need to be mentioned. These are the drip pockets where water gathers after running down the top and leaking into the top well. The customer located new pieces of waterboard, already die-cut to the proper size and shape. Frank simply covered them following the dimensions of the pieces and the old parts. A drip hose will be fastened into the bottom and passed through the floor pan of the car, allowing water to drain out.

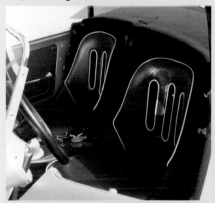

Custom interior in Austin-Healey Sprite. Custom vented seats. Detailed door pockets.

12 • The Convertible Top
Part Two—Making the Top

Photo 1. It will take three layers of vinyl tacking-strip to fill the tacking-strip channel of the rear bow. Install all three at one time.

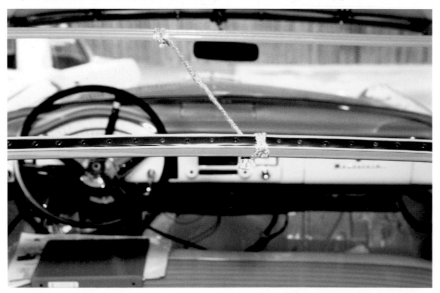

Photo 2. Keep the screws about 2 inches apart. Number 6 x 5/8 inch countersink, sheetmetal screws work well.

Part two of our three-part convertible top section describes the fabrication of the pads, rear curtain, top cover and bows, making this the longest chapter in the book! We divided it into four sections: preparing the pads, making the rear curtain, and fabricating and installing the top cover. We'll continue to stress the importance of making patterns for the more complicated parts. This is the key to the well-fitting top. Let's go right to work.

Bow Preparation

The Rear Bow

We must stress once again the importance of adjusting the top mechanism for alignment and window-fit. If the top is not in good adjustment and operating properly, you'll not be able to make the perfect fit or operate the top correctly after the cover is on. So, before you do anything else, adjust the top mechanism for optimum performance. If new seals are required, install them and make the adjustments with the new seals in place.

The top and pads are stapled to the bows. The header (front bow), back bow, and the corners of the two center bows must have a tacking-strip fastened to them. For this, we use the same vinyl tacking-strip described in the chapter on headliners. Originally, the cars of the forties, fifties and sixties used a fiber-type tacking-strip stapled to the bows. After 30 to 50 years this fiber has deteriorated. Few shops have staple guns of sufficient power to drive staples into metal. So, we fasten vinyl tacking-strip to the bows with screws and/or silicone cement.

Frank begins the bow preparation (or tacking-strip installation) with the rear bow. It requires three layers of vinyl tacking-strip to bring the level of the tacking-strip to the top edge of the bow. It's important to the finished appearance of the top that this be so. If, on your job, three layers of tacking-strip will still fall below the top of the bow, use strips of chipboard to bring it level. If the finished height is too high, grind the vinyl down to the level of the bow-edge after installing it.

Cut all three strips of vinyl extra-long, with the top piece longer than the bottom to allow for the radius in the corners. Anchor one end with one or two screws. At the other end, pull the three pieces of vinyl very tight and drive in another two or three screws, anchoring the other side. Then, every 1-1/2 to 2 inches, drive another screw. You want the tacking-strip extremely well anchored because tremendous tension is involved when the rear curtain, pads and top are all fastened to this one area. Finish by trimming the ends flush.

The Mercury (and all Ford products of this vintage) has a two-section rear bow. The part of the bow the vinyl sits on is not the outside of the bow. Consequently, when you drill through the vinyl and its platform, you're not drilling through the outside of the bow. Earlier model cars of the thirties and forties did not have this feature so you'll have to use silicone cement to glue the vinyl tacking-strip in place.

The Center Bows

With the center bows we find a problem: you cannot screw the vinyl tacking-strip to the bow. Because these bows are held to the mechanism with screws themselves, Frank was not able to lay the vinyl into the groove and cement it down. The tips of the

Photos 3 & 4. The two center bows are held on with screws from the back side. The screw ends must be ground away so the tacking-strip will lie flat.

Photos 5 & 6. Silicone cement will hold the tacking-strip tight. Just be sure to lay a good, heavy base for the tacking-strip to set in.

Photos 7 & 8. You need two pieces of tacking-strip in this area. The short one is for the pad. The long one retains the top to the header.

Photo 9. The rear bow must be anchored tightly in the correct location throughout the entire process of making and installing the pads and rear curtain. You'll need a factory manual, the old top or an authority to find the correct location for this bow.

Photos 10 & 11. Cut the pad base from top material. Staple it to the front, rear and center bows. Follow the indents of the bows on the inboard side for that edge. The outboard edge follows the edge of the frame rail.

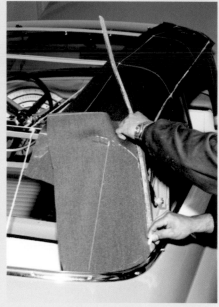

Photos 12 & 13. The rear pad locates in the radius of the back edge of the body. Cement the bottom to the tacking-strip and staple the top to the rear bow. Frank has located the inboard edge of the rear pad in line with the centerline of the side pad.

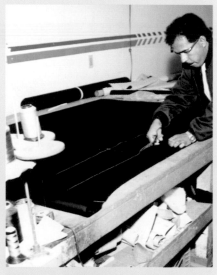

Photo 14. On the bench Frank refines the lines of his pad base and adds 1/2 inch for seam allowance on both sides.

Photo 15. Cut two pieces of bow-drill that will become the tops of the pads. These are sewn to the base, folded over and top-sewn. This will form the finished edge of the pad.

screws pushed the tacking-strip out of the groove. To overcome the problem, he ground the tips of the screws flush with the bottom of the channel in the bow. You can see this in photos 3 and 4.

After grinding the screw tips, Frank was able to force a single layer of vinyl trim into the groove. Note the dip in the bow where the tacking-strip lies (photo 6). This dip accommodates the thickness of the pad. The pieces of tacking-strip are for the pads only. The top itself is not stapled to this area. These pieces of tacking-strip are fastened to the bow with silicone cement. Lay a bed of cement in the channel. Force the piece of vinyl into this channel and allow it to dry for 24 hours before attempting to drive staples into it.

The Header or Front Bow

In the photos you see Frank installing a small piece of vinyl tacking-strip to the curved corner of the header. This is for the pad. He screws these in place using #6 X 5/8 inch countersink sheetmetal screws. These screws cause "humps" to rise in the vinyl. Frank grinds them down with the sander until the vinyl is level.

Frank installs another longer tacking-strip across the front of the header. This is held in place with metal tabs stamped out of the sheetmetal of the header. If any of these were missing, Frank would have used a screw in its place. The top is stapled to this strip. Like the rear bow, a great deal of tension is applied to this strip. Be sure it's well attached. With all of the tacking-strip in place, you're ready to turn your attention to making and installing the side pads and making the rear pads. The rear pads will be installed after the rear curtain.

Fabricating the Top Pads

Before you can begin to make the pads, you must overcome a perplexing problem: where to locate the rear bow. This is a problem on almost all vehicles, especially "The Big Three" of the years under discussion. You're in luck if you have the old top to work from. Even pieces of the rear curtain or the side pads will give you enough information. If none of this is available, as was the case for our demo Mercury, you have to go hunting for the measurement. You need to know the distance from the back edge of the body (the cutout for the top well) to the back edge of the rear bow.

After calling all his "experts" and not finding the numbers, Ron resorted to calling Acme Tops, a west-coast aftermarket manufacturer of convertible tops. Because of his long association (Read: He buys a lot of ready-made tops here!) with Acme, one of the sales staff went to the stock room, pulled a '57 Mercury top and measured the back curtain. Thanks, Acme! You saved the day.

When you have the correct location for your back bow, tie it in place with two pieces of rope. Be sure both ends of the bow are equidistant from the edge of the body. Leave the ropes in place as long as you can—preferably until all the pads and rear curtain are in place. The final preparation step is to be sure the aluminum-reinforced, rear tacking-strip is bolted in place with lag screws. All of the patterns for the rear of the top will be located off this piece.

Side Pads

The side pads are relatively simple to locate and make. In the photo series on pages 130 and 131, Frank has laid out a large piece of top material, stapled at the rear bow

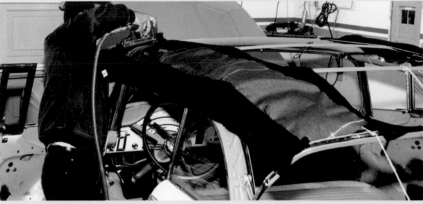

Photo 16. Return the pad to the exact location in which you marked it. Be sure all your witness and location marks line up.

Photo 17. Cut a 1/2 inch piece of polyfoam to fit exactly within the pad. It must also be cut short of the front and rear tacking-strips. This prevents bunching up on top of the tacking-strip.

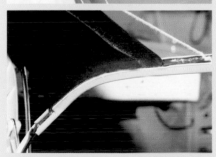

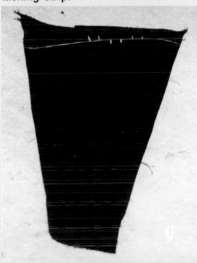

Photo 21. One of the rear pads. Note the witness marks that locate the bottom to the aluminum-reinforced, rear tacking-strip beneath the edge of the body.

Photos 18-20. Cement both the pad and the polyfoam. Lay the foam onto the pad base making sure the edges are correctly aligned. Cement one side of the pad top to the foam, then the other. Don't worry about cement overspray. The top of the pad will not be seen when the top cover is installed.

Photo 22. This very long piece of vinyl (actually two pieces sewn together) will become the pattern for the rear of the top and the rear curtain (also known as the top curtain).

Photos 23-25. The pattern material is cemented to the rear tacking-strip and stapled to the rear bow. It must reach from one rear frame-rail to the other with no wrinkles.

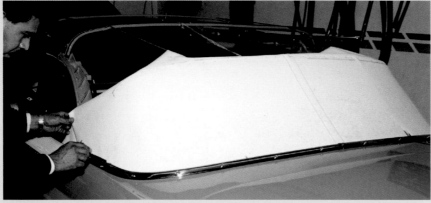

Photo 26. Location marks must be made at the rear bow, along the body edge, and over the rear tacking-strip. Note that Frank uses the seam between the two pieces as a centerline.

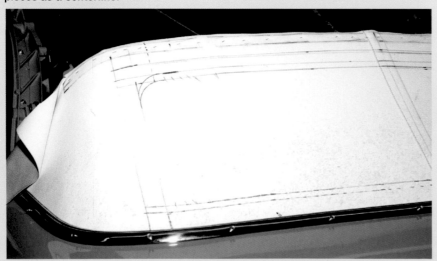

Photo 27. These are the lines that define the rear-curtain, the zipper, the reinforced bottom of the curtain, and the whole rear section of the top cover. Review the body copy for a description of each line.

and at the header. (The face of this material faces into the car.) The material is stretched tight enough to eliminate any wrinkles but not so tight as to distort the rear bow.

As we discussed, each bow is indented about 1/4 to 3/8 inch to accommodate the thickness of the pad so it will not stand proud of the top. These indents give us the exact size of the pad. Frank draws a line across the back edge of the rear bow. Then, making a mark at the edge of each indent, he can draw the inside line. The outside line follows the contour of the side rail of frame. A front cutoff line is scribed across the front tacking-strip in the header. This is now the base of the side pad.

Rear Pad

To locate the rear pad correctly, Frank first sprays a thin coat of cement on the rear tacking-strip. He cements the bottom of another piece of top material to the tacking-strip and staples it to the rear bow, directly over the pad. Frank previously located the center of the pad at the rear, and marked this location. From that centerline, he chalks a line on the rear pad, 90 degrees to the rear bow and down to the tacking-strip. The side of the pad follows the frame rail contour—up to the side pad.

Frank now gets into the car and on the front side of the rear pad outlines the tacking-strip in chalk. He'll also mark the tacking-strip where the edge of the rear pad falls. This is his witness mark for locating the edge of the rear pad. With this accomplished, he returns to the bench and trims the selvage, leaving a 1/2 inch seam allowance.

The pad tops are made of a thin cotton material we call bow-drill. This is a name from antiquity that's with us still. Bow-drill was originally used to cover the bows of buggy top—and the name has stayed.

Later, in the fabrication of the top, you'll see Frank use it again to make a covering for the two center bows.

The bow-drill is used to make two side flaps for the base of the pads we previously shaped. These flaps are sewn to the side of the pad, to be wrapped over the top after a layer of foam has been cemented in. Frank cuts two strips of bow-drill the length of the pad and 3/4 of its width. (A pad 8 X 72 inches would have two pieces of bow-drill 6 X 72 inches.) At the machine, Frank sews the bow-drill to the pads face-to-face. This puts the selvage edge inside the pad. Next, he folds each of the bow-drill pieces over the pad base and top-sews a seam about 1/4 to 3/8 inch in from the edge. This gives a nice finished appearance to the pad. This done, the same process is repeated for the end pads. Now the side pads may be installed.

Installation

Installation is very straight-forward. Cut two pieces of 1/2 inch foam the finished size of the pad. In the car, staple the pad to the bows in the exact position they were marked. Spray a thin coat of cement to the inside of the pad and one side of the foam. Place the foam on the pad and seal it down. Now, spray a coat of cement over the top of the foam and the inside of the inboard bow-drill flap. Bring this flap over and seal it down. In like fashion, cement the outboard flap over the inboard flap. It's not necessary to staple the ends closed because future stapling will take care of it. Most trimmers, however, place a strip of duct tape over the front edge to prevent it from "telegraphing" through the top.

The rear pads are set aside now, to be installed with the rear curtain.

Photo 28. Frank has the pattern out of the car and on the bench. The lines you see outline the rear tacking-strip and the location of the lag-bolt holes.

Photo 29. To use the pattern, Frank has cut it into its basic parts. The top piece is part of the zipper placket, the center piece is the rear curtain (with part of the top cover), the bottom piece is the reinforcement piece for the curtain. To the side is the pattern for the rear of the side panel.

Photo 30. Frank lays out the rear curtain pattern on a piece of top material. Notice that he has reattached the bottom of his pattern, separated in the previous photo. The mark he's making adds a stretcher to the bottom of the curtain.

Photo 31. This is the result of the outlines of the rear-curtain. The line above the tacking-strip location line defines the edge of the reinforcement piece.

Photo 32. Frank lays a piece of clear vinyl over his marked rear curtain piece and holds it in place with weights. If you don't have weights use tacks or staples. For the next few activities, these pieces must stay in exact alignment.

Photo 33. Frank cuts a piece of paper the exact size of the opening in the rear curtain and carefully tapes it in place with 1/4 inch tape

Photo 34. He trims the bottom of the clear vinyl a couple of inches above the bottom tacking-strip line and tapes it to the top material.

Photos 35 & 36. Frank trims the other three sides of the clear vinyl and tapes them in place.

Photo 37. At the sewing machine, Frank sews the clear vinyl to the top material backing. Here you see the top material on the bottom, a layer of clear vinyl over that and a paper pattern taped to the clear vinyl, outlining the exact opening of the rear curtain.

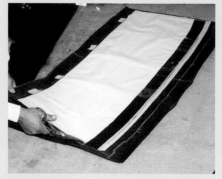

Photo 38. The next step is to trim the ends flush with the seam. The top and bottom are not trimmed.

Photos 39 & 40. This is the reinforcement piece. Frank outlines it exactly. He adds a 1/2 inch seam allowance at the top before cutting it out.

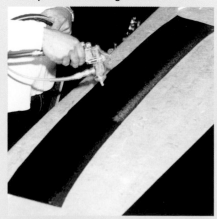

Photo 41. On the back side of the piece Frank sprays a layer of cement. He folds the edge over on the seam allowance to create a finished edge.

Photo 42. The reinforcement piece is sewn to the panel in line with the bottom of the paper pattern. Use a double seam here. Be sure the tacking-strip location lines on the reinforcement piece are in line with the corresponding marks on the panel.

Photo 43. Sew the zipper and zipper placket to the top.

Photo 44. Bind the raw edges at the side with binding tape. In this photo the curtain-panel has been turned over and Frank is sewing it from the back.

Fabricating the Rear Curtain

Making the Pattern

The rear curtain pattern is part of a larger pattern for the whole rear section of the convertible top. Look at the size of the vinyl Frank has cut in photo 32. (Actually, it's two pieces of material sewn together.) This will wrap from one frame rail to the other.

After cutting and sewing the piece, Frank will staple and cement it in place, with no wrinkles anywhere! This is very important. If the pattern is wrinkled or mislocated, the top will be too. Begin the installation by using the seam line as a centerline. Cement and staple it in place from the center out.

All vinyls are made with a cloth backing called Jersey (a generic name). By placing this cloth backing to the outside, Frank can mark on it with pencil. He uses a pencil so he can erase if he makes an error. The ropes holding the top bow erect should be left in place. Cut the pattern to fit around them.

The first two areas to locate are the rear bow and the rear edge of the body. We suggest using masking tape for witness marks on the body of the car. Frank used marking pen on the chrome. This comes off chrome with no problem. Long-term contact with paint, however, will cause a permanent stain.

The next step is to enter the car and outline the tacking-strip as you did for the rear pads. This locates the pattern within the car and could, if need be, removed then replaced in the exact same location. Thus, if the pattern fits perfectly, it's reasonable to expect the top made from that pattern will also fit perfectly. You now have a "canvas" on which to draw your rear curtain and back section of the top. Let's look carefully at Frank's "artwork" in photo 27 on page 132.

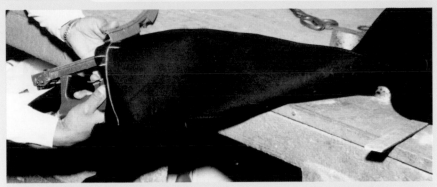

Photo 45. Frank begins the installation of the rear curtain by stapling the rear pads to the rear tacking-strip. Do not staple the sides of the pad. Like the previously installed pads, the rear pads must be padded with polyfoam. This will be done after the installation.

Photo 46. Now Frank can staple the rear curtain to the tacking-strip.

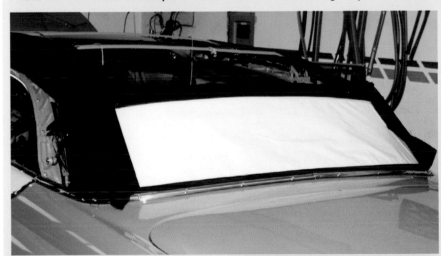

Photo 47. Frank has installed the rear curtain and pads in the car. The rear tacking-strip is completely fastened to the body and the top of the curtain is well stapled to the rear bow—as are the pads. Be sure all your marks are aligned.

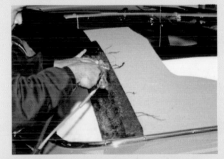

Photo 48. Fill the rear pads with 1/2 inch polyfoam just as you did the side pads. Like Frank is doing here, use chipboard or paper to prevent overspray.

Photos 49 & 50. The finished pads and rear curtain.

Photo 51. Snap a chalk line on the pad to locate the seam between the side panel and the top panel. Most vehicles have a locator mark on the header for the location of this seam. Transfer the distance between these marks in the front to the rear bow. If you have no locator marks, make the seam lie about 2 inches outboard of the side pad's inboard edge.

Photo 52. This pattern gives a roughed-out size for the side panel.

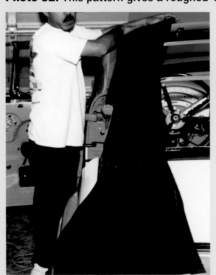

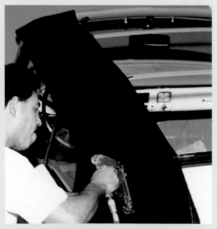

Photos 53 & 54. Frank locates the panel temporarily to the header and rear bow with staples.

Designing Rear Curtain and Back Section

In photo 27 at the top of the pattern we see the outline of the bow. This is simply a large witness mark for relocation. The first horizontal line down from the bow represents the zipper location for the rear curtain.

The zippered section is made of top material and will be sewn to the clear vinyl of the rear curtain. The second line locates the inside edge of the cutout in the rear of the top. That's why the curve connects to the vertical line. The line directly below that was an error. Frank should have erased that line, but had already worn out his eraser and could not find another. He therefore "lined" it out. Those are the hashmarks you see crossing this line out.

The last two horizontal lines are at the base of the pattern. The top line is an error. (Can you see the hashmarks?) The line closest to the body represents the end of the clear vinyl of the rear curtain. Below this line will be more convertible top material. The location of these lines is arbitrary unless you're attempting a "factory-original" restoration. If this is the case, the customer should supply the original top, the correct measurements with a factory manual or be willing to pay for your investigation.

Turn your attention now to the two vertical lines. The first, or one closest to the viewer's left, is the outside edge of the rear curtain and the inside edge of the rear top pad. The next is the inside edge of the cutout for the rear of the convertible top (as described above). There is one other short, dotted line to the right from the inside edge of the rear top bow down to the marked-out line of the opening. This witness mark locates the inside edge of the side top pad. These lines may be a bit confusing if you're new to the trim business. As Frank cuts and assembles, all will soon be made clear.

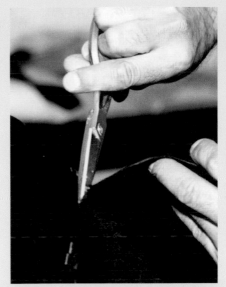

Photo 59. Besides outlining the finished edge of the top, Frank also adds two witness marks to locate the area where he'll anchor to the frame-rail.

Photo 57. Frank roughs-out the shape of the back to help this area lie flatter.

Photos 55 & 56. When you wrap the rear of the side panel around the rear pad, the top material will form a dart at the rear bow. Cut this dart along the line of staples retaining the side panel to the rear bow. Let the material fold over this cut.

Photo 58. With a friend to hold the top in place, outline the rear edge of the body. You'll use this line to locate the pattern for stapling the cover to the rear bow.

Photo 60. Using his pattern, Frank marks the cutting or trim line for the rear of the top. The two witness marks locate the seam between the side panel and the end piece.

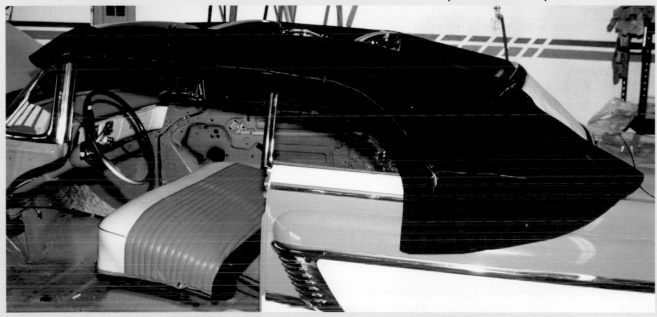

Photo 61. Frank now has everything laid out and is ready to mark the bottom of the side panel.

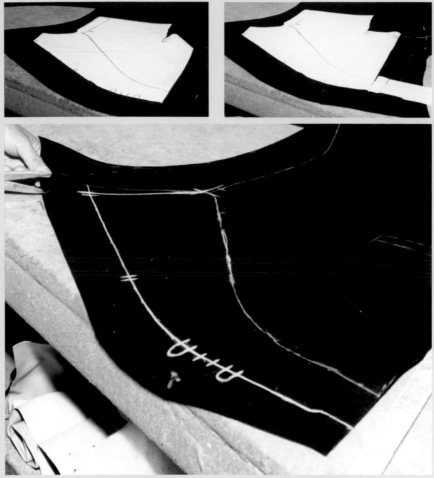

Photos 62-64. This is the pattern end from the original. It's been set in position with the line of the body over the corresponding line on the side panel. By adding the bottom part of the pattern over the body line, Frank can locate the line he needs to guide him while he staples the side panel to the rear tacking-strip. The last photo shows the finished line.

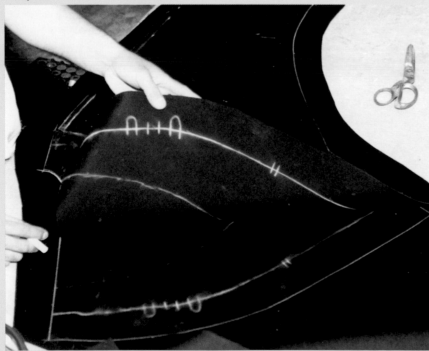

Photo 65. The passenger's side panel is made from the driver's side panel. The chalk marks will transfer with a little patting.

Cutting, Fitting and Sewing

In photo 29, Frank has returned to the bench and cut his pattern into the pieces he'll need for fitting. At the top, the pattern has been separated where the zipper will be. Next is the piece for the clear vinyl with the outlines for the opening in the rear of the top. Beneath this is the strip of top material that will be sewn to the bottom of the rear curtain and attach to the reinforced tacking-strip. The piece to the right side becomes part of the side panel at the rear.

Frank temporarily reattaches the bottom piece of the pattern to the pattern body. From this he lays out and marks a full piece of top material from the pattern. Over this he places a sheet of clear vinyl cut to the approximate size. He next cuts a piece of paper to fit the exact opening in the rear curtain. He tapes this to the clear vinyl with 1/4 inch masking tape. This serves two purposes: The first is to protect the clear vinyl as he moves it through the sewing machine. The second gives him an exact outline of where to sew when he cannot see a seam line below. As an added bonus, he can mark on it if he needs to locate something.

The next step is to trim the clear vinyl—without moving it from its proper location. He trims an edge, leaving a 1/2 inch seam allowance, tapes the edge to the top material and trims another. With four cuts he has the vinyl cut to size and ready to be sewn.

At the machine Frank sews all four sides of the clear vinyl to the top material. Where there is masking tape, he sews right over it. It will be easy to pull off after the sewing is done. When all four sides are sewn, he trims away the selvage on the two outside edges. Later, he'll bind these raw edges to give a nice, finished appearance. The basic curtain is together. A zipper must be sewn at the top and a reinforcing piece at the bottom.

Frank next cuts the reinforcing piece. You saw this as the bottom piece in photo 42 on page 134. Notice that he adds 1/2 inch to the top of the piece. This is cemented and folded over upon itself. The resulting finished edge will be the edge you see from outside the car. He sews this piece to the bottom edge of the clear vinyl, assuring himself that the marks outlining the location of the top bow are aligned with the similar marks on the back of the rear curtain panel.[1]

In a similar fashion, he uses the top pattern to cut out the zipper placket. This is sewn to one edge of the zipper. The other edge of the zipper is sewn to the rear curtain panel. Be sure the zipper pull is on the inside of the car. Unzipping the rear curtain for fresh air or to lower the top must be done from the inside of the car. The rear curtain is finished after Frank binds the raw edges at the sides. Now the curtain is ready to install.

Installation

If, like Frank, you were very careful to make everything exact and line up all your marks, the rear curtain and rear pads will fall into place the first time. Remove the tacking-strip from the car and bring it to the bench. This is usually a three-piece assembly. Begin by aligning the marks on the rear pads with the tacking-strip and staple them in place.

Don't staple the bow-drill. It's left alone for now. After installing the assembly of curtain and pads, you'll have to add polyfoam to the pads as you did the side pads. Be sure to cut out for the lag

[1] The panel is the sandwich of clear vinyl and top material. Later, when the entire job is finished, the last step will be to carefully cut out the top material from in front of the clear vinyl and remove the paper covering.

Photo 66. Finished shape of the dart. Some trimmers will sew this dart together. We recommend against this. Notice also, the seam-allowance witness marks for the end piece have been connected with one line.

Photos 67-69. Frank makes a reinforcement edge for the opening in the back of the top cover. This piece lies along the vertical edge. He coats both pieces with cement and lays the side panel over the reinforcement piece. The job is finished by trimming away the selvage. Leave 1/2 inch, however, at the top (on the panel itself) to seam to the end piece.

Photos 70-72. Frank chalks a line 2 inches in from the edge of the finished edge. To reinforce this area, he sews in flat pieces of material.

Photo 73. To form the end piece, Frank staples a strip of material in this location then uses his pattern to mark it out. Again, he uses witness marks to correctly locate things.

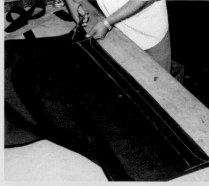

Photos 74-76. As with the other pieces, the end piece must also be reinforced. Frank uses the end piece as a pattern to make another piece. This is cemented to the end piece and trimmed to fit. Frank leaves a 1/2 inch seam allowance at each end.

screws that attach the tacking-strip to the car. Next, staple the rear curtain to the tacking-strip, making sure every mark is correctly aligned.

Take the assembly to the car. (A friend is very useful here.) Fasten the tacking-strip to the car with its lag bolts. If the lag-bolt holes are wide enough to allow for adjustment, be sure the adjustment is the same as when you made your original witness marks. Don't get things out of whack now! Tighten the bolts securely and turn your attention to stapling the curtain to the rear bow.

You have a witness mark at the top of the rear curtain that outlines the rear bow. Be sure this outline falls directly over the bow. It's a tendency for trimmers to pull the rear curtain as tight as they can to eliminate any wrinkles. Resist the temptation. There will be no wrinkles if you locate the curtain in the exact position. If you make the rear curtain too tight, the part of the original pattern that outlines the rear of the top will not fit in relation to the curtain. Stay with your marks. It's all going to work.

Staple the top of the curtain to the rear bow using your outline. Then, staple the rear pads to the top bow, continuing to let the bow-drill "flap in the wind." Cut a piece of 1/2 inch polyfoam to fit inside the pad from the edge of the body to the edge of the bow. As you did with the side pads, cement the foam in place, then cement the sides over the foam. Trim the selvage from above the zipper placket and the rear curtain is installed!

Well, the hard part is done and it's all downhill from here! You'll now make the top cover. This will be easy because you already have half the pattern. Installation will be a snap because of all your excellent location and witness marks. Are we having fun? You bet!

Making the Top

Locating the Side Panels

All convertible tops are assembled in four pieces: two side panels, a top panel and an end piece that covers the rear curtain zipper. There are specific locations for the pieces. We'll begin with the location of the side panels; then, what we'll now name as the rear panel; and follow with the top panel.

Our Mercury's front bow is stamped to receive the seam between the side panel and the top panel. This gives us one location for the edge of the panel. The second location was the one drawn on the original pattern. The rear of the side panel should align with the edge of the cutout in the rear of the top. Put this pattern piece back up to the rear curtain and make a witness mark for the location of the rear of the side panel. As long as the pattern is there, sketch its shape on the paper protecting the clear vinyl. Locate the seams for both sides.

Using a chalk snap-line, snap a line from the front mark to the rear mark along the pad, just as you see Frank and George doing in photo 51. This is the exact location of the seam between the side panels and the top panel.

To avoid wasting top material, use a piece of discarded vinyl to "rough-out" a piece about the size you'll want to cut for the side panels. It should be about 2 to 4 inches too big all the way around. On Frank's piece, he's made a mark at the rear bow. This will help locate the piece after it's been cut. He takes this piece to the bench and cuts out two side panels—one for each side of the top. Frank makes sure there is enough material along the bottom to reach down to the tacking-strip.

He places the side piece on the car and temporarily staples it in place at the front and at the rear

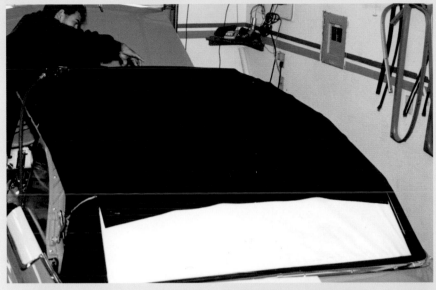

Photos 77 & 78. To fit the top panel, Frank cuts a piece a few inches larger than needed on all sides. He chalks lines to locate the front, back and centerline. Inside the car he draws outlines around each bow. Later, he'll cement and sew a strip of bow-drill to these areas to wrap around each bow.

Photo 79. This is the inside of the top panel. Note the lines for the bows and the centerline. By patting along one of the snapped chalk lines, Frank picked up that line. Now, he cuts away the selvage, 1/2 inch outboard of the line. The inboard line becomes the seam line.

Photo 80. To lay out the other side, Frank folds the material along the centerline and transfers all of his marks.

Photos 81-83. To make the cover for the bows, Frank lays out the pieces on a section of bow-drill. With masking tape, he outlines the area to be cemented. He also masks off the area around the bow outlines and sprays a layer of cement here. He then cements the two pieces together.

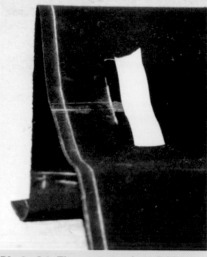

Photo 84. The next step is to fold the bow-drill back on itself to form a finished edge.

Photo 85. The bow covering is finished by running a seam down the center from one side of the top panel to the other.

Photo 86. Sew the side panels to the top panel with a 1/2 inch seam allowance. Then, sew another seam as close to the edge as possible.

bow, making sure his staple is in the exact center of the tacking-strip (the center front-to-rear). Now he pulls the material snug around the side of the car and the rear pad. This makes a pucker in the material above the top bow. Frank makes a cut with his scissors outboard of the center-line of the tacking-strip about 1/4 inch.

Then, he lays the selvage from the pucker over the stapled part of the side piece and places one or two temporary staples in it to keep it in place. He finishes the rough-fit by cutting away some of the material lapping over the rear curtain in the basic shape of the finished piece.

In photo 58 Pete holds tension on the material, keeping it smooth around the corner of the body. Frank chalks a line in the same area he penciled a line on the earlier pattern. Can you see what's taking place? From this body line, Frank can locate the pattern. The bottom of the pattern for this area shows exactly where to staple the material. Frank and Pete finish up by outlining the cutting, fitting and locating areas of the side panel.

Refining the Fit

The snapped chalk line on the pad transferred to the side panel. Frank had only to define it better with additional chalk marks. At the bench, he selects the pattern piece for this side, and, as described above, fits and locates for the tacking-strip.

All finished edges of a convertible top are reinforced with a 2 inch-wide strip of top material cemented or sewn to the edges. This will then be the next step in the fitting process. Follow the photos beginning on page 134 as Frank reinforces the edge of the cut-out over the rear curtain.

From his pattern he lays out the curved edge. Measuring out 2 inches he draws cutting lines.

In the first photo of this section you see a mark 1/2 inch in from the top edge. This is seam allowance to which the end piece between the two sides will be sewn.

After cutting out the piece but leaving the selvage around the curved edge, Frank coats the piece with cement. Likewise he coats the inside edge of the side piece with cement in the corresponding location. The two pieces are brought together with the edges aligned and sealed together. We suggest using a roller to seal the two pieces together because they will not be sewn together.

Around the edge over the window and quarter window, Frank draws a line 2 inches inside the line defining the edge of the side panel. This too, will be reinforced. However, it's not necessary to cement these pieces. They're sewn to the top. Frank needs only to lay large scraps beneath the sides and sew along the chalk lines. Then, he trims the selvage from each side of the two seams. After trimming the inboard edge, leaving a 1/2 inch seam allowance, the side panels are complete and ready to be fastened to the top panel and end piece.

Fitting the End Piece

Frank cuts a piece of material from scrap that fits across the width of the rear curtain and temporarily staples it to the top bow. With his pattern of this area, he lays out the lines defining the inside edges and the seam line. At the bench he marks out another piece with the backs together. This will be the reinforcement piece, so it is cut 1 inch narrower. This allows a 1/2 inch seam allowance for each end of the end piece. Remember this end piece is sewn to each of the side panels.

The two pieces are cemented together and the selvage of the reinforcement piece trimmed away.

Photos 87 & 88. Some trimmers turn the seam to the inboard side and top-sew it in place. To give a more "original" appearance to our job, Frank will cement the seam allowance to the top panel. Again, he masks the area where he does not want overspray. He folds the seam over on to the top panel.

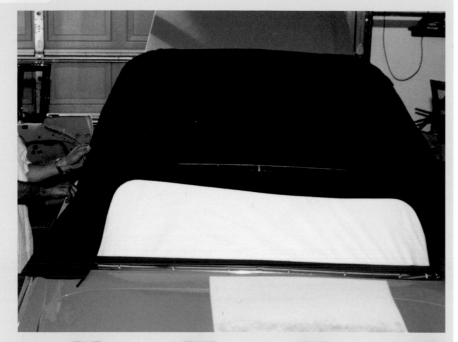

Photos 89 & 90. Frank lays the finished cover over the frame and lines up all the witness and locating marks. These are particularly critical at the rear bow. When correctly located, Frank removes the tacking-strip and staples the bottom edge of the side panels to it. He is equally careful here to make sure his location marks are properly placed.

Fitting the Top Panel

The final piece to fit is the top panel. Frank cuts a piece of top material large enough to hang over the front bow by about 6 inches and in the rear by about 3 inches. He marks one side of the top and then folds it in half to mark the other side. This, of course, means he must also have a centerline. The project begins by temporarily stapling the top panel to the bows.

Frank marks the front and rear and, by patting on the edge of the material, transfers the chalk line on the pad to the back of the material. Inside the car, he outlines the location of the two center bows. Now he can remove the piece from the car. The only trimming to do at the bench are the two sides. The marked side is trimmed 1/2 inch outboard of the chalked edge for seam allowance. Frank folds the top in half to locate the opposite side and trims away the excess.

Attaching the Bow Covers

This top will be fastened to the two center bows. This is not always the case nor, if Don recalls correctly, is it factory-original. It will, however, keep the top from "ballooning" or lifting when the car is driven at speed. To attach the top to the bows, Frank will fasten strips of bow-drill to the top. These will then be cemented to the bows. Watch as he fastens the bow-drill to the top (photos 81 through 85).

Frank lays out two strips of material the exact length he needs to fit the area of the bow he wishes to cover. Each includes a centerline. He measures the width of the bow and, using this measurement, lays out masking tape to that dimension on each side of the centerline of the bow-drill pieces. In this gap, he sprays a medium coat of cement and allows it to dry. While the cement dries, he moves to the top.

He masks off around the chalk marks he made locating and defining the width of the bows. To this area he sprays another coat of cement and lets it dry. Now, the bow-drill and top are brought together in the cemented areas and sealed together with a roller. After removing the materials, but before Frank sews the side panels to the top panel, he'll sew a seam down the centerline of these two pieces. Finally, upon installation, the bow-drill will be wrapped around the bows and cemented in place. This fastens the top to the center bows.

Sewing the Top Together

After anchoring the bow-drill pieces to the top, Frank will sew the two side panels in place, then the end piece. Follow him in photos on pages 142 and 143.

In the first photo Frank has folded the bow-drill back on itself. This will make a finished edge when wrapped around the bow. He makes one seam down the centerline of the bow starting at the edge of the top panel and finishing at the other edge. He does this for both pieces, folding back all four ends of the bow covers.

The next step is to sew on the side panels. This is done with a double seam, aligning the witness marks at the rear bow, two center bows and the header. The double seam begins with the seam 1/2 inch in from the edge—the normal seam allowance. Next, another seam as close to the edge as possible locks the edges together.

When both side panels are sewn to the top panel, Frank will turn the seam allowance inboard and cement it in place. Some trimmers sew the selvage in a flat-fell seam at this location. Frank says it looks more original to cement it. (The original and vinyl aftermarket tops lay the seam

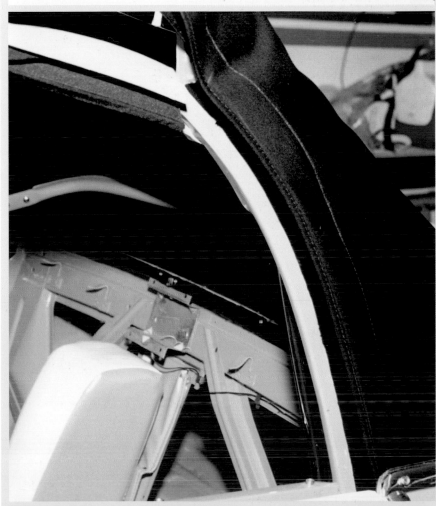

Photos 91 & 92. This flap, attached to the binding, is cemented to the top rail to prevent it from vibrating in the wind. Be sure to trim away the selvage before you install the seals for the quarter windows.

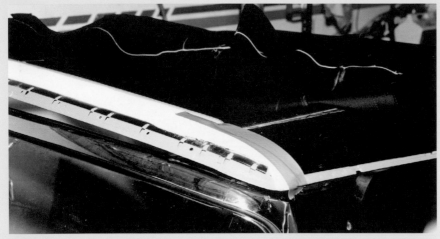

Photo 93. A strip of polyfoam prevents the texture of the header from telegraphing through to the top. The duct tape over the pad serves the same purpose.

Photo 94. Cement the top to the header then follow-up with staples. Notice that Frank has carefully aligned the chalk mark at the front of the header.

Photo 95. This is the location for the other flap (that was sewn to the binding). It's finished off just like the rear.

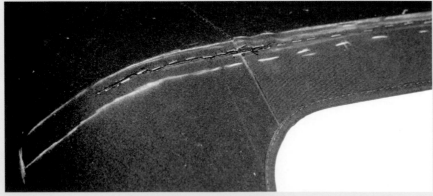

Photo 96. Here are the finished edges at the rear bow. Frank must keep his staples in a line, no more than 3/8 inch apart. Any more than this and the wire-on will not cover them.

over and heat-seal it to the top panel. Cementing works just as well.) Last, the end piece is sewn in place and its seams also turned and cemented flat.

It remains now to bind the raw edges. These are the edges along the side panels and around the rear opening over the rear curtain. Frank will use a cloth binding tape to do this. For us to note here, though, is the insertion of two pieces of material that will be used to hold the top to the rear frame rail and to the top frame rail over the wind wing.

Frank cuts four pieces of top material about 3 inches wide. Two of them will be long enough to fit into the length of the rear frame rail. See this in photos 91 and 92. The other two pieces are cut about 6 inches long and will attach to the front frame rail above the wind wing. Earlier, Frank marked these two locations on the side panels with witness marks.

As Frank binds the edges of the side panel, he slips the appropriate piece of material into its location, lying flat and facing into the top. He sews them into the binding and consequently, to the side panel in the doing. These four pieces will be cemented to their appropriate places, keeping the top from vibrating (in the wind) around these areas. This finishes the sewing of the top and it may now be attached to the car.

Mounting the Top

The two locating marks that are now the most important are the witness marks locating the seam between the side panel and top panel at the rear bow. Everything locates off here. Drive a couple of staples here through the top. At the front, pull the top tight, aligning the front witness marks or lines and drive in a couple more staples. Anchor the other side the same way. Be sure the bow-drill wraps are directly over their respective bows. The top should be smooth, flat, and lying fairly wrinkle-free.

Inside the car, remove the rear tacking-strip to which the rear curtain and pads are stapled. Fit the bottom of the top to the tacking-strip, carefully aligning all your witness and location marks. Now, staple it down all around. Inside the car, return the tacking-strip to its original location. There should be no wrinkles in the rear-quarters of the top. If there are, check your marks to be sure everything is located correctly. Ninety-nine percent of the time, if there are wrinkles in this area, it's the result of mislocating. The other one percent is poor fitting or sewing. (Check for these too!)

Locate the strips you sewed into the binding. Cement the rear strips to the rear frame rail as shown in photos 91 and 92, page 145. Trim the excess. At the front of the top, cement a narrow piece of 1/2 inch polyfoam to the header. Along the tacking-strip, spray a layer of cement and a corresponding layer on the inside of the top. Pull the top snug, not too tight, and cement the front to the tacking-strip. At the rear, temporarily staple the top panel to the rear bow. Check for wrinkles and be sure the bow covers are still in place.

If the top is looking good, anchor the top panel, front and rear, with staples. Then anchor the rear piece and trim the selvage. At the front, staple the top to the tacking-strip to secure it in place. Cement the "wings" you attached at the binding to the top frame rail, just above the wind-wings. Now you can attach the top to the two center bows.

The object is to cement first one side of the wrapping to the bow, then the other. Finally, you'll trim the selvage. In the photos, Frank has taped the "wings" of the wrap to the top. This allows him to spray the cement without the pieces getting in his way. Notice also he uses

Photos 97-99. To cover the bows, Frank cements first one side, then the other, trimming in between. He uses masking tape to hold the cloth up out of the way and chipboard to prevent overspray. To emphasize his careful installation, notice how the lines, chalked in during the original fitting, are perfectly realigned with the bows.

Photo 100. Before cementing the edge of the top under the header, Frank installs the chrome trim.

Photo 101. Now Frank can cement the flap of the top to the bottom of the header.

Photo 102. Here's the finished header with all of the weatherstrip installed.

a piece of scrap chipboard to prevent getting cement on the top.

He sprays one side and the bow, wraps that side around the bow and trims the selvage. He sprays the other side and the now-covered bow, wraps this over the bow and again, trims away the selvage. The finished job is neat, tight and there's no stray cement on the top material. Note how accurately the chalk lines follow the now-covered bow.

Finishing the Job

The Header

Our Mercury has a chrome reveal molding across the front. It is held in place with molding fasteners fixed with nuts beneath the header. Most cars, however, don't have this luxury. The top wraps around the header (without staples) and cements to the underside of the header. The front of the top is then finished with a large welt (1/2 inch rubber tube covered with top material).

On our top Frank fastens the reveal molding to the header. He sprays a coat of cement to the header and material and wraps it around the header, trimming the excess. The last step at the header is to install the weather seal.

The Rear Bow

You must now install a piece of wire-on across the back-bow to cover all the staples. The most successful way to do this is to fasten one end just past the dart on the side panel. At the other side of the car, pull the wire-on tight and anchor it on the outboard side of the other dart. Carefully align the edge of the wire-on with the edge of the bow and staple it in place. Use a soft mallet to force the edges of the wire-on closed.

With the addition of chrome tips to cover the bare ends of the wire-on, the job is finished except for the rear curtain.

Rear Curtain

Inside the car, very carefully cut away the top material in front of the clear vinyl. Keep the cut as close to the seam as possible without cutting into it. Outside the car, tear off the paper. You may need to relax the top a bit to get behind the rear opening.

Congratulations! You worked your way through this extra-long chapter. We hope your next top is the best you've ever made.

Summary

In this information-packed chapter you've followed Frank through the process of making pads, a rear curtain, and a full convertible top. The best trick you learned was making and fitting the pattern across the back. Here, you designed the rear curtain and the back end of the top. By knowing the relationship between the rear bow, the edge of the body and the tacking strip, you can fit, sew and install the top with no wrinkles. There were no wrinkles in the pattern—why would there be wrinkles in the top?

Take your time with top building. Getting it right the first time will be faster for you than refitting and installing three or four times.

Photos 103 &104. To anchor the wire-on correctly, staple one end to the top. Then, at the other side, pull the wire-on tight and staple it down. Drive staples into the wire-on from one end to the other.

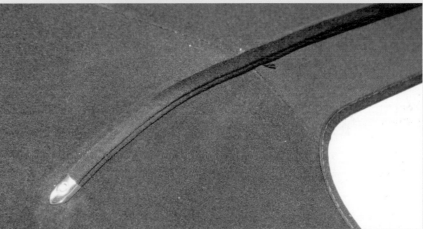

Photo 105. With a plastic, rubber, or leather mallet, close the wire-on. Finish with a chrome tip.

Photos 106 &107. Here's the finished top. There's not a hint of a wrinkle or poor fit anywhere.

We're now ready to put the finishing touch on our new convertible top. A nice boot to cover it and the mechanism in the down position will look very nice. It should be made from the same vinyl as the interior of the car.

A good boot serves more than an aesthetic purpose. Besides looking good, it protects the inside of the top from ultraviolet rays. The exterior of the top material is well protected from UV rays with UV-inhibiting chemicals. The inside of the material is not. It also prevents trash from being thrown into the well—not to mention people inadvertently dropping cigarette butts in there.

In the days when everyone smoked, it was not uncommon for a passenger in the rear seat, with his arm over the seat and a cigarette in his hand, to have that cigarette either slip or be blown out of his hand and into the top well. Before the driver could stop, raise the top and find the burning cigarette, it had put a hole in the top, pad or rear curtain. Not a pleasant experience! Today, far fewer people smoke, and almost no one smokes in their own or their friends' cars. However, the top boot remains something of an "institution" and should be one of your skills. Now let's finish this Mercury.

Fabricating the Liner

Fitting the Body Piece and Arms

A good top boot consists of three major pieces: a liner made of top material, a layer of polyfoam and an outside cover of vinyl or other finishing material of the customer's choice. Our Mercury

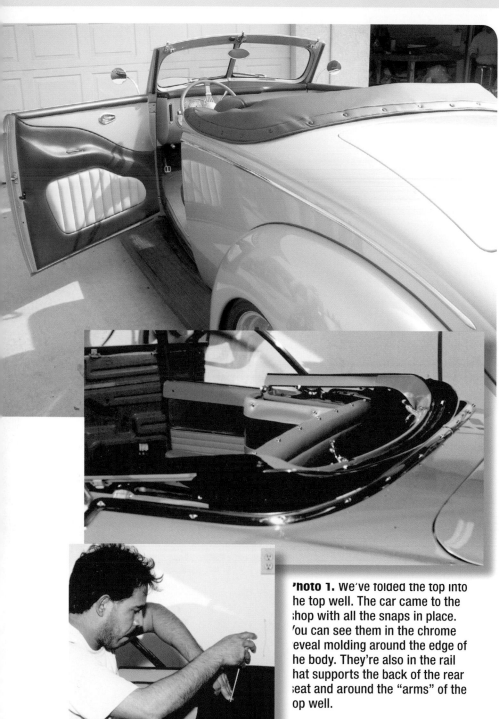

Photo 1. We've folded the top into the top well. The car came to the shop with all the snaps in place. You can see them in the chrome reveal molding around the edge of the body. They're also in the rail that supports the back of the rear seat and around the "arms" of the top well.

Photo 2. To hold the front of the boot liner, Frank removes three of the male studs, makes corresponding holes at these locations, then replaces the studs through the holes.

top is made this way. The vinyl selected for the exterior was the same used for the top well and interior of the car. Before any fitting begins, however, be sure all the male halves of the snaps are in place. If the car didn't come to you with these, install them now. All of the original holes should be there unless body work eliminated or covered the holes. With all of the snaps in place, you can begin the project by fitting the liner.

The liner is made in three parts: a center section and two end pieces. The center section covers the area from the back of the rear seat to the rear of the well, and from the inside edge of the quarter-panel to the opposite side. The two end pieces define the area from the forward-most part of the folded mechanism to the rear of the well. Frank begins the job with the centerpiece, fitting not from a pattern this time, but with the actual material.

He cuts a piece of top material several inches larger on each side than the finished size. As usual, he starts with a centerline matched to the centerline of the car. To anchor the front, he removes three of the male snap fasteners and uses the studs to hold the front in place. The rear is fastened tight with 1 inch masking tape. We'll call this the body piece.

The first places to fit are the lines at the end of the body piece. This line travels from the farthest outboard edge of the seat back to the center of the radius of the body at the rear of the top well (photo 4). The front and rear are easily fit. Just follow the outside edge of the chrome reveal molding around the rear of the top well. Across the front, at the forward edge of the rear seat back, draw another line. You can draw all four of these lines first, or follow Frank's method. As usual, he works only to the middle. At the bench he folds the

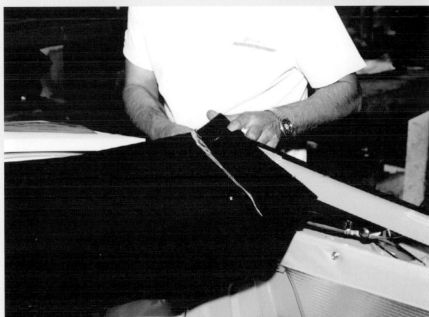

Photos 3 & 4. The first fitting line Frank makes is from the outboard edge of the seat back frame to the center of the radius of the body at the rear of the top well. This will be a seam line rather than a cutting line.

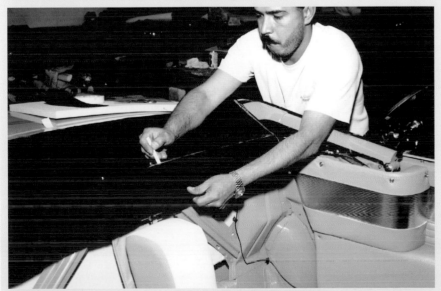

Photo 5. To make the front line of the boot, mark along the forward edge of the back cushion frame rail. If your vehicle is not constructed like our Mercury, make this line at least 1/2 inch forward of the snap-studs. If you can squeeze out more, do so.

Photo 6. The rear line follows the outside edge of the chrome reveal molding.

Photos 7 & 8. Frank makes the "arm" from a separate piece of material. Like the body, he holds it in place with masking tape. Notice the close fit around the rear quarter-window.

material over on itself and makes the unmarked half from the marked side.

Sometimes, even when you've done your very best to make the top lie in the well correctly, it seems to develop a will of its own and will stick up more on one side than the other. If you're having this problem, you may want to fit each side of the top boot independently of the other. Whether fitting half or all, the next step is to fit the top of the "arm"—that section where the side rails fold and lie.

Cut another piece of material large enough to fit from the rear edge of the main body piece to well past the front of the "arm," and wide enough to hang over the body (outside the rear quarter window) and over the inboard side of the "arm" section of the well. If you're fitting all the parts for the reasons described above, then cut a piece of top material for the other arm. If you're able to fit one side from the other, just fit one arm now and use that as a pattern for the other.

Fitting the material for the arm begins by imitating the diagonal line of the liner, from the radius to the outboard edge of the seat back. If your job is like ours, you may need to sew a dart into that area to get rid of a pucker. (See this dart arrowed in the finished product, photo 15.) The arm and body will be sewn together along the line you've just created. Make witness marks to ensure a good seam. Continue the outboard line up to the rear quarter window, then follow the inside of the window to the end of the arm area of the top well. The line now follows the top edge of the well, back to join the front edge of the body piece.

Fitting the Facings

There are two pieces, parts of the arms, that remain to be fitted. One is at the end of the arm and the other is a band (facing) sewn to the arm to retain the cover to the inside area of the arm portion. These are best seen in photo 13.

Look at photo 10. Here you see Frank fitting the end. Next, he'll fit a band about 2-1/2 inches wide around the inside of the top well part we've been calling the arm. Later, as seen in the finished photo, he'll place three snaps in the facing to retain the cover to the top well.

As you fit these two pieces, be sure you make plenty of witness marks. You can get into a lot of trouble without them. Now we're ready to trim our fitted parts and make the polyfoam pad that goes between the liner and outside covers.

Trimming the Pieces to Size

At the bench, you'll now trim things to size and for sewing. Begin with the body piece. If you've fit only one side, fold it in half along the centerline and transfer your chalk marks by patting around the edges—as we've done before. Trim the selvage from the front and back on the chalk line. You need not leave a 1/2 inch seam allowance here. There must be seam allowance on the sides to join with the arms.

Transfer the chalk marks from the arm you just fit to a new piece of material. Be sure the witness marks transfer also. Trim the selvage on the chalk line around the outboard side. Along the front and inboard sides, leave seam allowance for the end piece and facings.

In a similar manner, duplicate the end piece and trim the selvage, leaving seam allowance on all sides.

Roll out the vinyl, face-up on the bench. Lay out all seven pieces of the liner face-up on the vinyl. Mark around the liner pieces and cut them out from the

vinyl. Be sure you transfer all the witness marks.

Preparing the Foam

Now we'll laminate 3/8 inch foam to the finished pieces. This is done by spraying a coat of cement to the polyfoam and material then laminating the two together. The problems arise in where to trim.

Trim the polyfoam flush with all edges except where there will be seam allowance. Trim the foam so it does not get sewn into the seams between the body piece and the arms. Then, trim away around the seam allowance for the facing and end pieces.

When it comes to sewing the liner pieces to the vinyl, there must be no polyfoam sewn into the seams. When you bind the edges, however, you'll be binding liner, vinyl and polyfoam.

Sewing It Together

Let's sew all our pieces together. Begin by edge-sewing each piece of vinyl to its respective liner piece laminates. To edge-sew the material means to sew all around the piece as close to the edge as possible. Then, sew the darts.

Sew the arm pieces to the body, matching the edges and witness marks. Turn the selvage edges inboard and top-sew the selvage to the body. You now have the three main pieces of the boot sewn together. The next step is to sew in the end pieces. Again, be sure to align the witness marks. Sew in the end piece, then top-sew the selvage to the body. Be sure the selvages face into the body, not into the end piece. You must now sew in a decorative seam around the outside edge.

Draw a line about 1-1/2 inches in from the edge, around the outside of all three edges of the assembly. Draw a similar line around the inside edge, up to the edge of the arm. Do not mark along the edge of the inside arm. You'll later be sewing the facing to

Photo 9. Frank marks out the rear of the body piece and arm at the same time. His line continues around the chrome reveal molding up to the rear quarter window. It then passes inside this window. Be sure to leave enough room so the window does not rub against the boot.

Photo 10. Frank carefully locates the end piece. Note all of the witness marks he uses. We count seven on this one small piece. After fitting the end, Frank will fit the facing.

Photo 11. Frank trims the top material liner body. The front and rear are trimmed on the line. The ends are trimmed leaving seam allowance. The arms will be sewn to the ends while the front and rear edges are bound.

Photo 12. Here's the arm you saw Frank fitting in the previous photos. Now he's transferring this fitted piece to the material to make the opposite arm.

Photos 13 & 14. Frank has now assembled the top-boot and is in the binding stage. On the reverse side, he'll trim away this selvage from the binding.

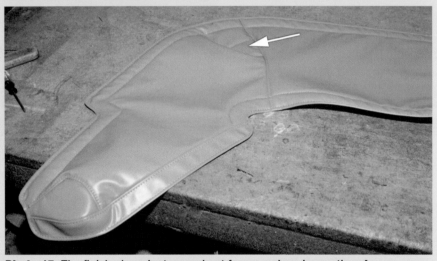

Photo 15. The finished product spread out for your close inspection. Arrow indicates dart.

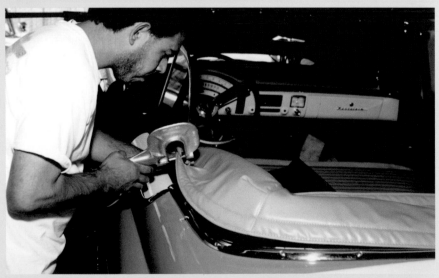

Photo 16. The shop's portable snap-fastener installing tool. They're very handy and save a lot of time. If you haven't invested in one of these yet, start saving your money. They're worth every cent of their low cost.

this area. At the sewing machine, run a stitch along these two scribed lines.

The last step of the assembly is to sew the facing to the inside of the arms. Align the witness marks and sew the facing to the arm. Top-sew the selvage to the facing.

Sewing on the Binding

The last sewing step is to bind all of the edges—front, sides and rear. Cut strips of vinyl as long as possible, 1-1/4 inches wide. Bind the edges of the cover as you would any other binding job. Trim the selvages as close to the thread as possible. This finishes the assembly of the top boot. The last step is to install the snaps.

Snap Installation

Take the newly finished boot to the car and locate it over the top and top well. Frank used three male snap studs as anchors to hold the boot in place while he fit the body. Now he has only to punch holes through the vinyl to locate the female half of the snap. He installs these three caps (female half), and fastens the front of the boot to the rear-seat frame. Again, with masking tape, he secures the boot to the car.

Stretch the boot tight and hold it in place with masking tape or duct tape. It's very easy now to see the male half (stud) of the snap pressing against the vinyl. If you can't see them, you can feel them with the tips of your fingers. With chalk, mark the location of each stud. Then, with your portable snap fastener, install a corresponding cap for each of the studs. When all of the caps are installed, you've finished the top boot. Congratulations on a job well done!

Summary

Our top boot finished off the convertible job nicely. It should have been a relatively easy job. Here are the important things to remember: To achieve a smooth-looking finish, the boot is made of three layers of material: vinyl, polyfoam and top material. If the top sits in the car perfectly square, you can fit one side, fold the material on the centerline and mark the other half. If, as many tops are, one side of the top does not fold into the well level with the other side, fit the material at both sides.

Laminate the polyfoam to the liner of top material. Fit the vinyl for the outside of the boot using the liner pieces as patterns. Edge-sew all pieces together. To achieve the best fit, turn all the selvage edges to the center and top-sew. Make a decorative seam, 1-1/2 inches in from the front and rear edges. Sew in the end pieces and facing, followed by binding all the raw edges.

Secure the top to the car with snaps—and drive away in good health.

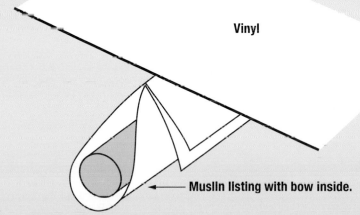

Photos 17 & 18. Our finished top boot installed on the Mercury. Frank had to rework the arm to get rid of those wrinkles—a result of the top pads having been folded incorrectly when the top was originally brought into the down position.

How to make a listing

Vinyl

← **Muslin listing with bow inside.**

Listing is a 3 inch wide strip of muslin folded in half and sewn to a piece of vinyl or fabric. Rod or wire can be inserted through loop. If you use a fastener such as a hog-ring to loop over wire, material can be fastened to frame so fasteners can't be seen.

14 • The Roadster Top

Welcome to a very interesting chapter! It's neither the easiest chapter nor the hardest. It does, however, incorporate all of the interesting techniques we've discussed thus far. You'll fit, cut, sew, make patterns, locate witness marks, and do all the other intricacies of custom auto trim. You'll learn one new technique in this chapter.

The cover for the demonstration roadster is made in three pieces, as was the Mercury convertible we just finished. The three pieces of the roadster top, however, look nothing like the three pieces of the convertible. The top pieces of this roadster go from side-to-side while the panels of the convertible gained their length from front-to-rear. It would be possible, of course, to make the roadster top look exactly like the convertible top. But then, it would look like every other roadster on the street—and who needs that?

We go back now to Pete's side of the shop and watch him as he puts a good looking cover on this recently completed top. We'll follow as he makes a cover for the outside; then, as an added bonus, we'll get to watch him make a headliner.

Photo 1. Here's our demo top. It's made of aluminum and ready to be covered.

Photo 2. To start the foaming project, Pete takes the largest measurements in both directions. Here, he measures from side-to-side. He'll cut the foam a few inches larger as it must wrap around the edges.

Making the Roadster Top Cover

Covering the Top with Foam

This top, although made of aluminum and steel, is designed to look like it was a soft top. It even has two "bows," made by wrapping aluminum over a framework of bows.

We'll call them bows throughout the chapter, as a means of identification—front bow, back bow, or first and second bows. With this in mind, we'll begin by covering the top with foam.

Just about everything we do in custom upholstery begins with polyfoam padding. Once again, we'll use closed-cell foam as the base upon which to build. Watch as Pete works up the foam for this special aluminum top.

He begins by measuring the width of the top along the back bow, then, from the back bow to the front. He'll cover this top in two pieces. The second piece, of course, is the rear of the top—from the back bow to the base. After cutting the foam, he cements it to the top with about 1 inch of overhang beyond the back bow.

Using a yardstick, he draws a cutting line on the foam that imitates the seam in the metal beneath it. He then trims away the selvage. Notice in photo 9, he's trimming the foam at the same angle as the back panel. This allows the back panel foam to lie flat without a bulge at the seam.

When he cements foam to the back panel, he lets the top edge sit above the surface of the first piece of foam installed. He'll trim the selvage created by this, flush with the existing foam. As usual, he sands all the seams and little wrinkles to make a perfectly smooth base for the cloth (or vinyl). There remains only to turn the top over, wrap the foam around the frame, and cement it in place. Careful trimming and sanding finishes the job.

Cutting, Fitting and Sewing

Before Pete sets about cutting up top materials, he wants to make some location marks on the polyfoam so he'll be able to fit the material properly, then locate it on the top exactly as it was fit.

Photo 3. The foam is installed in two pieces: one over the top and the other around the rear. This is also the way the cover will be made. Pete applies cement just in the area he'll be covering.

Photo 6. Trim the foam on the same angle as the rear of the top. The foam then becomes an extension of the rear of the top.

Photos 4 & 5. After cementing the foam to the top, Pete carefully trims the foam just above the rear bow. This must be done carefully as the second piece of foam will butt up against it. You don't want any gaps to telegraph through the top material.

Photos 7 & 8. When you foam the back, leave a little extra around the top bow. Later, you'll trim this off, parallel to the top. The finished foam will then have the same shape as the aluminum.

Photos 9 & 10. Finish the foam seams with a little scuffing. Likewise, knock down any wrinkles, lumps, or bulges that might have occurred.

Photos 11 & 12. Wrap the foam around the frame and cement it in place. Taper the edges, shaping it into the frame by sanding the edges to a feather edge.

Photo 13. Pete tries the now-foamed top on the roadster. He's checking to be sure the fit has not changed with the addition of the foam, especially around frame edges.

Photos 14 & 15. Pete lays out lots of lines on the top to help relocate the cover after it has been fit. Each bow is outlined, a centerline is made and check marks laid out at equal intervals from the centerline.

To do this, he draws lines on the top indicating the front and rear bows. He very carefully scribes a centerline.

Finally he makes equally spaced witness marks along the bow lines, measured from the centerline out. As with all our projects, Pete will fit one side of the top, fold the material over, and form the opposite side from his original marks.

Notice in photo 18 how Pete fits the edge of the material that will wrap around the top frame and be cemented inside. If this seam were to be left straight, he would not have enough material to wrap around the inside curve.

After fitting the centerpiece, he fits the front, then the rear. He now has three pieces to be sewn together. Compare these three pieces with the convertible top in the last chapter. There, the seams ran from front-to-rear. Here, Pete's seams run side-to-side. If the Mercury convertible top frame was made just a little differently, Frank could have made the Merc top just like Pete is making the roadster top.

At the bench, Pete better defines his lines and witness marks, then folds the material on the centerline and marks the opposite side. Now he can trim the whole thing.

Sewing the top is very straightforward. The three pieces are first sewn together, matching all the marks. Then the material is turned to the outside and each seam top-sewn, creating a flat-fell seam. Now Pete is ready to cement the top to its frame.

Cementing the Cover

Here the process gets a bit "sticky." The cover must be cemented to the frame with all the seams straight. Working around the corners of the rear presents challenges we've not met yet. It can be done but you must exercise some care and caution.

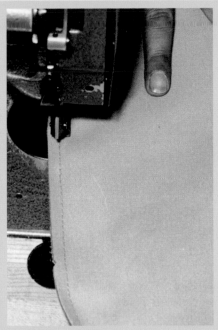

Photo 16. Fitting begins with the centerpiece between the front and rear bows. Pete will transfer all the marks he made on the foam back to the fabric.

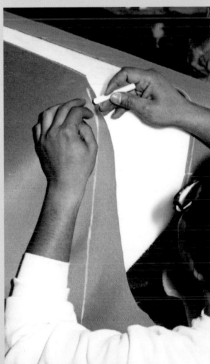

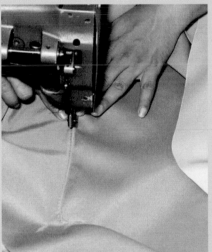

Photos 17 & 18. Continue the chalk line down the bow. There is a seam line here where you joined the polyfoam. At the radius, wrap the fabric around the frame and continue the line. You'll do this again with the front piece. Later, when these two pieces are sewn together, you'll be able to wrap the cover around the frame with few or no relief cuts.

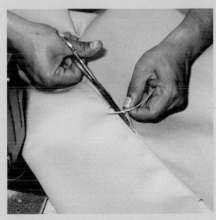

Photo 19. Finished trim. Note that all the locating and witness marks have transferred to the fabric.

Photo 20. As usual, Pete folds the material at the centerline and fits one side from the other.

Photos 21-23. At the machine, Pete sews the top together. After making the seam, he turns the top over and top-sews it. This is called a flat-fell seam. The selvage is turned to the rear. When all the seams are finished, trim away the selvage from the top-sewn seam. You want as little bulk as possible.

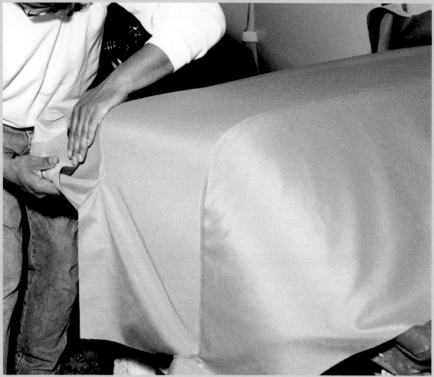

Photo 24. Pete "test-fits" the top before cementing it in place.

Photos 25 & 26. Cementing the top begins at the center, then works first down the back and finally out to the front.

Photo 27. It's of the utmost importance at this step to be certain the seam and locator marks are correctly aligned with one another. Be sure the seam is perfectly straight. If you're off here, the whole top will be off.

Photo 28. Here, the center of the cover has been completely cemented to the top. To cement the rear section, Pete will have to lift up this corner. This is why the cement must not be allowed to adhere the two pieces together. To prevent this, the cement must be dry to the touch and as little pressure applied to the outside of the fabric as possible.

Begin by spraying a coat of cement just in the section between the front and rear bows. In a similar manner, spray a corresponding coat to the inside of the cover in the same area. Allow the cement to dry well. It must pass the Kraft-paper test. However, it must not be sprayed on the night before and expected to be ready for you the following morning. This will be too dry and tight adhesion will not occur.

When the cement is dry to your satisfaction, fold the center section of the material (between the first and second bow) back on itself. Align the seam with the line drawn on the top and carefully press just the center part of the seam onto the cemented line. Pull the seam tight from one side, adjust the witness marks to align, and press that half of the seam into place. On the other side of the top, repeat the process. Now the seam is anchored.

Very carefully smooth out the center section of the cover over the foam. Be careful not to press too hard on any one place. You may have to lift the cover after it's in place. If you caused the cement to adhere tightly, when you lift the material you'll tear out pieces of the foam. When Pete lifts material, he lays the back over the center section so he can see the seam for the rear bow. He pulls first on the diagonal at one side, then the diagonal on the other. Finally he pulls at the center.

The object of this exercise is to get the seam for the rear bow to line up (with no wrinkles) over the locating line you drew over the rear bow. Work carefully to get the seam line straight and all the witness marks in place. The rest of the fit depends on how well you locate the center of the top.

When you think you've got it just right, be sure the back part of the cover is lying over the top, exposing the back of the material and the rear of the top. Now spray a coat of cement to both sections and allow to dry as before.

Carefully begin pulling (or rolling) the back of the cover down over the polyfoam. It gets a bit tricky in the corners as you can see in photo 30 as Pete struggles to get all of the wrinkles out. Pete doesn't use this trick, but here's Don's suggestion for the first time you do this.

Cut a piece of chipboard to fit neatly into that corner and wrap around the curve. It should be about 10 to 12 inches wide. Lay it up against the seam and roll the material over it about 3 or 4 inches. Now the fabric and polyfoam can't cement themselves together. Slide the chipboard out a bit, allowing that 3 or 4 inches to make contact. Roll the cover over the chipboard a little farther and slide it (the chipboard) out. Working carefully this way, you should be able to get the material smoothly around the corner. Work both sides simultaneously.

Pete was able to get the back down successfully (as you will too) and can now turn his attention to the front of the cover. It works just like the rest. Spray on the cement—both sides, let dry, and stretch it out. In photo 33 you can see Pete really getting into it! When the top is successfully cemented in place, give it a good rub-down to make sure the cloth and polyfoam adhere well to one another. Turn the top over and finish off the cover.

Trimming the Inside

The most important part of trimming the inside is at the radius around the openings for the driver and passenger windows. You'll most likely have to slash the material at this radius to get it to lie flat. If, however, you're very careful in fitting, it may lie perfectly flat without any cuts. Unfortunately, Pete was not that accurate with his fitting. He had to relieve the material in this area.

The other area in which to pay attention is along the front header.

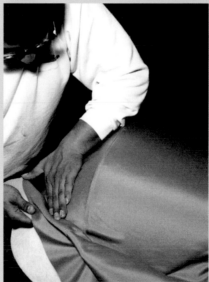

Photos 30-32. This corner takes a bit of wrestling to get all of the wrinkles out. If all your locator marks were exact, this corner will fit. Yes, it fits here and the cover looks great.

Photo 29. Pete lifts the corner and begins applying cement to the rear of the top.

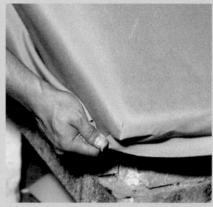

Photo 33. Go get 'em, Pete. Stretch it out there!

Photo 34. This is what Pete was trying to do: stretch the material out for this dart to fall on the corner.

Photos 35 & 36. Cementing the cover to the inside is a simple step. The problem is to avoid having the material bunch up in the corners, creating a problem with the fit between the top and car.

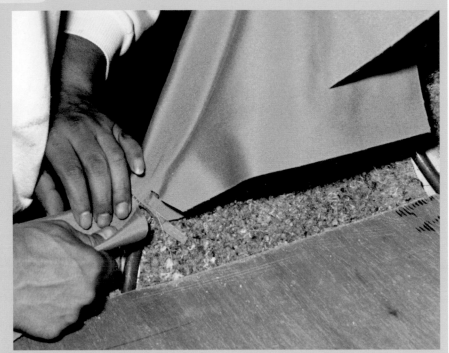

Photo 37. Pete hoped his fitting would have been perfect in this radius. Unfortunately, it wasn't up to his usual standards. A few slashes in the material relieved the tension and lets the material lie properly.

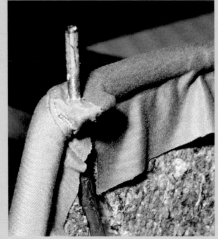

Photos 38 & 39. Here's where the material tends to bunch up or get too thick—at the front and rear corners. Staple or cement one side of the material, cut away the selvage, and wrap the other side over the cut edge.

Photo 40. See how close together the slashes are made to wrap the inside of this radius. Without this many slashes, you run the risk of tearing the material.

Carefully cut away all excess material in the corners. Any bulk here will cause a gap between the header and the top of the windshield. If the gap is too wide, the customer will not be able to fasten the top to the windshield frame.

In a similar manner, avoid any bulk around the rear edge of the top—for the same reason. The top must sit flat around the back. The last area to consider is the cutout for the rear window. Reference photo 40 to see how Pete handled this problem.

In the photo you can see that Pete made many very fine slashes in the material at the radius of each corner. In so doing, he can wrap the material around the radius with none of the cuts extending into the visible portion of the material—and there are no torn areas. If you try to get by with just two or three cuts, the material will usually tear. When it tears it always goes out past the radius to where it can be seen from the outside. Take the extra time to make enough cuts to get the material to lie the way you want it. The top is now ready for a headliner.

Making and Installing the Roadster Top Headliner

Fitting

When it came time to make the headliner for the top we just finished demonstrating, Don found himself flat on his back with the worst flu of the season. Fortunately, on his return to the shop, another roadster top came in for a headliner. Pretend then, if you will, that we picked up right where we left off.

By now, you should be able to glance at the photos and say, "Yeah, I see how that's done. You just make panels, cover them and stick 'em in." And, you'd be absolutely right. Let's watch Pete do just those things.

Hc begins by fitting a panel pattern across the back and making a cutout for the window. Next, he makes a pattern for the sides. There is no pattern for the center. This area is foamed and covered as we would any large panel.

When the patterns for the sides and rear are finished, Pete transfers them to panelboard, cut out and covered in foam—just as he might have if these were to be door panels or any other type of panel we've discussed. Now he's ready to foam and cover the center.

Pete does this operation just as Frank did on the Willys. Pete, however, did not have to install any paneling in this area. The fiberglass of the top is smooth enough to allow the foam to be cemented directly to it. He carefully cements both the polyfoam and fiberglass, bonding the two together.

In the final step before covering things, he checks the fit of the rear and side panels after foaming the top. The 1/4 inch foam takes up 1/4 inch of space. However, Pete wants to be able to force the panel down into the foam to assure a tight, gapless fit. If he's able to press the panel into the foam and have it still fit around the edges, then the panel is ready for covering. If he loses any of the fit, a couple of licks with the sander and he's back in business.

Covering the Top and Panels

Pete will cover the inside of the top and the panels as we have demonstrated several times before. One trick we've not looked at, however, is the "blind-tacking" finish along the front edge. Photo 49 demonstrates this technique.

Pete begins by laying the material for the headliner

Photo 41. Pete will make a headliner for this top. Unlike the previous top, this one is made of fiberglass over a wood frame.

Photo 42. This headliner will be made of panels covered in headliner material. We could have covered it in one piece as we did the Willys or make bows and cover it like the '57 Ford.

Photos 43 & 44. Pete makes patterns of the rear section and both sides all at one time.

Photo 45. To fit the window, punch holes with a trim pin, around the perimeter of the window, from the outside.

Photo 46. Lay the foam into the top and cement it in place—just as you would for any other project. Finish by trimming and sanding. If the customer wanted it, you could carve a design into the foam at this point, just as you would on a door panel.

Photo 47. Pete test-fits the side panel for continued good fit. The addition of the foam could raise the panel a little. However, the panel will be forced down into the foam to close any gap. Any further fitting can be done with just a bit of sanding.

Photo 48. Ron and Pete check the headliner material before cutting. Always do this, looking for flaws in the fabric or material.

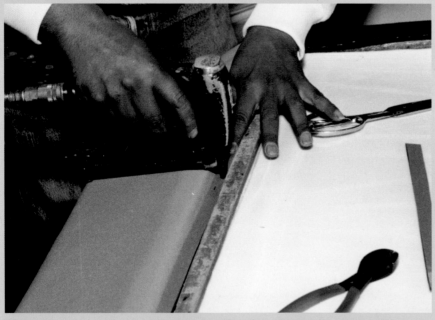

Photo 49. Pete is "blind-tacking" the headliner into the top. He staples the material, face-down, into the front of the top. This is followed by stapling a piece of Masonite over the edge. When the material is folded back over the Masonite tacking-strip, it hides all the fastening beneath.

face-down in the groove between the front of the top and the plywood header you see in the photo. The top material is stapled to a wood member beneath this groove. Next, Pete cuts a piece of Masonite to fit into the groove. Using heavy staples, he staples the Masonite into the groove, over the fabric. Now, when he lays the fabric back over the Masonite and header piece, the material will be face-up and he'll have a straight, tight, front edge to the headliner with no signs of how it's held in place. We call this blind-tacking.[1]

Installing the Rear and Side Panels

At the beginning of the chapter we said you'd learn a great new trick. Here it comes. Pete must now fasten these three covered panels to the inside of the top. You'll have noticed in the photographs that there are no snap fasteners to be seen on any of these panels—and it doesn't look like they could be successfully cemented in place. Well, Pete is going to nail them to the wood frame on which the fiberglass has been formed.

It's a very simple process. Pete selects the finest brad or finishing nail available at the hardware store. (Brads and finishing nails have no heads.) For this job he selects a # 2 X 1-1/4 inch finishing nail. He will drive this through the material, foam and panel into the frame below. Because the finishing nail has no head, he can pull the material over the nail, and the hole in the fabric closes over it. In photo 55 you see him using a trim pin to catch the material and draw it up and over the nail.

The only precaution to add is this: Most nails and brads are covered with oil to prevent

[1]Blind-tacking is one of the skills borrowed from furniture upholsterers. This is how the outside back and arms of your sofa are covered.

rust. Driving one of these nails through fabric always leaves a tiny, black oil-ring stain. To prevent this, wash the nails with lacquer thinner first. In the furniture upholstery shops where this trick is used all day long, they store these nails in a bottle of lacquer thinner. It cleans them and prevents rust at the same time.

Another Fastening System

As a demonstration, Pete installed one of the panels as he would have on the aluminum top used in the earlier demonstration. That top had no wood frame members. In this type of installation, Pete would have left one side of the panel open—the side around the window. Working from behind the material, over the foam, he would have screwed or pop-riveted the panel to the frame member, making sure the panel was drawn tightly to the frame. Then, with a very thin putty knife, he would force the covering material into the narrow gap between the panel and the top. The tight fit would hold the fabric in place.

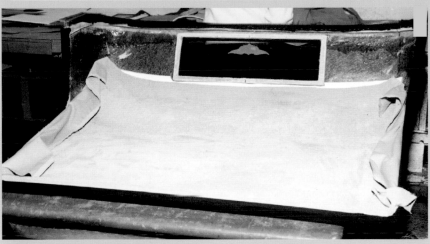

Photo 50. This is the covering, cemented to the top.

Photo 51. Pete has now added the back panel.

Photos 52 & 53. Covering the side panels is just like covering any other panel. Foam is cemented to the panel board, sanded smooth, and the edges tapered. The cover is then cemented to this, wrapped around the panel and cemented or stapled to the back.

Photos 54 & 55. To fasten the panels to the frame, Pete drives finishing nails right through the material and panel into the wood behind it. Then, with a trim pin, he pulls the fabric up over the top of the nail. The material then closes around the hole. Be sure to wash the nails with lacquer thinner first, removing the oils used to prevent rusting.

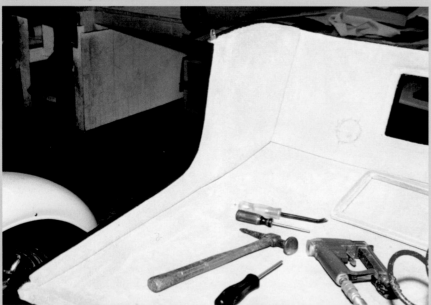

Photo 56. Here's the finished panel. You can't see the nails or the holes.

Summary

You should now feel like an old hand at this custom trim business. In this final chapter we brought to use everything you've learned so far. The most important trick in custom upholstery is to make patterns that exactly fit the area you're working on. Here, you can make mistakes, throw things away (losing only pennies and minutes), and work until you know the finished product will fit perfectly the first time.

To get this perfect fit to go from the pattern to the finished product, you learned the importance of using witness marks and location marks. Location marks show you exactly where a finished piece goes. Witness marks help you join two or more "things" together in the exact manner in which you fit them.

In this section we stressed again the importance of good foaming techniques. Use lots of layout lines. Trim the foam so it follows the same contour of what you're covering. Use sandpaper to knock down the high spots.

Good luck with all your new projects. We hope they all come out perfectly the first time!

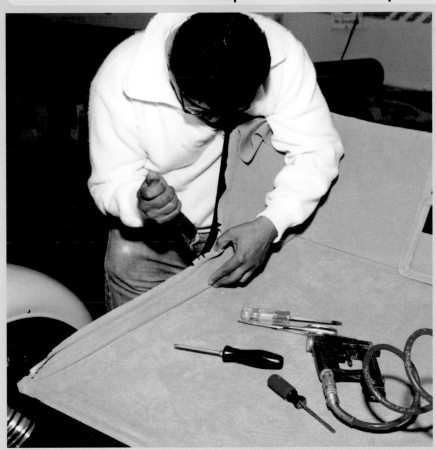

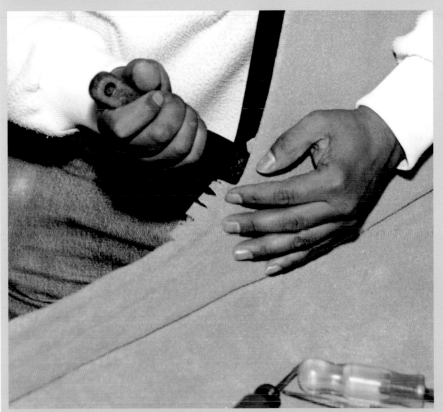

Photos 56 & 57. Another installation method is to leave the inside of the panel open. You can then get behind the material and fasten the panel to the frame with screws or pop-rivets. Using a thin putty knife, force the selvage edge of the material into the gap between the panel and the top. The tight fit will hold the material in place.

15 • Trimming a Dune Buggy

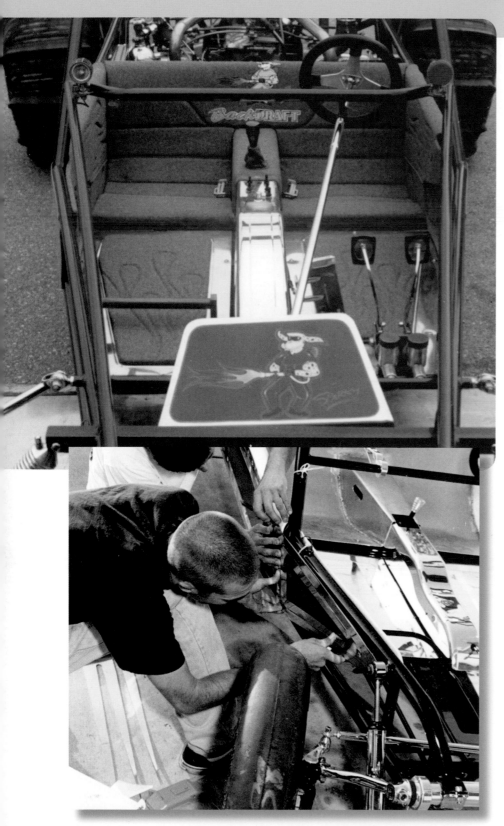

About 100 miles south and east of Ron's shop on the Yuma, Arizona and California border, lie the great Yuma sand dunes. They are the largest sand dunes in the world, outside of those in the Sahara Desert of northern Africa. Sometime in the early '60s, people began to take old Volkswagens (because of their air-cooled engines), cut the body off the pan, put wide tires on the back and use these contraptions to go exploring around these dunes. For lack of a better term they were called dune buggies. By the time the first one was finished and operating, folks began to make improvements. Today, the dune buggy is an engineering marvel and the monetary investment can exceed that of a fine European luxury sedan.

Like the street-rod enthusiast, the "buggy buyer" wants an interior to reflect his or her personality and add to the overall ambiance of the vehicle. So they bring it to Ron who gives them just what they've been hoping for.

In this chapter we'll follow Ron and his gang as they fabricate an "interior" on a very fine, two-passenger rig whose owner wants it ready for springtime fun.

Panels

Most of what comprises a dune-buggy interior is a group of panels: one on each side of the buggy; one each as a driver and passenger footrest (what would be carpeting in a car); panels around the seat area; and two curved panels that are the seats. For this section, we'll look mostly at the two side panels, comparable to door panels in a regular automobile.

All of the panels in this dune

Photo 1. Ron and his helper remove the exterior panels from the buggy as the first step in the trim operation. When the interior panels are installed, the foam and fabric will wrap around the top rails (the one under Ron's left arm). When the exterior panels are replaced they will cover the raw edges of the fabric and foam.

buggy—seats included—are made to be removable. This allows the owner or service people to access wiring and plumbing. In most cases everything is held to the frame with Velcro (glued and pop-riveted to the frame), Auveco fasteners (as used on door panels in previous chapters), and a few screws. Ron uses as few screws as possible because he (and the customer) likes the trim work to present an unblemished appearance. The job begins with Ron and a helper removing the vehicle's exterior side panels.

This exposes the buggy rails around which the material covering the panel will be wrapped. On this rail Ron runs a long strip of Velcro. When the interior panel is finished it will be installed with the top edge of the fabric wrapped around the rail and fastened to the Velcro.

Making Patterns

Pattern making begins with chipboard as usual. Pieces of chipboard are cemented together to make a panel large enough to cover the selected area. The chipboard is clamped to the frame with spring clamps. Ron marks the chipboard with a pencil using the frame rails as his guide. He then cuts out the pattern and transfers it to 1/8- or 5/32 inch plywood. For a full discussion on this process, refer to Chapter 2, Pattern Making.

Fabricating and Covering the Panels

After marking the plywood to correspond to the pattern, Ron cuts the panel with a saber saw and sands the edges smooth. He then test-fits the panel to the area to be covered and makes any minor adjustment necessary. When he's satisfied the fit is good, he makes plans to fasten the panel to the buggy.

Photo 2. As usual, Ron begins by making patterns for the panels. Chipboard is far cheaper than plywood so make sure your pattern is correct before you begin to cut.

Photo 3. Ron drills holes for the clips that will retain the inside panels to the vehicle. Next, he'll put the panel in place then drill through the existing holes, into the plywood. This is the reverse of the way Juanito drilled the clip holes for the Willys door panels.

Photo 4. Here's the plywood panel cut to the basic shape. Ron checks to make sure the fit is right before he proceeds further.

Photo 5. This cutout will eventually house a map pocket. The screw is a temporary holding device and will be replaced with a clip.

Photo 6. Ron and his helper have installed a layer of foam. Now they check the fit again and mark where the foam will be trimmed.

Photo 7. Ron does the final trimming at the bench to get an accurate line.

Photo 8. As usual, he sands the entire surface of the foam. This rounds the edges and provides "tooth" for cement.

Photos 9 & 10. To locate the insert, Ron begins with the panel in the car. This way he's assured of locating it correctly. At the bench he refines his lines and will cut away the excess foam to reveal the sculpting.

Photo 11. On the driver's side are a series of electrical switches that would otherwise be covered by the panel. Ron will make a cutout in the panel to access these switches. Here, he has cemented a piece of the tweed from the panel onto the body. Photo 29 shows the finished product.

Photo 12. Ron must now fit the top edge of the fabric to wrap around the top rail and fasten there with Velcro.

Photo 13. Backside of finished panel showing Auveco clips Ron used.

The side panels of the demonstration buggy are attached with Auveco clips just as the Willys door panels were attached. Because most of the buggy's wiring runs through the frame tubes, Ron tries to avoid drilling holes into the tubes unless he's pretty sure there's no wiring inside.[1] Most clip holes are drilled through the sheet metal. Again, Ron is extremely careful. He doesn't want to drill any holes for his clips that will not be hidden behind another panel. The holes he drills in the buggy will be covered (concealed) when the exterior panels are replaced.

The next step is to cover the panel with a layer of closed-cell foam, round the edges and scuff the surface to help the cement bond. Now comes the fun stuff.

In the photos you can see the design Ron has for the sculpting he will do to the panels. By peeking ahead, you can see that not only will he sculpt the panel, but he also makes a contrasting-color insert. The seats and panels for this car are covered in gray tweed while the inserts are made of a hot-pink body cloth matching the pink trim on the car's frame rails. The rest of the car is a deep burgundy.

Ron returns the panel to its place in the buggy and snaps it in. Then he lays the insert pattern over the foam, adjusting it until he feels it's correctly placed. This is a subjective decision based solely on what is artistically pleasing to the eye. He holds it in place with a few pieces of masking tape, then removes the panel and takes it to

[1] If Ron must drill through a frame or rail member he knows holds wiring, he wraps masking tape around the drill bit, just up from the tip the thickness of the tubing. By wrapping eight or 10 layers of tape around the bit he creates a "stop" that only allows the bit to pass through the metal then go no farther. He could also use a drill-stop collar that set-screws to the bit at the desired depth.

the bench. Here, he marks around the pattern, then cuts the foam away.

Covering the panel is straightforward and done as in all the other demonstrations. Covering begins in the middle of the panel where the sculpting is.

Ron applies a coat of cement to the foam and to the fabric. He gives it plenty of time to dry so the material may be lifted after contacting the foam if adjustments are necessary. As always, he's very careful to get the material tightly into the sculpted-area grooves without breaking down the foam edges. When the material is fully attached to the panel surface, Ron turns it over and cements the edges to the back—except along the top edge.

Returning the not-quite-finished panel to the car, he again snaps the panel in place, wraps the foam and material around the rail and clamps them down. Now he marks the edge where the Velcro will be fastened. This done, he returns the panel to the bench and sews Velcro to the edge of the material (but not to the foam edge).

Forming the Pocket

By now I'm sure you've noticed the large pocket at the front of the panel. This is very simply made as follows.

Ron cuts two pieces of material—one about 4 inches bigger than the hole, the other about 2 inches larger. The large piece will be for the front of the pocket and the smaller for the back. He then sews a length of 1/4 inch bungie cord (elastic shock cord), into a hem in the top of the larger piece. He then "gathers" the material evenly along the bungie cord. Next, he places this over the hole, staples the two ends of the bungie cord in place and finally staples the sides and bottom.

As he staples the bottom he forms the excess material (the

Photo 14. Sculpted panels ready for the inserts. Note the transmission "hump" was covered first in foam, then wrapped with a single piece of tweed. No fitting or sewing was necessary.

Photo 15. To make the map pocket, Ron begins with a piece of material about 4 or 5 inches longer than the opening. Into this he hems a piece of 3/16- or 1/4 inch bungie cord.

Photos 16 & 17. Next, he "gathers" the fabric until it just fills the area of the opening with the top edge just below the top edge of the panel. He staples both the bungie cord and fabric to the panel, "gathering" (or pleating) it along the bottom.

Photo 18. To make the backside of the pocket he staples a flat piece of material directly over the top of the pleated material. Notice it is stapled on all four sides.

Photo 19. The finished pocket ready to hold emergency supplies.

Photo 20. Ron finished this part of the panel by sewing Velcro along the top edge. A corresponding hook or loop strip will be fastened to the top rail of the car.

Photo 21. Here is the insert—cut from plywood and covered with closed-cell foam. Ron used the same pattern for the insert as he did for the area he earlier sculpted.

Photo 22. Pete jumps in to help by covering the inserts. Here he's applying cement.

Photo 23. Pete must carefully wrap the cover around each "flame." This is very touchy because there is very little material to work with.

result of "gathering" it along the bungie cord) into pleats. This gathered and pleated material, supported by bungie cord along the top, can now be pulled out and used as the front of the pocket.

The final step is to staple the smaller piece of material over the pocket material to form the backside of the pocket. This material is stapled to the panel without any gathering. Now the pocket is complete and ready for maps, sunscreen lotion and of course, that most important tool of any desert expedition, the bottle opener. Ron now turns the panel over to George Torres who will make and install the insert.

Making the Insert

If you recall from above, Ron had already sculpted the area where the insert will be. George will copy the pattern for the insert onto a piece of panelboard. He'll then cut it out and cover it.

After cutting the insert, George checks the fit. It should fit loosely into the sculpted area so when it's covered the fit will be snug. The second step is to cover the insert with foam—the same as used on the panel. Again, this is sanded over the top to ensure a good glue bond. Finally, the new insert is covered, cementing it to the top and around the back.

Check photo 24 to see how George treats the tapered ends of the insert. Notice that they are not wrapped around the panel and cemented to the backside. They're left hanging out to later be wrapped around the main panel and stapled in place. Note that this is much like you saw done on the Ford sedan delivery door panels. There, a tail was left on the trim panel, a hole was drilled through the panel and the tail inserted through the hole to be stapled on the back. Both of these techniques create sharp, well-defined "arrow tips" on inserted panels.

To finish the inserts, George must cement them in place.

Photo 24. Notice each flame tip has been left loose. It has not been wrapped around the panel as the rest of the material was. These ends (or tails) will later be wrapped around the main panel.

Photo 25. After Pete finishes the inserts, George prepares to place them into the sculpted area of the panel. Note the masking tape to keep cement from getting on the panel proper.

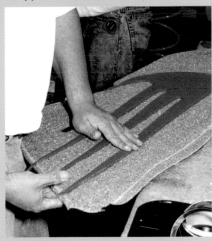

Photo 26. Starting to look good. George has the insert cemented in place.

Photos 27 & 28. "Tails" from the insert are wrapped around the main panel and stapled in place. This gives an excellent finished appearance.

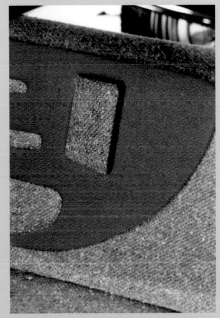

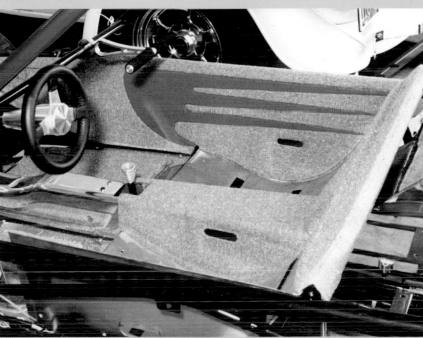

Photo 29. This cutout provides access to electrical switches. It's an attractive "fix" for a real problem.

Photo 30. Finished panel is exceedingly handsome and reflects the "techno-rod" styling of this dune buggy.

Photo 31. The second step in the process of making the panels to make heel or carpet pads for the driver and passenger. These will reflect the design of the side panels. We join the party after the patterns have been made and the panels cut out.

Photo 32. Unlike the pads in a car, these pads will be retained to the floor with regular Auveco door-panel clips.

Photo 33. Notice how Ron uses the pattern from the side panels to make the sculpting for the heel pads. He uses the last two-thirds of the "flames." Use this trick when you want to maintain consistency of design throughout your project.

Photo 34. Here's how it looks in the semi-finished state.

Photo 35. Ron cuts a piece of chipboard for the insert. Notice that it has been cut to fit over the heads of the clips. When the insert is cemented in place it will lie flat rather than show a lump where the clip is located.

Photo 36. With the chipboard foamed, Ron prepares to cover it.

Notice in photo 25 that he used masking tape to prevent cement from getting on the main body of the panel. As with fastening arm rests to door panels, George also staples the inserts to the panel by stapling through the panel into the insert. George is careful to use the correct length staple so the ends won't poke through the foam and material.

Heel or Carpet Pads

Here, we have basically a repetition of what was done with the side panels but the inserts are made from the same material as the pad.

The job begins by making a pattern to fit the area to be covered. This pattern is then transferred to panelboard and the piece cut out. Next the snaps are installed. Usually four are enough. The second step is to apply the foam.

Look at photo 33 to see how the insert pattern from the side panels is used to draw the inserts for the heel pads. Using only the back half of the pattern, Ron transfers it to the foam and carves away the surplus.

Now Ron is ready to make the insert. This time, instead of panelboard he'll begin with chipboard. Refer to photo 35 to see how Ron cut away small circles in the chipboard for the insert to allow the chipboard to lie flat over the snaps. This important step assures that the insert won't have lumps in this area.

Ron covers the chipboard now with foam and scuffs the top. He then covers the foamed chipboard with the same material as the heel pad. The final step is to cement the insert into the covered heel pad. The finished results are seen in photo 37.

Seat Frame

Around the back of the seats is a rolled bar that finishes the area of the seat frame from which the shoulder harnesses are attached. This area must be trimmed, leaving holes for that harness.

Making the Frame Panel

George Torres has the responsibility for making this panel so we will follow him as he puts it together. As usual, he begins by making a pattern, transferring the pattern to panelboard and cutting it out. In photo 38 you can see the cutouts for the shoulder harness and the location of the snaps. In that same photo, George has begun foaming the panel. There are now two layers of foam rubber: 1 inch on the bottom and 1/2 inch on the top. This is for artistic purposes. It could be foamed all in 1 inch or all in 1/2 inch. Ron feels it looks better this way because the 1 inch foam ties in nicely with the foam in the seats. When George has the panels snapped in place, Ron will begin the covering operation.

Covering the Frame Panel

Ron will make a "slipcover" to go over this panel. A slipcover means it only has one edge (seam) around the top rather than a "boxed cover" which would have a facing between the front cover and the back cover.

He places the material on the panel, just as he would if this were a seat, and marks around it. Although you don't see it in the photograph, he also marks the areas to be cut out for the harnesses.

At the sewing machine Ron sews facings into the four holes for the harness, then sews the front to the back. When finished, he turns the cover inside out and sprays on a coat of cement. He also sprays on a coat of cement over the panel. After the cement has dried, he wraps the cover over the panel, pulling the facings of the harness

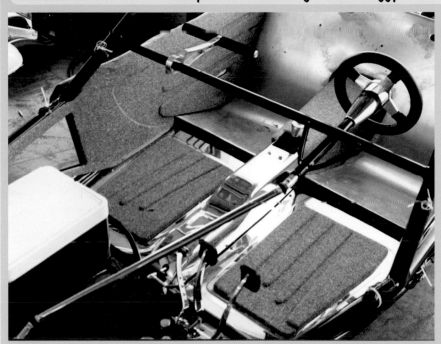

Photo 37. Finished product has a deep sculpted effect and really looks nice. The customer wanted the insert made from the same gray tweed as the panel. This keeps it from "competing" with the side panels (unfinished in this photograph).

Photos 38-40. To foam the pad that goes behind the seats, George follows the same procedures. He cements the foam to the panel, trims it with the saw or knife and then shapes it with a sanding disc in a die grinder.

Photo 41. As a design consideration, the seat-frame panel is foamed with two different thicknesses: 1 inch on bottom and 1/2 inch along the top.

Photo 42. Close-up of seat frame back. A rolled bar along the top adds height to the back. Below that is a piece of 1-1/4 inch tubing. Note the two bolts with self-locking nuts mounted to the tube. These retain the shoulder harnesses that pass through the holes directly above them. Beneath the bolts, along the length of the tube a strip of Velcro loop has been cemented to hold the cover in place. In this photo the seat-frame panel, with its foam, has been snapped in place. Note the clip indicated by the arrow.

Photo 43. Ron fits a slipcover for this panel just as he would a seat cover. This will be a simple front and back with no facing between them.

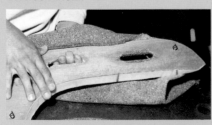

Photo 44. Here's a good trick. When you have very little material to grab hold of to pull it tight around a curve, don't pull it from the back, push it from the front. This reduces the possibility of pulling the woven threads apart.

Photo 45. Ron stitches the front and back together and installs the Velcro loop to the back edge of the cover.

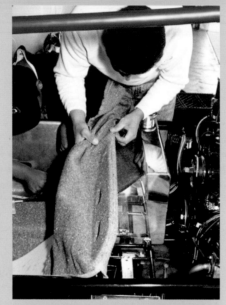

Photos 46 & 47. The tricky part: Ron must slip the cover over the panel and frame, cementing it as he goes along. This is somewhat akin to cementing a pillowcase to a pillow. The secret is to let the cement get very dry first. Then align things with a very delicate touch. If you don't use much pressure while you work, you can lift the cover from the foam without tearing it. To seal it down, rub it briskly. Once rubbed, however, you'll never be able to lift the fabric without tearing the foam.

holes through their respective exit points in the panel. The finished job is seen in photo 48. The harnesses have not yet been installed.

Making and Installing the Seats

Seats for a dune buggy are a little unusual and a bit different from any of the seats you've seen made before. Because there is a solid-aluminum pan beneath them, the "frames" of the seats need not be made strong enough to support a passenger. Therefore, Ron can make the seat "frame" out of chipboard! Let's watch as he and George do just that.

Seat Frame

George begins by making a pattern of the seat area. He had to wait until the frame panel had been partially made and installed. This gave him the inside curve as you can see in photo 50. To retain the seat to the car, George will use three Velcro strips.

First, he must locate the Velcro strips that will be in the car. The location of the most important strip is the one in the center of the seat radius. The closer this strip is to the exact center of the seat radius, the better the chipboard conforms to the curve.

The locations of the Velcro strips in the car are transferred to a piece of chipboard. Then more strips are sewn to the chipboard. As you know, Velcro comes in two "sides," one made of hooks and the other of loops. It does not matter where the hook or loop is attached, only that one side gets the hook and the other the loop. After the Velcro is attached to the chipboard "frame" George locates the pattern, marks around it and cuts the "frame" to the correct shape.

To get the curve, George first sprays a coat of cement to the "frame" and to the 1 inch foam he'll use as padding. After they're dry, he draws the "frame" into a curve tighter than what the finished product would be. He then places the foam, curved to correspond to the frame, in place and presses it tight. The reason for starting with a tighter curve is because of a phenomenon called spring-back. Everything that can be bent has some "memory" of being flat. No matter how tightly it's bent, it tries to return to its flat state. Therefore, any time you wish to bend something into an arc, it must be bent past the desired radius so that when it tries to return to its original state, it returns to the arc you originally wanted.

To finish the seat George trims the foam to the "frame," sands away any rough edges, and has a seat that's ready to be covered. Could anything be simpler?

Covering the Seat

Pete jumps in at this point to help get out this rush job. Covering the seat is almost as simple as making it. Pete cuts a piece of material about 2 inches wider and longer than the seat it will be covering. This is then bonded to a layer of 1/2 inch scrim-back foam (it has the netting on the back so it will hold a stitched seam).

Pete then lays out the same "flame" pattern on this cover as Ron and George used on the panels. Rather than sculpting the flames, he sews through the fabric and foam creating the "flame" in a raised figure.

Pete next lays this piece on the seat, marks around the outside edge, trims away everything but a 1/2 inch seam allowance. He then fits and cuts two side facings, a top facing and a front facing. The front facing is made wide enough so he can sew a strip of Velcro to it and let it hang down as a flap.

Photo 48. The finished job—as usual, it looks like it was sprayed on.

Photo 49. George begins the seat fabrication by making a pattern. Here he's fitting it around the as-yet-unfinished seat-frame panel.

Photo 50. Looks good, George!

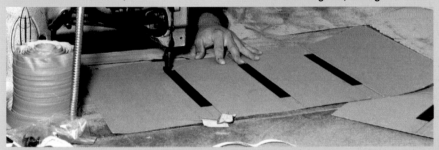

Photo 51. Chipboard seat "frame" is retained to the body of the car with Velcro. George is sewing three strips to the chipboard that will become the seat.

Photo 52. Center Velcro strip must be carefully located directly in the center of the radius. This pulls the seat in tight to the body pan.

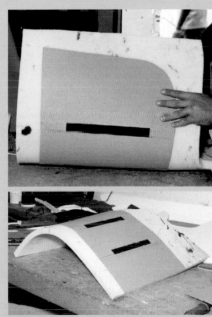

Photos 53 & 54. Cementing the chipboard and foam together while both are held in a curve creates tension causing the "sandwich" to keep this curve.

Photo 55. George finishes by trimming the foam and sanding it flush to the chipboard.

Photo 56. Test-fit shows he's done the job right.

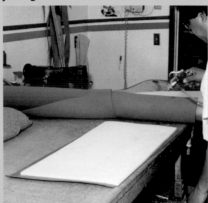

Photo 57. Pete jumps in to help cover the seat. Here he's spraying cement to the foam prior to bonding foam to fabric.

Photo 60. Velcro retainers are sewn to the cover at the top and bottom. Bottom is just above Pete's right hand.

Photos 58 & 59. He deftly sews a "flame" pattern into the seat material, then sews facings around the front. This makes the cover that he cements directly to the foam and chipboard of the seat.

Photos 61 & 62. Front and backside of the finished seat, ready to install.

Later, when the seat is placed in the car, this flap will be fixed to another strip of Velcro fastened to the car. If you look back to photo 50 you can see the Velcro attached to the frame below the seat.

As if he were sewing up a cushion, Pete sews the four pieces of facing to the main body of the seat. Now, he will cement this cover to the seat "frame" and the job will be finished. So far, the car is shaping up nicely.

Covering the Cooler

For most explorers of the mighty Yuma sand dunes, a cooler for refreshments is not an option, it's a necessity and like any other part of the car, it must look good as well as work well! Pete will put together a nice cover for it in the same material as the rest of the car.

First, pieces are cut for the top and four sides. These are then sewn to foam to give that nice padded effect. The pieces are fitted, one to the top and one each for the sides. The sides are left long so a piece of bungie cord can be hemmed in around the bottom.

The four sides are sewn together. The top is then sewn into the sides just as you would sew together a cushion cover. Finally, Pete finishes by sewing the bungie cord into a hem around the bottom and pulling the cover over the cooler.

It's just a small trick and one for which Ron doesn't even charge the customer. It's just one of those neat things that sets Ron's shop apart from the others and brings back repeat customers.

Summary

This chapter has delved into some very new and involved ideas in panel making. Review chapters two, four and five which cover pattern making, door panels and specialty panels—all used in this section.

Dune buggy upholstery is practically all panel making using Velcro and Auveco fasteners to hold them in place; even the seat covers began as panels. The emphasis on panel making has been two-fold: hiding the fasteners and covering raw edges. Most buggies will have exterior metal panels to cover the edges of your upholstery work. Some edges, though, must be hid by making a "slip-case" cover pulled over the panel or burying them beneath or behind some feature where they will not be seen. As always, make inexpensive patterns from chipboard before committing yourself to the finished materials.

When working with closed-cell foam there are two things to remember: Always scuff the outer surface to give the cement some "tooth" on which to bind. Then, allow plenty of drying time. If the cement is well cured the material can be lifted without damage to the foam, that is, until pressure has been applied. Once pressed tightly together you will tear the foam if you attempt to peel away the material.

Drilling holes in dune buggy rails is very risky unless you know there are no electrical wires or hydraulic plumbing where you intend to put a hole. Therefore, use a collar on the drill bit so it only penetrates the rail. If you don't have a collar, eight or 10 wraps of masking tape around the bit will serve the same purpose.

The important part of seat building is getting the curvature correct. Every piece of material that can be bent wants to return to its original straight form. To overcome this "memory" it's necessary to over bend the chipboard and foam. Make one or two samples before jumping into the real thing.

Finally, trimming out a dune buggy, racecar, or other unusual vehicle will test your skill as both artist and craftsperson. We're sure you'll find many new ways to improve on our example.

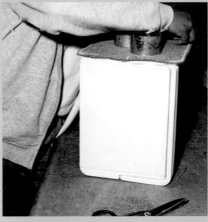

Photos 63-67. Pete cuts, fits and sews a cover for the customer's cooler. It's held to the cooler by sewing in a piece of bungie cord around the bottom. It simply pulls over the top and snaps into place.

Dune buggy seats: hard-look with flames in gray and red tweed material.

Photo 1. The process begins by removing what's left of the old cover and tracing its outline on a piece of chipboard. George carefully removed the binding so the selvage edge could be included in the outline. Unseen in this photo are the two witness marks George made to indicate the location of the fold lines.

Photo 2. Using the witness marks he made above, George draws a line representing the two edges where the original cover folded. With a razor blade (or any sharp object) he scores the top layer of the chipboard along this line. This allows him to fold along these two lines, leaving a crisp, well-defined edge.

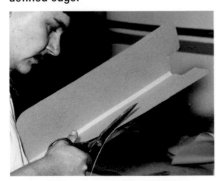

Photo 3. You can see how well the chipboard folded along the scored lines. Now George carefully trims the edges straight and square.

Photo 4. From the local auto-parts store, Ron bought a small mirror, designed to be double-taped to a sunvisor or other surface. You see this in the lower right-hand corner of the photo. This mirror will be installed into the sunvisor. George outlines it on the chipboard, then cuts away the part that would cover the glass. The plastic edges will remain covered.

Photo 5. He tests for fit and finds his cutout is just right. Notice that it's about 1/8 inch wider than the glass. When the fabric is applied, the wrapping around the edges will add just enough thickness to bring it even with the glass.

Recovering old sunvisors has always been a problem for the trim shop. Trying to manipulate a big sunvisor through the sewing machine while binding an edge too thick to fit comfortably under the foot has driven many trimmers to early coronaries. At Ron's shop they've come up with a superb method for all of the sunvisors made before the early '60s. We're all still working on those ugly, molded and padded things they produced from around 1960 on. Maybe by the second edition of this book we'll have solved the problem. For now, though, let's watch George and Ron make a couple of fine new sunvisors for our '57 Ford.

Photo 6. Using the chipboard as a pattern, George outlines the area of the mirror location within the original sunvisor base. He makes another outline, a cutting line, a little larger than necessary. This gives him a bit of room to adjust the mirror for a perfect alignment with the cutout in the chipboard.

Photo 7. Although the saber saw is almost bigger than the sunvisor, George skillfully removes the area in which the mirror will sit.

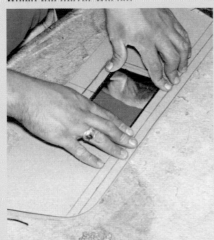

Photo 8. As usual, everything is test-fit before committing it to the finishing touches. Here, George has the mirror sitting in the sunvisor with the chipboard wrapped around it. So far, it looks good.

Photo 9. The next step is to cover the chipboard with 1/4 inch closed-cell foam. To make allowance for the extra radius of the polyfoam around the double-folded center, George lays the chipboard cover over the edge of his bench—one side of the "wing" on the bench, the other at a 90-degree angle to it. He then wraps the cemented foam around the radius.

Photo 10. He reverses the chipboard and wraps the other side.

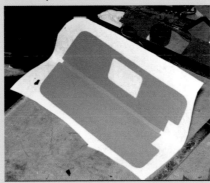

Photo 11. Finished, the polyfoam covering looks like this. Now, when it's wrapped over on itself, there won't be any excessive stretching at the fold.

Photo 12. Trimmed and ready to be covered. To cover the chipboard, George works as you've seen him do before. He sands the polyfoam, and in this case bevels the outside edges. This removes bulk at this location. Cement is sprayed to both the material and polyfoam, the cement is allowed to dry, and the material applied. Finally, he wraps the material around the edges and cements it in place.

Photo 13. With the chipboard covered, George wraps it around the sunvisor frame. He installs the mirror in the cutout and begins cementing around all the exposed surfaces.

Photo 14. This is the backside of the sunvisor. You see the back of the mirror with cement sprayed over both the sunvisor frame and the sunvisor cover. Now George will close it up.

Photo 15. At the machine, Ron runs a seam around the edge of the cemented "sandwich," about 1/4 to 3/8 inch in from the outside edge.

Photo 16. Here's the finished sunvisor seen from the mirror side. George will wash the cement overspray from the mirror glass before he installs it in the car.

Photo 17. The view from the backside. A very nicely finished sunvisor—and no one had to struggle!

17 • Covering Reveal Moldings

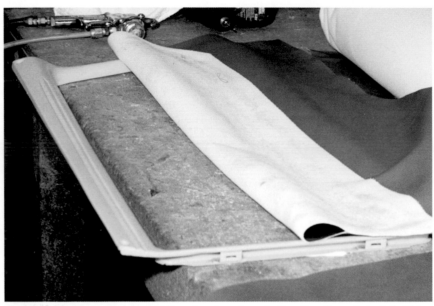

Photo 1. The important part of the planning stage is the direction of stretch. This project works best if the stretch is with the length of the molding. To start, cut a piece of material that will cover the full molding. Apply a light coat of cement to the fabric and molding. Allow the cement to dry well before joining the two.

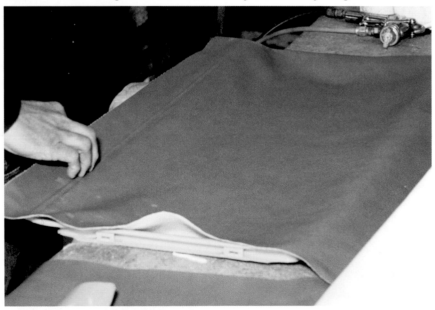

Photos 2 & 3. Ron begins by working the bottom of the molding. Notice that he defines the groove right away. He starts with his fingernails and finishes with the end of a pair of long-nose pliers.

A fine finishing touch to any custom interior is to be able to cover the reveal moldings from around the windshield, backlite and side windows. (For those of you with lots of trim experience, you may be accustomed to calling reveal molding, garnish molding. Both terms are absolutely correct and interchangeable. Reveal molding is the term most commonly used in automobile manufacturing.)

With a little explanation (and a lot of stretching) you should be able to cover your customer's reveal moldings in vinyl, leather or even fabric (although fabric is the least desirable). Ron does the job on covering the reveal molding for our '57 Ford.

Photo 4. The next step is to rough-cut the center. Leave plenty of material for wrapping around the molding.

Photo 5. Yes, it does look like Ron has a lot of excess material. It does, however, go away. It's useful to have this excess material when you reach the corners.

Photo 6. Ron works the material over the exposed surfaces first. Later, when all the wrinkles are gone, he'll wrap the material around the back of the molding and cement it in place.

Photo 7. Here's the trick. Ron stretches the material as tight as it will go. This pulls all the wrinkles away from the flat part of the molding and leaves them on the outside.

Photos 8 & 9. Ron continues to work the wrinkles away from the visible areas of the reveal molding. In the first photo, he works them over the edge with his thumbs. In the second photo, he stretches the material with both hands prior to wrapping around the frame.

Photo 10. It's looking good now. Be sure there's enough cement in the concave areas to hold the material flat to the metal. This area will lift if the cement does not bind it tightly.

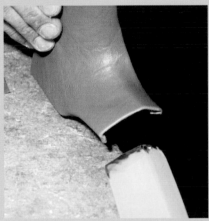

Photo 13. Here's the finished reveal molding. It looks like the cover has been sprayed on.

Photo 11. When the material lies tight and smooth over all exposed surfaces, you can then begin to cement the vinyl or leather to the back. If you try to pull the material around the metal and cement it to the back in one step, you'll never get rid of all the wrinkles or mold the material into the compound curves.

Photo 12. This is the base of one of the two risers that frame the inside of the windshield. It connects to the reveal molding that covers the union between the instrument panel and the windshield. This photo shows how Ron has ground away paint (and some metal) so that, when covered, these two pieces will still join together. The piece on the right must slide into the piece on the left when both are covered.

Photo 1. Meet Catherine Barley, "The Vinyl Lady." She arrives in her station wagon, loaded with vinyl dyes and repair materials. She's even equipped with all the power tools she needs to get the job done quickly.

Photos 2 & 3. The process turns out to be very simple. On the very small scratches she applies a drop or two of instant glue. Next, with 400-grit wet-or-dry sand paper, she gently sands over the scratch and glue. This closes the scratch and sands away any fibers or bits of material left standing. It works with both leather and vinyl.

Photo 4. Catherine goes around the car, repairing each scratch. To repair about 10 scratches took less than 10 minutes.

Every trimmer has had the terrible misfortune of somehow damaging the leather or vinyl of a newly upholstered piece of interior. The most common is jumping into a car, plopping your behind into the seat, and discovering you have a pair of shears in your back pocket! The second most common problem is to drag a finished seat or panel over a sharp object on the bench. In the past, the only resolution to the problem was to replace the damaged panel. The wonderful world of science has come to our rescue in the form of a new skill we call vinyl repair.

This trick has been around since the mid-sixties but is only now a real solution to some of these problems. In the early days, the repair was long, involved and usually more visible than the original problem. Now, minor scratches can easily be removed in only a matter of minutes. Larger repairs take only a little longer. Of course, great tears still require the old-fashioned repair: replacement.

While working on the book at his shop, Ron got a call from one of his customers to tell him he wished to sell his car and would like a few repairs made to freshen the interior. Among the needed repairs were a few scratches in the leather. To solve this part of the problem, Ron called on Catherine Barley, affectionately known as "The Vinyl Lady" to make the necessary repairs. She arrived in a few hours, ready to perform her magic.

Photos 5 & 6. The second step is to clean the leather around all the repairs. In the photo, she sprays the leather with a non-detergent cleaner and wipes away the excess. This removes any oils from skin, cleaners, waxes and even mold-release agent. This prepares the leather to be dyed.

Photo 7. Before she can spray any dye, the material must be perfectly dry. She uses a heat gun to rid the leather of any remaining moisture.

Photo 8. Here begins the artistic part of the job. Catherine must now mix her vinyl dyes to match the color of the leather (or vinyl) exactly. She tried hard to explain how she did it, but neither Don or Ron thought they could jump right in and mix the colors—even after her excellent explanation.

After three or four attempts, she hit it dead on. In the photo she's matching her test (on a piece of chipboard) to the seat. When she has it just right, she sprays a coat of dye over the recently repaired area. Any minor scratches left by the 400-grit sand paper will be filled in with the dye.

Photo 9. To speed the drying process, Catherine uses the heat gun again. In less than 20 minutes she had all the scratches repaired.

During our discussions, Catherine explained she could also repair things like cigarette burns and minor tears. On the tears, she asks the trim shop to cement a patch to the back of it. This closes the tear and supports it, then, it can be handled in the same way as a burn.

Catherine has bottles of clear vinyl she can use to fill voids. She also has small sheets of vinyl with grain embossed into them. On a burn, she sands away any ash and raised vinyl. Then, she applies a few drops of liquid vinyl to the remaining hole or void in the tear. When the vinyl has dried for a couple of minutes, she applies the embossed side of her vinyl patch to the repair. The embossing is transferred to the semi-wet vinyl, reproducing the grain pattern around it. The repair is finished by spraying the repair with vinyl dye.

We asked Catherine if there were others like her and where could they be found. She replied there were none like her, but there were many who could do this type

of work. She suggested any trimmer needing this type of help should call a local new-car dealership that sells their used cars from their own lot. The used-car dealer requires the services of a vinyl-repair expert on a frequent and ongoing basis. He or she will direct you to them.

Photos 10 & 11. Ron wanted Catherine to dye some of the parts of the Willys to match the leather. Here, she has matched the color of the leather exactly and has begun to spray the speaker grille and door-opener reveal moldings. Check the photo of the finished speaker panel on page 50 to see how well she did her job.

Photo 1. Here is the pattern resting on a piece of beige leather. Like all of the patterns in the industry, it, too, is made of chipboard. We sure hope the world never runs out of chipboard trees! All along the length of the pattern are holes Jack has punched for the thread to pass through. He says he hasn't time to count all the holes. We think he's holding back.

Photo 2. The process begins by laying out the pattern on the leather, marking around it, making a dot for each hole the thread will pass through, then cutting out the cover. Next, with a leather punch, Jack punches out each dot. This gives him all the holes he'll need to stitch the cover. In this photo he's punching the last few holes.

Photos 3 & 4. Wherever the leather is folded back upon itself, Jack grinds away enough of the backside to prevent a lump beneath the fold or seam. Jack is drawing a line at the end of the leather that marks the seam allowance. This seam joins the two ends of the cover.

Photos 5 & 6. Using a high-speed die grinder, Jack grinds away the back of the leather, right up to the line. He's removed about half the thickness of the leather.

Photo 7. Now he sews the two ends together. The seam is right on the line to which the leather was removed.

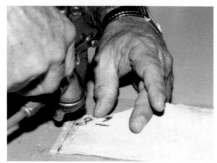

Photo 8. To ensure the seam selvage will not bunch up when the cover is installed, Jack cements the selvage edge back upon itself.

The fastest-growing part of the hot rod market today is manufacturing interesting and exciting new steering wheels. They've done just about all they can do with "rims" (wheels). The best of these are covered in the same material as the rest of the interior, or in a black or neutral leather. The best in the business, on the west coast, doing this covering is Jack Anderson, who does work for Ron's Shop.

Jack, a former NASA engineer, uses his engineering skills full time in his major interest: cars. Jack can make a pattern for anything with his fancy CAD program running on his powerful computer. For nearly every steering wheel available, OEM or aftermarket, Jack has made a pattern. This allows him to quickly cut, assemble and sew a beautiful leather cover. We called on Jack to watch him cover an aftermarket wheel going in one of Ron's cars—a 1957 Chevrolet.

Jack gives away all of his secrets on these pages—except how he gets all of the little holes in his pattern to line up. He says anyone with an engineering background, or infinite patience, could make a pattern like his. We'll let you be the judge. Perhaps you're the one with enough patience.

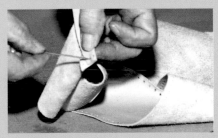

Photos 9 & 10. A very neat job indeed. Here is the front and back side of the seam.

Photo 11. In a similar manner, Jack grinds and cements the selvage at the edges of the folds that will wrap around the spokes.

Photo 12. With a trim pin, he relocates the holes for the thread after cementing the folds. The operation has filled them with rubber cement.

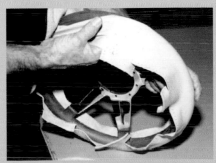

Photo 13. The cover is ready to be installed on the wheel. Notice how well it wraps in this and the following photos, even before it's sewn. This is the result of Jack's pattern. It was made about 1-1/2 inches shorter than the actual circumference of the wheel.

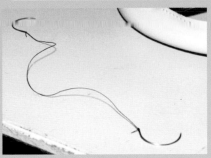

Photo 14. Another of Jack's tricks is to attach a curved needle to each end of his thread. This eliminates the need for two lengths of thread. Also, he ties the thread to the needles. This prevents it from slipping through the eyes. Now, he can begin sewing the wraps about the spokes.

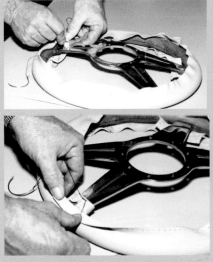

Photos 15 & 16. Picking up the hole on each side of the wrap, Jack takes two wrapping stitches to start. There is some strain here and the double stitch helps prevent the thread from wearing. Note how each end of his thread is passing out of the hole, ready to form the cross stitch.

Photo 17. He now makes three cross stitches ending with another double stitch at the base of the wrap. The threads are next passed beneath the leather and glued to the steering wheel with a drop of super glue.

Photo 18. The spokes are now wrapped and Jack can proceed with sewing the remaining seams.

Photos 19 & 20. The stitching along the length of the wheel is done just as they wrap around the spokes. A double stitch begins the seam. Then, the remainder of the stitches are cross stitches, ending at the next spoke with a double stitch. Herein lies the engineering of the pattern. There must be an equal number of holes on each side of the leather, each the same distance from its neighbor. Without this type of accuracy, some stitches would be longer than others and he would end up with one empty hole.

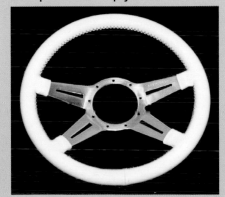

Photos 21 & 22. The finished wheel on the bench and in the car. Great job, Jack!

Suppliers

Adhesives

3M Industrial Adhesives
3M Center Bldg., 21-1W-10
St. Paul, MN 55144-1000
(800) 362-3550
www.mmm.com/adhesives

Alpha Systems, Inc.
5120 Beck Dr.
Elkhart, IN 46516
(574) 295-5206
www.alphasystemsinc.com

Astrup Co.
2937 W. 25th St.
Cleveland, OH 44113
(800) 786-7601
www.astrup.com

Consolidated Admiral
(wholesale trade only)
P.O. Box 382
Woodbury, NY 11797
(516) 921-2131
www.consolidatedadmiral.com

Hahn Systems
4629 Clyde Park SW
Wyoming, MI 49509
(616) 534-0702
www.hahnsystems.com

Russell Products, Inc.
17989 Commerce Dr.
Bristol, IN 46507
(800) 545-5620
www.russellproducts.com

Button-making Equipment

Fasnap Corp.
23669 Reedy Dr.
Elkhart, IN 46514
(800) 624-2058
www.fasnap.com

Handy Button
Machine Co.
1750 N. 25th Ave.
Melrose Park, IL 60160
(708) 450-9000
www.handybutton.com

Carpet, Auto

Auto Custom Carpets
P.O. Box 1350
1429 Noble St.
Anniston, AL 36201
(800) 352-8216
www.accmats.com

Blacksmith Distributing
(trade only)
1801 Cassopolius St.
Elkhart, IN 46514
(800) 551-0134
www.blacksmithdistributing.com

Consolidated Admiral
(wholesale trade only)
P.O. Box 382
Woodbury, NY 11797
(516) 921-2131
www.consolidatedadmiral.com

Custom Auto Interiors
247 S. Olive Avenue
Rialto, CA 92376
(909) 877-9342
www.customautointeriors.com

LeBaron Bonney
P.O. Box 6
Amesbury, MA 01913
(800) 221-5408
www.lebaronbonney.com

Original Parts Group
5252 Bolsa Ave.
Huntington Beach, CA 92649
(800) 243-8355
www.opgi.com

Consoles

The Accessory House
5156 Holt Blvd.
Montclair, CA 91763
(909) 621-5953
www.accessoryhouseonline.com

Consoles, Overhead

The Accessory House
5156 Holt Blvd.
Montclair, CA 91763
(909) 621-5953
www.accessoryhouseonline.com

Custom Auto Interiors
247 S. Olive Avenue
Rialto, CA 92376
(909) 877-9342
www.customautointeriors.com

Hoosier Van Conversion and
Truck Accessories
52904 County Rd. 13,
   Unit B17-5A
Elkhart, IN 46514
(800) 592-7600
www.hoosiervan.com

Convertible Tops

Acme Auto Headlining Co.
550 W. 16th St.
Long Beach, CA 90813
(800) 288-6078

Bill Hirsch Auto
396 Littleton Ave.
Newark, NJ 07103
(800) 828-2061
www.hirschauto.com

GAHH Auto Tops
8116 Lankershim Blvd.
N. Hollywood, CA 91605
(800) 722-2292
www.gahh.com

LeBaron Bonney
P.O. Box 6
Amesbury, MA 01913
(800) 221-5408
www.lebaronbonney.com

National Auto Mall
200 Everette Ave.
Chelsea, MA 02150
(617) 889-0600

Robbins Auto Tops
321 Todd Ct.
Oxnard, CA 93030
(805) 604-3200
www.robbinsautotopco.com

Fabrics

Astrup Co.
2937 W. 25th St.
Cleveland, OH 44113
(800) 786-7601
www.astrup.com

B & M Foam & Fabrics
3383 Durahart St.
Riverside, CA 92507
(951) 787-0221

Bill Hirsch Auto
396 Littleton Ave.
Newark, NJ 07103
(800) 828-2061
www.hirschauto.com

Consolidated Admiral
(wholesale trade only)
P.O. Box 382
Woodbury, NY 11797
(516) 921-2131
www.consolidatedadmiral.com

Custom Auto Interiors
247 S. Olive Avenue
Rialto, CA 92376
(909) 877-9342
www.customautointeriors.com

GAHH Auto Tops
8116 Lankershim Blvd.
N. Hollywood, CA 91605
(800) 722-2292
www.gahh.com

J & J Auto Fabrics Inc.
247 S. Riverside Ave.
Rialto, CA 92376
(909) 874-3040
jjfab@sbcglobal.net

Keyston Bros.
(nationwide wholesale only)
9669 Aero Dr.
San Diego, CA 92123
(858) 277-7770
www.keystonbros.com

LeBaron Bonney
P.O. Box 6
Amesbury, MA 01913
(800) 221-5408
www.lebaronbonney.com

Three Rivers Supply
(wholesale only)
477 W. 7th Ave.
West Homestead, PA 15120
(800) 245-0220

Velcro Laminates Inc.
54835 CR 19
Bristol, IN 46507-9466
(800) 235-1776

Veteran Company
(wholesale only)
5060 W. Pico Blvd.
Los Angeles, CA 90019
(323) 937-2233
www.veteranco.com

Fasteners

Astrup Co.
2937 W. 25th St.
Cleveland, OH 44113
(800) 786-7601
www.astrup.com

Atlas Supply of Texas
700 E. Parker St.
Houston, TX 77076
(800) 392-8527
www.atlassupplyoftexas.com

Au-ve-co Products
Auto-Vehicle Parts Co.
7 Sperti Dr.
Covington, KY 41017
(606) 341-6450
www.auveco.com

Consolidated Admiral
(wholesale trade only)
P.O. Box 382
Woodbury, NY 11797
(516) 921-2131
www.consolidatedadmiral.com

Eastwood Company
260 Shoemaker Rd.
Pottstown, PA 19464
(800) 345-1178
www.eastwood.com

Fasnap Corp.
23669 Reedy Dr.
Elkhart, IN 46514
(800) 624-2058
www.fasnap.com

Velcro Laminates Inc.
54835 CR 19
Bristol, IN 46507-9466
(800) 235-1776

Headliners

Acme Auto Headlining Co.
550 W. 16th St.
Long Beach, CA 90813
(800) 288-6078

Bill Hirsch Auto
396 Littleton Ave.
Newark, NJ 07103
(800) 828-2061
www.hirschauto.com

Consolidated Admiral
(wholesale trade only)
P.O. Box 382
Woodbury, NY 11797
(516) 921-2131
www.consolidatedadmiral.com

LeBaron Bonney
P.O. Box 6
Amesbury, MA 01913
(800) 221-5408
www.lebaronbonney.com

Original Parts Group
5252 Bolsa Ave.
Huntington Beach, CA 92649
(800) 243-8355
www.opgi.com

Insulation

Quality Heat Shield
3873 Carter Ave., Suite 202
Riverside, CA 92501
(951) 276-1040

Leather

Bill Hirsch Auto
396 Littleton Ave.
Newark, NJ 07103
(800) 828-2061
www.hirschauto.com

Consolidated Admiral
(wholesale trade only)
P.O. Box 382
Woodbury, NY 11797
(516) 921-2131
www.consolidatedadmiral.com

GAHH Auto Tops
8116 Lankershim Blvd.
N. Hollywood, CA 91605
(800) 722-2292
www.gahh.com

Garrett Leather
(trade only)
1360 Niagara St.
Buffalo, NY 14213
(800) 342-7738

LeBaron Bonney
P.O. Box 6
Amesbury, MA 01913
(800) 221-5408
www.lebaronbonney.com

Veteran Company
(wholesale only)
5060 W. Pico Blvd.
Los Angeles, CA 90019
(323) 937-2233
www.veteranco.com

Parts

The Accessory House
5156 Holt Blvd.
Montclair, CA 91763
(909) 621-5953
www.accessoryhouseonline.com

Original Parts Group
5252 Bolsa Ave.
Huntington Beach, CA 92649
(800) 243-8355
www.opgi.com

Rod Doors

R.W. and ABLE, Inc.
P.O. Box 2160
Chico, CA 95927-2160
(800) 510-7478
www.roddoors.com

Seat Belts

Juliano's Hot Rod Parts
321 Talcottville Rd.
Vernon, CT 06066
(860) 872-1932
www.julianos.com

The Truck Stop
dba Specialty Conversions
1889 Commonwealth Ave.
Fullerton, CA 92833
(888) 870-2358

Seat Covers

Original Parts Group
5252 Bolsa Ave.
Huntington Beach, CA 92649
(800) 243-8355
www.opgi.com

Seat Frames

American Metal Fabricators
55515 Franklin St.
Three Rivers, MI 49093
(269) 279-5108

Atwood Mobile Products
57912 Charlotte Ave.
Elkhart, IN 46517
(574) 522-7891

C & L Upholstery
12913 S. Marquardt Ave.
Santa Fe Springs, CA 90670
(562) 921-6545

Glide Engineering
10662 Pullman Court
Rancho Cucamonga, CA 71730
(909) 944-9556
www.glideeng.com

Seats

Cerullo Performance Seating
2881 Metropolitan Place
Pomona, CA 91767
(909) 392-5561
www.cerullo.com

Recaro
3275 Lapeer Rd. West
Auburn Hills, MI 48326
(800) 873-2276
www.recaro-nao.com

Tea's Design
2038 15th St. N.W.
Rochester, MN 55901
(507) 289-0494
www.teasdesign.com

Sewing Machines

Consolidated Sewing Machine
131 W. 25th St.
New York, NY 10001
(212) 741-7788
www.consew.com

Keystone Sewing Machine
833 N. 2nd St.
Philadelphia, PA 19123
(215) 922-6900
www.keysew.com

Quality Cow
221 West Ord
Grand Island, NE 68801
(800) 431-0032
www.qualitysew.com

Upholstery Supplies

American Upholstery Supply
1355 N. Marion St.
Tulsa, OK 74115
(800) 331-3913
www.atrim.com

Astrup Co.
2937 W. 25th St.
Cleveland, OH 44113
(800) 786-7601
www.astrup.com

Custom Auto Interiors
247 S. Olive Avenue
Rialto, CA 92376
(909) 877-9342
www.customautointeriors.com

Eastwood Company
260 Shoemaker Rd.
Pottstown, PA 19464
(800) 345-1178
www.eastwood.com

Keyston Bros.
(nationwide wholesale only)
9669 Aero Dr.
San Diego, CA 92123
(858) 277-7770
www.keystonbros.com

LeBaron Bonney
P.O. Box 6
Amesbury, MA 01913
(800) 221-5408
www.lebaronbonney.com

Peachtree Fabrics, Inc.
1400 English St. N.W.
Atlanta, GA 30318
(800) 732-2437
www.peachtreefabrics.com

Upholstery Tools

Eastwood Company
260 Shoemaker Rd.
Pottstown, PA 19464
(800) 345-1178
www.eastwood.com

Index

A Sweet '55

'55 Chevy Bel Air features factory Lexus seats front and rear, with modifications to fit. Upholstery work includes custom dyed leather to match the car's paint.

Headliner includes hand made custom chrome bows for a '50s nostalgic look. Trunk panels are molded around the wheel wells and the floor has a unique center carpet insert.

Photos this page: E. John Thawley III